BEYOND AMBIGUITY

Manchester University Press

ANGELAKIHUMANITIES

editors
Charlie Blake
Pelagia Goulimari
Salah El Moncef
Timothy S. Murphy

general editor
Gerard Greenway

Angelaki Humanities publishes works which address and probe broad and compelling issues in the theoretical humanities. The series favours path-breaking thought, promotes unjustly neglected figures, and grapples with established concerns. It believes in the possibility of blending, without compromise, the rigorous, the well-crafted, and the inventive. The series seeks to host ambitious writing from around the world.

Angelaki Humanities is the associated book series of
angelaki – journal of the theoretical humanities.

Already published

Evil spirits: nihilism and the fate of modernity
Gary Banham and Charlie Blake (eds)

The question of literature: the place of the literary in contemporary theory
Elizabeth Beaumont Bissell

Postmodernism: what moment?
Pelagia Goulimari (ed.)

Absolutely postcolonial: writing between the singular and the specific
Peter Hallward

Disclosed poetics: beyond landscape and lyricism
John Kinsella

Polysituatedness: a poetics of displacement
John Kinsella

Late modernist poetics: from Pound to Prynne
Anthony Mellors

The new Bergson
John Mullarkey (ed.)

Subversive Spinoza: (un)contemporary variations
Antonio Negri, edited by Timothy S. Murphy, Michael Hardt, Edward Stolze and Charles T. Wolfe

ANGELAKIHUMANITIES

BEYOND AMBIGUITY
Tracing literary sites of activism

John Kinsella

Manchester University Press

Copyright © John Kinsella 2021

The right of John Kinsella to be identified as the author of this work has been asserted by them in accordance with the Copyright, Designs and Patents Act 1988.

Published by Manchester University Press
Oxford Road, Manchester M13 9PL

www.manchesteruniversitypress.co.uk

British Library Cataloguing-in-Publication Data
A catalogue record for this book is available from the British Library

ISBN 978 1 5261 6006 5 hardback
ISBN 978 1 5261 9121 2 paperback

First published 2021
Paperback published 2025

The publisher has no responsibility for the persistence or accuracy of URLs for external or any third-party internet websites referred to in this book, and does not guarantee that any content on such websites is, or will remain, accurate or appropriate.

EU authorised representative for GPSR:
Easy Access System Europe – Mustamäe tee 50, 10621 Tallinn, Estonia
gpsr.requests@easproject.com

Typeset
by Cheshire Typesetting Ltd, Cuddington, Cheshire

To Gerard Greenway and in memory of Urs Jaeggi

Earth Hymn
'Guardian and friend of the moon, O Earth, whom the comets forget not,
Yea, in the measureless distance wheel round and again they behold thee!'

(Samuel Taylor Coleridge, from 'Hymn to the Earth', imitated from Stolberg's
  'Hymne an die Erde')

Drag me, wanderer, down town quickly for Capital's light show –
The Quay, wanderer ... where I trip over my own feet trying to reafforestate,
Where the makers of city deny their impact via tendrils reaching out
Into zones they designate as resources. Where I can locate is reduced
To a place in my head I don't own, built up over millennia, an ugly
Portraiture of self and lines of descent. But I continue on foot,
Attempting to plough a furrow through concrete, open out to winged seed
Flying in from a different timeline, ready to defy conditions and rise to the sun.

Guide me, wanderer, down town, avoiding Capital's light show –
For there's plenty of praise here if I can discover how to trill
Without it costing you an arm and a leg, this banter around the river,
Twilight sails softly billowing as relaxed as Margaret River white wine.
This jigsaw puzzle of presence, giving room to manoeuvre? Were
It just a few words, a snippet of text, a 'that was then, this is now'
Scenario ... you know, easy come, easy go? And yet, your plates shift,
And you belch and shudder under the strain of holding us up.

Drag me, wanderer, down town quickly for Capital's light show –
A farce, wanderer ... a glimmer of glass and skyworks, a pat on the back
For 'healthy competition'. Earth, *developers* are not your friend – I have heard
Them laughing at you as I've passed under their boardrooms, their dead nests
Scanned for bugs, an exterminator ever at the ready, serving hand over foot,
  speculating
At their beck and call. A little sparkle has appeared in some eyes, as solar-
Engineers sell their vision of futures trading, glittering sulphate reflectors
In the canopy, crown decline the sepia over the black & white of ancient footage.

Guide me, wanderer, down town, avoiding Capital's light show –
Learning to walk through the cloud and let flow and flow through,
Not like The Verve's video for *Bitter Sweet Symphony* – maybe Richard
Ashcroft would have walked *around* cows or sheep or kangaroos
If he'd been walking around here, chanting to himself? I have seen
Echidnas trundle with such determination down the hillside, beak
Set towards a veining of termites up an old York gum trunk. In childhood,
I worried so much about *scale* looking out over things from the treehouse.

Drag me, wanderer, down town quickly for Capital's light show –
Quick smart, wanderer ... along the familiar beat, the worn lines in sand
I can barely read, struggling for skills. I come from out where the winnowing
Is glitter in the air, where pollens shake down where they can, confused
As origins, looking for purchase. They struggle with *political economy*.
An asteroid passes between the moon and the earth, coming out
Of the shadows as an affront to science, to observation, to glocal©
Denial rolled into ball-bearings. A gravel road, a secretive mine. Trucks!

Guide me, wanderer, down town, avoiding Capital's light show –
Across hot and cold reservoirs, this Carnot cycle of my unplaced body
That still leaves a stain, something uncomfortable, best written-out
Of records that change as needs be anyway. Roots feeding roots –
Surely no surprise in the co-operative take on dwelling, the walls
And surveillance cameras of wealthy streets a haul from quarry holes
In the blue soul of Hills rock? Each year fewer red-tailed and fewer
White-tailed cockatoos, their calls streamers of naming dispersed by aerosols.

Drag me, wanderer, down town quickly for Capital's light show –
High light, wanderer ... squelching froglets' vulnerable tenacity against the
    cutting
Edge; terms of trade are the toxic wooden floors of metal containers and the
    harbour
Chock-a-block with points of purchase, reaching out; these pilgrimages
For some, not for others, distant mountains expanding to crack and fall down
End of days, night person I am, foraging among the pale tubers. No claims.
    Nothing.
You, wanderer, are the wanderer – I am not setting my teeth into granite, but
    watching.
Guide me, wanderer, down town, avoiding Capital's light show!

(John Kinsella)

Villanelle In Memoriam Urs Jaeggi

You'd have broken the form down into fragments
of speech, questioned the mechanism, undone the quotes
that bind the philosopher to a position, a circumstance.

I will remember *for us* the interplay of documents
and voice in the East Berlin Literaturhaus, the notes
of breaking the form down into fragments.

I will remember for us the non-alignments
of syntax and image, freeing picture house endnotes
that bind the philosopher to a position, a circumstance.

I will remember Deleuze and Guattari enjambments,
the wolf in a shadow of the tower – unlearning rote,
as we broke up the form and followed the fragments.

I will remember the depth of ink and the dénouement
of a rocking horse in your Berlin flat, later of Zurich and litotes,
refusing to bind the philosopher to a position, a circumstance.

For more than a quarter-century we worked by increments –
our 'Tractortatus' trying to respell propositions and essences – afloat
on your sculptures of consequence, lines worked into fragments
freeing the philosopher from a position, all circumstance.

(John Kinsella)

CONTENTS

List of figures	*page* xi
Prefatory comments	xii
Acknowledgements	xviii
INTRODUCTION: LOCALITIES	1
PART ONE	10
How does the activist cope with ambiguity?	11
Resisting the compliant text	22
The truth should be in blurbs, encomiums, references, letters of support and launch speeches etc.	32
PART TWO	51
An Unambiguous Response to Helen MacDonald's Article 'The Forbidden Wonder of Birds' Nests and Eggs'	52
How do poems come out of conversations?	55
On being an ethical vegan for thirty-three or so years …	57
No pets but surrounded by animals – proximity sensors and warnings	63
Dream pastoral inversions: re-approaching pastoral fraughtness through questions of Australian rurality	74
PART THREE	86
Celebrating Fay Zwicky	87
A dissenting imagination: disambiguations	91
Places we do or don't go to not only *in person*, but also *in writing*	96
'Precise poems' are more ambiguous than we might think: on Judith Wright's *Collected Poems*	108
On Georgina Arnott's *The Unknown Judith Wright*	122
On Alison Whittaker's poetry collection *Blakwork*: a letter to an editor	124
Non-ambiguous: dispossession and culpability – on Ambelin Kwaymullina's *Living on Stolen Land*	126

Contents

On Glen Phillips's *Collected Poems 1968–2018: In the Hollow of the Land*	127
A poet's personal appreciation of Les Murray (in memoriam, April, 2019)	130
IM Bruce Dawe, 2020	132
Sinews – on Siobhan Hodge's *Justice for Romeo*	135
On Matt Hall's poetry collection, *False Fruits*: habitation and the 'Consonant Feather'	138
On Kim Seung-Hee's *Hope Is Lonely*	140
On Philip Neilsen's MS *Wildlife of Berlin*	145
On Omar Sakr's *The Lost Arabs*	147
On Paul Kelly's 2017 album/CD *Life is Fine*	148
The polyphony of voices brought together	151

PART FOUR — 156

The inherent reciprocities of memoir-making: on the memoirs of Evelyn Shakir and George Ellenbogen — 157

PART FIVE — 173

On an innovative poet's book, never published: introduction to Scott Patrick-Mitchell's *Vade Mecum* — 174

PART SIX — 178

Working with Urs Jaeggi	179
On *Textures of Ambiguity*	191
On my own, my language is not alone	204
Rocks can burn, too: and there's nothing ambiguous about it	205
Poetry can lead to speculative 'realist' fiction: the inspiration behind *Hollow Earth*	209
On Spenser's stanza 'Virtue gives itself light'	210
Consuming rebellions and the need for non-violent protest	213
Extinction Rebellion is too much about image and not enough about its own impacts	221

PART SEVEN: TOWARDS 'CONCLUSIONS' — 223

Disembodying and re-embodying the poem as act of acknowledgement of land rights and a rejection of 'property': on acts and actioning of environmentally concerned poetry	224
Resist! Against cruelty – emphasis without violence	231
Conclusion to *Beyond Ambiguity* and a triptych of poetics	237

LIST OF FIGURES

1	The author aged 11 in his younger brother's herpetarium holding a bearded dragon with another bearded dragon sunning itself on a chunk of wood.	*page* 73
2	Demapping Jam Tree Gully at the start of August, concentrating on the southwest corner.	78
3–12	Drawings: ink on paper by Urs Jaeggi.	182
13	London (2016), by William Yeoman. Photo provided by William Yeoman.	196
14	Fremantle (2016), by William Yeoman. Photo provided by William Yeoman.	198
15	York 1 (2016), by William Yeoman. Photo provided by William Yeoman.	200
16	York 2 (2016), by William Yeoman. Photo provided by William Yeoman.	202
17–18	Burnt Rocks near Walwalinj, York, 2012. Exfoliated granite due to extreme heat from fire. Photos Wendy Kinsella.	207
19	Cover image of the *Australian Poetry Journal*, 9.1, *Resist!* Image provided by Jacinta Le Plastrier – *Publisher of Australian Poetry Journal*. Design by Stuart Geddes.	236

PREFATORY COMMENTS

This book is intended as a follow-up to my books *Disclosed Poetics: Beyond Landscape and Lyricism* (2007) and *Polysituatedness: A Poetics of Displacement* (2017), both published by Manchester University Press. I tend to think and work in units of threes, so I guess this volume is a kind of conclusion, the final in a trilogy of hybrid creative-critical works dealing with issues of spatiality and temporality in the context of place-study poetics. But it's not a neat categorising or tying off because so many threads lead into these works and hopefully fly out of them in the search for (often elusive) anchor points. In recent years I have been collaborating on book-length hybrid critical works with Russell West-Pavlov, which necessarily overlap in their interests and concerns with this series, and in more directly creative writing works with fellow poets, which have significantly affected my perceptions around acts of collaborative practice. From the outset, I acknowledge all these interactions, and celebrate them.

The essential purpose of my work is to challenge familiar topoi and normatives of poetic activity as they pertain to environmental, humanitarian and textual activism in 'the world-at-large': to show how ambiguity can be a generative force when it works from a basis of non-ambiguity of purpose. The 'disambiguation' is a major difference with all other critical works on generative ambiguities: I state that there is a clear unambiguous position to have regarding issues of justice, but that from such a confirmed position ambiguity can be an intense and useful activist tool. There is an undoing of an apparent paradox of text in terms of 'in the real world' activism. It becomes an issue of consequences arising from creative work and positioning. Whether in discussing a particular literary text or 'event in the world', I make use of creative texts at *specific* sites of a broader, intertextual and interconnected activism.

With this volume, my concern is to push definitions beyond the lexical into the 'field' – theory is only useful if it has practical reifying applications for *just* outcomes. 'Ambiguity' is an issue of polyphony of doubt for me, and in this book I hope to discover (I don't claim to have achieved) various points on which ambiguity can turn a situation from an activism (textual or at the physical site) to a resolution, and also bring certainties of resolution into doubt so that we never relax into a complacency of 'success' (mass extinction shows success can only ever be relative).

A key generative notion is the creation of poetic texts that allow multiple entries and exits, that offer up varied and shifting meanings, that change according to context. That is the joy of the poem. But as an environmental and social-justice activist, I am interested in precise interpretations of rights issues: that bit of bush should NOT be damaged, those human rights MUST be respected. The apparent contradiction between the vague and the precise, especially as it is found in the disturbing binary of 'didactic' or 'lyrical' aestheticising, is a distraction from cause and effect, to my mind.

These 'qualities' *can* co-exist in a poem and offer up at least the illusion of discovery of 'purpose' (the poem is against war, the poem is affirming of love over hate, the poem is showing nature as beautiful and industry as damaging etc), and also hold their ground, keep their 'opinion' ultimately hidden. So, behind the obvious messages and motifs, the poem itself holds other opinions/views, sometimes contradicting the initial or overt or obvious (intended) impression.

Beyond the ambiguity lie certainties. Rights and wrongs. I believe in things in specific ways. Readers may not agree, but the fact that I have a set of what I consider to be beliefs – and that I write with these in mind – is relevant to how my text is used and interpreted. This is not a desire to homogenise, to redirect to how I see things, but for there to be an understanding of sharing and exchange in acts of writing and reading, reading and writing. The wonder of collaboration is the merging of difference and sameness, of making something that has its own life beyond its creators. Ambiguity is exponential in this, as collaborators can of course never fully participate in the feelings and thoughts of the other – there is always the hidden or undeclared textuality, and the textuality the author is unaware of.

But there's also a pact, an agreement of at least semi-common purpose in a conscious and willing collaborative creative (critical) act, and it is this consciousness and mutuality that takes a collaboration beyond its surface ambiguities to allow 'something to come of it', for a reification. However, there's also something immensely generative through the likelihood that 'difference' (between collaborators, their voicings) sublimates and embeds innumerable other slippages and ambiguities. We can and can't know what our collaborator is doing and thinking as they introduce their words into the text.

Put simply, it is from this understanding that we set off on a journey through myriad texts that in their juxtapositions and elisions speak through and against each other with shifting levels of fluidity and abruptness. A collage, yes, but always written and drawn together with a singular unambiguous purpose that is understood to be ripe ground for generating unforeseen ambiguities. Is this a book written against William Empson's *Seven Types of Ambiguity*?[1] No, it's not. In fact, though it profoundly affected me when I was in my late teens, Empson's

---

1 www.ndbooks.com/book/seven-types-of-ambiguity/.

has little more than residual bearing on this book. If nothing else, I reject the system and the organisation. I am not seeking to move beyond ambiguity, I celebrate it. I am seeking to enter into the certainty of dubiety, if you wish. I know my opinions, but also know language has its ways beyond my control. I am glad for it. So, to be clear, I believe there's an ethical position to be taken over an issue that is primarily non-ambiguous, but that the creative expression of that position might well be generatively ambiguous. *Beyond Ambiguity*, however, is interested in the limits of both positions. There is a point where all ambiguities fail to be generative in the face of crisis, injustice, and planetary collapse. But as writers, as artists, as creators of asides to the site who reach *into* the site, we will necessarily engage with and proliferate ambiguities. It is the paradox that I explore through reifications and sublimations in what follows.

De-pastoral poetry of return: a statement to a friend

There are many discussions to have around 'poems of return' in relation to the theft of land from First Peoples. The pastoral is a definitive colonial construct – a colonial relationship to land that unambiguously seeks to usurp in practical terms and ambiguously in textual terms (play of voice, privileging of 'working' voices) – land for those working it, but also land in terms of those ruling over it. In the Australian context, pastoral is a deletion as well as a framework for myth-building and maintaining the occupation of place. It's too easy to get distracted by Virgil when the modern pastoral is a machine of aesthetics, capital and dispossession on a global scale.

I am looking at a de-pastoralising 'return'/'hand-back' poetry ... of course, there's no concrete 'handback' to be made in truth, because the land inviolably remains Aboriginal land, and the colonisers don't have anything to hand back because it's not theirs to hand back and never was, for all the claims, surveys, occupation, dispossession: theft. What I mean is a de-presencing, a de-occupying via acts of legal acknowledgement that the land was stolen and ALL belongs to First Peoples.

I am trying to write an *acknowledgement poetry* of 'return' of stolen ideas and knowledge and real 'returns' of land, and the space embodied in the poems written on that stolen land. This is a very serious thing for me, and I am working out how to write and enact it, but it's a start. The poems are ambiguous (I am told), but the moral-ethical purpose is entirely unambiguous. There is a right and a wrong in this, and, as one with 'settler heritage', I have a particular responsibility to act. And part of that acting is writing poems of address – but without permission from Aboriginal people when I refer to their lives and country, I am pushing ambiguity beyond the ethical. There are respectful ways of consulting – it enhances purpose through art.

I am de-spacing my own presence in language on usurped ground – return can take place in many ways and should, all concurrent. To reiterate – because reiterations are part of the poetics – the space of the poems is also stolen territory when it's written by non-First Peoples on First Peoples' country. I need to address this and I am. I cannot cope with the deceptions of 'landscape', the ambiguities of making a creativity while making no restitution. Writing, art practice, can too easily become a performance of activism while actually seeking to avoid real change – change that stops access to its very making. Ambiguity in this case becomes a *pretending*. While these injustices continue and get redefined so *so* many of us can pretend the issue of land is being addressed adequately – it is not.

So, a scenario: I see a native bird my son would also have loved to have seen as well, but he is absent. I am viewing it on stolen country (boodja), but also on *its* land. I wish land/country to be returned to its people, Noongar Aboriginal people, and also for the land to be acknowledged as the bird's as Noongar people know (and tell us). I am there, I am part of the moment, my son is absent. There is an unambiguous politics of presence, and yet there is an ambiguous (but sincere) relationship to the moment and its wonders. How is this to be written? Should it be written? I have the compulsion to write it while asking these questions. Can the poem be a site of negotiation (with or without an audience, with an Elder, with a community)? Is the poem enacting a site in which presence can also be part of an act of *deprescencing*? The poem is a field of contradictions, but it is being written 'knowingly'. I write, I try to ask and answer the questions within the poem-making.

And about 'Western Spinebill Sighting and the Absence of Tim'

Though Alfred Jarry's 'pataphysics' lurks behind the banksias of the following poem, really the question is: how does the western spinebill hold on in a narrow band of protected bushland that is being degraded by suburban overuse – leisure that erodes? Banksia blooms are unforgettable in all stages of their blooming, even in their death. The 'crumbling banksia' is sadly a comment on a death before its time as the eco-system comes under pressure from development, the colonial legacy. The Noongar name is 'Mangkatj': to learn more, go to Noongar Elder Neville Collard talking about them at http://whadjukwalking trails.org.au/media/swamp-banksia/.

Western spinebills ('booldjit' in Noongar language) are an exquisite honeyeater becoming less and less common.[2] They are suffering from the same environmental pressures as the banksias (which are defoliating, dying), though the bird illnesses they suffer are 'different' from plant illnesses, of course, but their 'intersectionality' is being collectively disturbed and destroyed.

Tim, our son (fourteen at the time), is concerned about their fate, as he is about the well-being of all birds and their habitats. He so wanted to see one that afternoon on the edge of winter, knowing we'd be 'waiting' for him at Bold Park nature reserve, but was at the Goethe Society (we came a long distance down from the country so he could attend), doing his language exercises. I created

---

2 See: www.climatewatch.org.au/species/birds/western-spinebill.

the poem to take the moment to him because he couldn't *be there*, but it also includes the critical scrutiny of the politics of colonial observation and invasiveness, which he'd expect.

The liminality of this poem is about the vagueness of 'hold' on what is seen, and what rights 'we' (he and I) do and don't have (largely don't have) in seeing, and about the portending of weather and loss and vulnerability. What can the poem do in the face of the degradation of habitat, of the rights of banksia and spinebills? How is this regionality of presence so afflicted by a global as well as local degradation (climate, extinction)?

Western Spinebill Sighting and the Absence of Tim

Tim is at a Goethe Society lesson
held near the Indian Ocean – he will
be conjugating and declining and – I know –
thinking of birds. He will feel excluded

when I tell him that I saw a western spinebill
at one of his favourite places on earth – Reabold Hill.
Had he been there he would have observed it closely,
listened carefully, and recorded all details in his bird book.

The spinebill would have been 'protected' inside a poem.
But in his absence I will meet the responsibility –
here it is, the bird, with agency intact, of itself.
As the sun set – and you can never see too many

suns setting into an ocean – a light shower
of rain fell and the elderly banksia candles
guttered. And the curved beak of the spinebill
portended the weather – longer days, but cold

and out of synch till they turn viciously hot. It knows,
Tim, as you know. How can we reset, recalibrate? How
can we ignore the restraints of that all-too-convenient
'pathetic fallacy' construct? And thus it flew again

into another, crumbling banksia, a banksia held together
only by half-light, then suddenly melting into night,
taking the spinebill with it into a deceptive peace,
adding more truth to a pataphysics than it warrants?

Retaining the memory of encounter is part of the drive to make the poem, but there's also the possibility of an obfuscation of seeing due to doubt about 'rights' to see – a semi-intentional 'forgetting' as a result of guilt about making an incursion into another creature's life-patterns outside of 'survival necessity'. This, for me, is part of the failure of aesthetic intent. I would argue that aesthetics consumes both certainty and ambiguity of and in perception, and if it has any generative 'essences', they reside in paradox and uncertainty, not in delineated outlines that can readily be mimicked, value-added, mass-produced, or, indeed, individualised to meet consumer (self) desiring. Violence and beauty, as played out in the Western game of aestheticising damage, are contested in this work, as they are in tangential ways in all my *modes of seeing* that have come out of colonialism and its adaptations, a Westernised education, the Westminster system which I rejected young as a pacifist anarchist, and so on and on … Ambiguity in aesthetics is diversion – aesthetics are inadequate as a means of rectification of achieving justice outside a path of delay and avoidance. That's not to say aesthetics can't have moral purpose, but that they can hinder us in their perceptions and portrayals of 'beauty' and 'order' as we reach towards unambiguous justice. I propose an anti-aesthetic ambiguity that uses Western structures as tools of undoing (I think ironically of the brilliant band Einstürzende Neubauten – 'Collapsing New Builds' and the anti-aesthetics of Blixa Bargeld) to reach towards unambiguous ethical outcomes. Aesthetic ambiguity is not adequate as a mode of decolonising restoration and respect.

All URLs were active as of 6 December 2020.

ACKNOWLEDGEMENTS

I would like to thank Gerard Greenway and Matthew Frost for their support over the decades in seeing this trilogy of activist poetics works into publication – publishing is a collaborative process, and a book grows through interaction. In the same way, I would also like to thank those I have conversed with for so long over issues pertaining to the interests of this work, including Nicholas Birns, Tim Dolin, Tony Hughes D'aeth, Philip Mead, Charmaine Papertalk-Green, Tracy Ryan and Russell West-Pavlov. And thanks, as always, to Paul Clarke and the production team at MUP, with a special thanks to Rachel Evans for her copy-editing work. I would also like to thank Dan Disney and Sarah Bailey for copyediting input at certain points. I am grateful to Curtin University for a Curtin Research Fellowship, which allowed me to work intensely on issues outlined in the introduction of this work, and for their facilitating interactions with colleagues and literary activists around the world. I acknowledge publications in which parts of this work first appeared (often in different or slightly different forms), which include: *Magma, The Conversation, Meanjin, Arena, The Australian, Westerly,* Judith Wright's *Selected Poems* (Carcanet, 1992 and also in my *Spatial Relations,* Rodopi, 2013, Vol. 1) and *Collected Poems* (Fourth Estate, 2016), *Granta, Australian Poetry Journal, Temporariness* (with Russell West-Pavlov, Narr, 2018), *New Directions in Contemporary Australian Poetry* (eds Disney and Howard, Palgrave, forthcoming), and *Mutually Said* blog (Kinsella and Ryan, http://poetsvegananarchist-pacifist.blogspot.com/). And thanks to Harpercollins (4th Estate), University of Western Australia Publishing, University of Queensland Press, and the various poets who have given support regarding some of the material in this volume. And I always acknowledge the traditional and custodial owners of the lands I so often inhabit and write about – the Ballardong Noongar people, the Whadjuk Noongar people, the Yued Noongar people and the Yamaji people. I do not feel that there is such a thing as the authorially 'exclusive' or unique text, but rather that I am part of many ongoing conversations and that what I write is an articulation of participation in activist literary discourse. Activism is participation, not ownership. This is, I hope, a work of communalism.

INTRODUCTION: LOCALITIES

In some ways, this book aims to develop textual and literary mechanisms – a *poetics* – for dialogue and exchange between different 'communities', in order to enhance positive communication and empathy, and lead to 'conflict' resolution, seeking 'common ground' for social and cultural interaction. This might be subtextual in most instances, but the suggestions are as relevant as the overt statements, and if this generates ambiguities, it also generates multiples points of departure from a status quo (of text, of reading, of context), from the nexus or tangled webbing of communications – it offers nodal points,[1] zones of agglomeration and coalescence, moments beyond the ambiguities.

Community, for the purpose of this document, is interpreted as a relatively 'localised' group of people with shared life-experiences, who often act in

---

1 Throughout this work, I use 'nodal point' as a temporal spatial terminology, with a subtext in the movement of concepts through branches (also consider 'mesh analysis'), and 'spatial networks' – conceptualised as points of choice (sometimes contradictory)/different pathways/alternatives/diversity/digression in occupation and presence of place. Terms that relate to crossover, intersection, vectors, graphs, and Venn Diagrams enact similar topologies of spatiality, of topography. The 'context' for this usage might be found in my earlier evocations and applications of this term in *Disclosed Poetics* (2007) and *Polysituatedness* (2017) but also in other of my critical works. It should go without saying that I am conscious of both feminist usages and contexts, and 'urban planning', 'transport networking' (and hubs), mapping, as well as 'physics' usages of 'intersectionality' and nodes – but the usage herein, whilst respectfully acknowledging the discourses that exist around such terms, is somewhat different in that it operates as subsets of ambiguity, and seeks its clarifications by coming out of those uncertainties. This does not mean it's not concerned with those other usages, especially in feminist discourse, but rather it subtexts spatiality out of the physical sciences (etc.) as point of departure. In the same way, I refer to the interlinked nature of my 'experimental' fiction writing as operating within an expanding parallel circuit. The issue is primarily one of spatiality, though, of course, all evocations are relevant in interpreting intent. In my case, it would be more relevant to say that I think of, say the 'hubs' as bushland and forests, maps as control mechanisms to be de-mapped in order to protect environment and respect peoples, and so on. Such nodal points always have polyvalent referentialities and ethical and political drivers. I think in terms of spatial 'nodalities'.

the mutual interest of that group, but also have different concentrations of sharings and interests, of common purpose and/or the mutual understanding of coping with difference and specificities. In many ways, community shares a language of comprehension, but not necessarily a literal language in common (though it can). Community is further differentiated in terms of those groupings of people sharing a geography and living facilities (say, in a village, shared buildings, locals laws etc) or as cultural groupings that move across geographical and physical boundaries (a demography of interest and advocacy, such as environmental interests in the international reduction of coal usage). There are internet communities, too, but they are less a concern for this book because the power-suck required to facilitate them is inimical to the *de-tech* undercurrents of this utterance. This is not to deny or attempt to delete their existence, especially as they are often extensions of 'on the ground' communities, but rather to consider community in non-digital ways (again).

The core principle here is the notion of exchange between communal and individual voices privileged in how they are received and heard outside their own communities, and those who are only (and often barely) heard within their own communities, struggling to be heard in a way that can implement positive change for themselves, their communities, and humanity as a whole. This basic issue is posited against a backdrop of environmental damage and compromise, of a marginalising discourse around issue of 'space' and 'place', and the wealth-flow toward already-wealthy communities.

'Place' studies largely emerge from the privileged learning enclaves of universities, and frequently fail to access the place-knowledge of communities that may not have access to means of 'broadcasting' what makes their 'local' knowledge relevant, dynamic and essential to themselves as well as to the wider world. Just as more 'local' knowledge is retrieved, recorded, contextualised and re-articulated through scholarly research – as we find in Australian Indigenous studies, where authority of source is shifted from the academic researcher to the community member, and I would maintain this as a positive model – I believe that we can take this principle further, by staging the 'research' discussions in 'the field', 'on location', and respectfully and non-appropriatively enacting that knowledge in literary contexts. And by this I do not mean exploiting Indigenous knowledges! In the same way, a broader model of locality might bring about a dialogue between different communities as well as different 'occupations' of localities. By 'a broader model of locality', I mean not only where we live or maybe come from, or where our family is located or is from, but where we are at a given time, with gradations of depth in interaction depending on time spent, input made 'into' that locality, and so on.

I wish to notionally (it's there, if not labelled!) extend my idea of the 'polysituated' self, in which no one person is of one place only, but rather is constituted by many places and is a nexus for many locations and place-inflections into the transnational, and into notions of communal belongings. In doing so, I am seeking to reconsider the comparative and inter-communal ways we deploy 'place', 'locality', 'space', 'belonging', 'alienation', and 'temporariness'.[2] It is essential to this book that we understand the limitations of internet dissemination (and dispersal and dilution) of knowledges, while at the same time being able to work with the medium if activist needs demand, but the irony of the 'energy-suck' and consequences of hardware manufacture more often obfuscate an environmental (and justice) outcome than deliver it.

I come to all of this through the focalisation of 'literature', in general, and poetry in particular, and often illustrate my arguments using such texts – I investigate, 'review', offer commentary on aspects of said texts, and offer 'opinions' pertaining to their contexts of writing and reading. But this book has an array of interwoven threads that are inter-disciplinary and certainly cross-genre, and range from creating what amount to *psychogeographic* (an appalling elision of complexity to my mind) 'maps' to 'unmapping' colonial imprints (see my works on this in *Activist Poetics: Anarchy in the Avon Valley*, and also in *Polysituatedness*).[3]

The book seeks to be multifaceted and polyvalent (as outlined below), but ultimately revolves around that single question: can literature, especially poetry, be used as a means of generative, restorative dialogue between different and sometimes opposed communities in different places, and also between different communities sharing a geography?

By approaching this problem with the belief that it is so, through a number of collaborative and individual critical and creative activities, I seek to confirm this belief, but also to create (further) textual means of enacting this rapprochement. Another core element of the 'problem' is what I term 'international regionalism' – a process of opening lines of international communication while respecting regional integrity. I have discussed this notion in many places (see *Disclosed Poetics*, *Activist Poetics*, *Spatial Relations* Vols 1 & 2, *Polysituatedness*, and also *Temporariness*), but do not articulate it much further here, as it is essentially the 'drive' behind all my work, not the specifics of this book in itself.

Central to this book is the interface between the creative and the scholarly – my ongoing concern, if not obsession. I just don't believe in the separation of modes of considering and discussing 'the world'. In clarifying the obvious

---

2 See 'temp(ə)rərɪnəs (Narr, 2018), a book I co-wrote with Russell West-Pavlov. As the book description goes: '*Temporariness* is a scandal in our culture of monumentalism and its persistent search for permanence. Temporariness, the time of the ephemeral and the performative, the time of speech, the time of nature and its constant changes – these times have little cultural purchase. In this volume two practitioners and theoreticians of time, space and the word embrace the notion of temporariness – seeing in it a site for a renewal of ways of thinking about ourselves, our language, our society and our environment. This collage of fragmentary genres approaches the notion of mitigated presence to build an atlas of intersections attentive to our own temporariness as the site of aesthetic and ethical responsibility. There are few (if any) books that explore these issues in quite the same way.'
3 John Kinsella, *Activist Poetics: Anarchy in the Avon Valley*, edited with an introduction by Niall Lucy (Liverpool University Press, 2010).

relationships between scholarly research work and writing in creative forms such as poetry or fiction, we not only contest the boundaries of genre and enliven them ('faction' is just one example), but even more relevantly, we will show that, rather than being anomalies or digressions, the conversations between scholars and creative writers are essential, constantly visible, and generative.

In the local, the visitor and the 'local' share some things in common, yet in others they are strongly differentiated. And locality is a matter of perceived degree. Where do the Indigenous local and non-Indigenous overlap – or not? And how might we further exchange, and take part in dialogue, to increase overlap (and is this desirable?) through creative acts? How much is the act of reading a text a visiting of that text? A visiting that means one doesn't damage in 'taking away'. It seems an ambiguous relationship, but it's not. I do not believe in copyright but I respect the integrity of cultural knowledge and do not consider myself as having a right of access to cultural spaces outside my own – rather, I believe in acts of permission, or staying respectfully distant. But appropriation too easily takes places unawares, and I think the act of reading creates an awareness of the act of writing, and a respectful conversation can take place between reader and text that allows each to grow.

These are questions we might ask when considering the temporal and spatial co-ordinates of belonging, and of what I term 'temporary locality'. The locality in terms of the earth itself, and also the conceptual locality of the text itself. As we move through different places, how much do we become part of them, and how much do they become part of us? How much will this book rub off on you and how much will you ignore or hope to forget or just feel indifferent to? Through such distracted considerations, can we – concretely – better structure discourse of exchange and tolerance that might result in fairer and more just arbitrations between people/s who have greater and lesser degrees of connections with that place, with the land itself? In other words, can reading practice help in real issues of rectifying wrongs and injustices? I believe it can.

Thinking over Hölderlin's poem, 'Evening Fantasy', and issues of welcome and hospitality, the 'unwelcome' is more often true for reasons of bigotry, yet also through genuine fear of loss as a consequence. Pivotal here is unravelling the guest-host codes into a meaningful manner of greeting and exchange without loss of identity.

A key aim is to create a focal point for literary and academic collaboration: for 'collaboration' to be a thing-in-itself, and to develop a critical language of collaborative intentions, approaches and outcomes. Too often, creative writers and literary scholars work alongside one another without their practices being linked in any concrete or knowledgeable way. Writers argue that scholars need the writing to critique; scholars argue that until death and time have given 'space' to consider an author's work in retrospect, no clear sense of its worth emerges.

I am arguing that poetry and literature in general live in their activist moment, the impactful moment of creation and original dissemination, as much as in the effect they have on cultures/readers at a later date, when they are absorbed and reconstituted. I believe scholars and writers *need* to work in collaboration on the same projects with their different outcomes in dialogue being applied to real concerns in the community: environmental (the degradation of a river system, of bushland, pollution, rising sea levels, loss of habitat), social (housing, homelessness, sanitation, public open space, walk trails) and cultural (literature across language difference, different cultures sharing space/proximity, what constitutes 'nation' and its consequences).

My book *Per Se*,[4] with Russell West-Pavlov, blends and blurs the lines between critical essay, creative response, mapping, visual imagery and collaborative dialogue. There are slight overlaps here, but they are suggestive rather than concrete. But I like to think of them as 'active' and part of the nexus of discussion. These facets of my critical and creative endeavour are deeply interwoven, and collaborative work is at the core of my practice. I have collaborated with many other writers, artists, musicians and academics over the last three-and-a-half decades. This book draws on these experiences, but focalises the actual act and mechanics of collaboration, for instance the aspects of my quarter of a century on-and-off collaboration/s with sociologist-novelist-poet-sculptor-artist Urs Jaeggi.

I am always collaborating, and always critiquing the nature and workings of these collaborations and creating comparative models. To understand the process is to understand the purpose. Methodology, as well as socially, ecologically and artistically generative outcomes, are tied to praxis itself. The ambiguities of sharing and creating works together take us beyond the ambiguities into reified activism. Into textual enactment.

This book, and the activities and activisms it hopes to stimulate, will hopefully contribute to an entirely new approach to creative thinking on 'locality per textuality', and ambiguity of text as a tool to concrete activist modes of intervention (and an understanding and accountability for the array of consequences of such actions) and an empathetic ecology in which poetry and literary texts become tools for analysing where we live, how we live and how we might improve our interactions with 'space'. The methodologies implied in the variegations and diversions and distractions of topoi and modes of expression in the process of making and reading this work *could* have application on all levels of 'being', from environmental healing through to resolving international differences over shared use of space. Sounds like a big claim, but it's not intended as such – I feel that poetically orientated textuality offers tools of positive intervention on a constant basis, if we want to use them as such. As I've said time and time again, poetry *can* stop bulldozers.

Regarding the vast body of spatial and place theory crossing many disciplines that pre-exist this book (and indeed the trilogy taken as a whole), the templates, approaches and models suggested or interacted with here *might* help extend

---

4 John Kinsella and Russell West-Pavlov, *Per Se* (Narr, 2022).

and synthesise a diverse array of material into a pragmatic critical discourse of activist textual intervention, but more importantly allow it to be a functional way of performing within the space of a poem/text itself. So rather than existing as theory alone, it would be embodied in the prosodic elements of poem-making as much as any other 'device' such as metre, rhyme, stanzas, mnemonics, the mimetic and the figurative.

This is not really a work of extensive critical analyses of texts, but rather an analysis of the affect and effect of encounter with texts which I have lived or spent time with in places (from the very local to entire countries) with which I have either direct or indirect association. A number of other threads become active throughout this consideration, such as 'history', 'ethics', public-private concerns, articulation of personal subjectivity in the face of greater social movements, and political connections and differences. I use the 'essay'/'article'/'review'/'fragment'/'speech'/'commentary' approach, as it helps create fluidity and flow that simulate the 'journey' aspect of the text. I have spent my entire adult life journeying, always returning to my 'home' in the Western Australian wheatbelt, around which this book ultimately 'circulates'.

Yet I have also had long-term homes and belongings in Cambridge, UK, in Ohio, in West Cork, Ireland, and I am increasingly connected to Tübingen in Germany. But other 'strong' points on my compass have included the islands of La Réunion, the Cocos-Keeling Islands (where I lived for a stretch in the mid-1990s), and many other zones/places. Though mostly not directly (and often for 'permission' reasons) they all feed into the 'locality' of this book – the nexus of its international regionalism, making nodal points, breaking away from those same points over time.

In a sense, this book has aspects of a mental 'travel narrative' that takes in the well-trodden ground of the 'awakening of the artist's imagination', but with the crucial difference that I wish to undo such motifs, to radicalise the way such journeys actually have an impact on cultural, literary and physical environments, what they appropriate and leave as residue. It's not a simple, polite picture of growth, but one that has consequences in sometimes hard-to-determine ways. As an activist poet, I have always been concerned with how a text might bring generative change without denying the rights of place, without acting as a colonising force in itself while trying to undo colonial urges and gestures.

I am also interested in considering how features of the land (primarily 'Australia' in this case) prompt certain approaches to writing: responsive, critical, ritualistic, imaginative and activist. This is yoked with a general transcultural poetics – in my case, a fascination with how poetries arise out of cultural differences as a means of bridging conversations, of creating dialogues between different cultural ways of seeing – to make for reading a world literature as an organic, interactive means of communication.

Ultimately, though this is part of an ongoing journey of literary encounter for me, I constantly try to undo motifs of exploration, 'retracing' and unravelling lines of colonial intrusion – lifting the trails out of land, sea and air. Hopefully, the book critiques this form of conceptual movement in its colonial manifestation as an empathetic act with transitional movements of people through migration of necessity and refugee dislocation.

Another subtext throughout the whole will be 'sites of protest' or maybe nodal points of activism. Over my life, I have made many points of contact with 'place' through activism and trying to create conversations between different local rights issues. For example, anti-war protests in Ohio and Perth, Western Australia segue with 'Occupy' protests in London and Cambridge, and all cross-talk in poems and literary writing. Though not the direct questions of this book, always when I comment on a 'local' text I am thinking comparatively in terms of *how* reading literatures of those places has affected these interactions and articulations of resistance. I am interested in where conversations across cultural spaces meet, how we establish nexus points and matrixes of literary sharing, especially as they emanate from points of contact in landscape (e.g. Kenyon College, Cambridge and so on). The section of the 'conversations' between Evelyn Shakir and George Ellenbogen in their respective memoirs is pivotal in this attempt. I have long been interested in spaces where, say, Hebrew and Arabic writers can share textuality, and how this reflects on a non-state issue of sharing and co-existence (I am an anarchist pacifist who tries to work outside 'states', as a constructive means of discussing people in place). I try to consider divisions as acting as *points de repère* rather than separations, and I find such traces in these wonderful memoirs written in English.

What I am essentially looking to do is undo 'linear' modes of reading texts. I learnt to speed-read when I was thirteen – diagonally across the page where text runs left to right. This contesting of the manner of writing, of the rules by which writers operate in telling their 'stories', is done at the point of interaction with text. Where I have, in the past, written of a 'polysituatedness' of place, I wish to unread texts through the momentum of changing locations of reading.

So, a text I read before travelling to a place – say, about Baudelaire travelling to Mauritius and La Réunion in 1841 – is read in wheatbelt Western Australia, then 're-read' in-situ (another of my favoured terms) in order to destabilise an overall response. Readings of a text are often as conforming as the writing (the act of writing *is* a conforming act, even if the intent and content are 'radical') according to the patterns of national and group languages, and I want to decode the control mechanisms that make our readings necessarily prescriptive and 'adhering' to the language environment in which we are operating. No text says what we think it says, is my basic contention, and the drama of reading needs to be scrutinised, the theatre of expectation we create in engaging with literature challenged. As readers, we are performing as much as writers.

'Movement' in and through this book is about destabilising referents in order to consider them in different lights – for writer and reader, I think. I am arguing for something outside (or beyond or even contrary to) mimesis as the actuality of texts – they do not imitate a reality, they are the servants of the falseness of the reality that the machines of control foist upon us. The text knows it is perpetrating untruths to maintain the terms for its own existence and persistence.

Texts, even deplorable ones such as those by de Sade, conjure a reality to which they seek to make us subservient, as does the speculative, in which verisimilitude takes us along for the ride that can't be 'real'. In essence, in (re)identifying place as the authentic grounds of the text, I am challenging the grounds for 'literature' itself. The damage to environment, to land, will continue as long as we valorise the art over its sources.

In this *unreading*, which becomes a generator of ambiguities, we are compelled to move beyond because unravelling to their unambiguous origins gives us truths we can't use without sending them back through a process of ambiguity to create figurative language that can escape the comprehensions and oppressions of the censors, of the corporate state. I propose reading against epiphany, against catharsis (which too often serves subjectivity, but not the biosphere!), and against conclusions, and rather look to dismantling of texts into component parts of experience and place, but also beyond, to encounter their ambiguities as a stage on the journey towards justice, and so we can better understand *why* they were constructed (as such) in the first place. I am arguing for a counter-literary reading of 'literary' texts. Open text has a very different meaning in this unmapping of the literary geography of 'the world', even where a handful of points on the globe come into reading-view.

Though this book is about quite 'localised' English-language texts, I *am* an enthusiast for a world literature with regional inflections. I am interested in interacting with local community where appropriate and where 'wanted' and welcome, and in considering how such interactions affect the way we read a literature of landscape, and also how things like what one comes across in a local bookshop (they still exist) can affect the way those (un)readings behave/function/occur. And though 'the world' is in many ways absent from this book, it is eternally subtextually present with a conscious decolonising 'reading of'. Being in a specific place at a specific time does, obviously, change our interaction with its textuality. Being absent and not writing about it, but thinking of 'that place' when writing of another (or a text in another place), doesn't mean it is absent from the moment or the text being written. That has positive (acknowledgement) and negative (infiltrating, consuming, appropriating) connotations. For a time in the mid-1990s, I lived on the Cocos (Keeling) Islands, one of the most isolated places on the planet in terms of distance to other human habitation. Reading nineteenth-century 'explorer documents' while *on* the islands, and reading Charles Darwin on reef formation, and writing poems and the thinking that went into writing a novel (eventually to become *Post-colonial*), and the 'collecting' of local stories (with permission, in consultation with locals, and in order to contest official colonial versions), all entirely changed my view of the place and what is or isn't 'literature', and what that might mean in terms of reading texts elsewhere. Something slipped, something destabilised. I don't discuss this in this book, but I have in other works (the novel *Post-Colonial …* and in *Temporariness* with Russell West-Pavlov … and other textual zones), but the 'experience' of being there and writing of there necessarily affects my writing of all place. 'Non-presence' is no marker of 'absence'.

As a gesture of solidarity for an oppressed people whose struggle is ongoing and whose situation is dire, I am going to add a statement here regarding the Rohingya people. This is a preface I wrote for the anthology *I Am A Rohingya: Poetry from the Camps and Beyond*. To place such a document of support as this in the context of this nodal point-aspiring book seems to me a just and positive act – my purpose is to prioritise the situation of the people in the camps, and to bring attention to the superb poetry coming out of such need and distress. The needs of people in distress, of communities under pressure, and the well-being of the biosphere are the only reason for a book such as this to exist; it has no other worth.

> *I Am a Rohingya* implores the world to listen to the spirit of a people who have experienced and continue to experience some of the worst human rights abuses, but who, even under extreme duress and the constant reality of violence from the Myanmar state, know the spirit and intactness of their voice, their right to be a people and to live in the land that is their home. The suppression of the Rohingya by the machinery of British colonialism, then the military dictatorship, and the failure of post-dictatorship government to arrest the attack on the Rohingya, and what is essentially an apartheid condition, have brought the people to speak out of their refugee camps along the border with Bangladesh, and to hope in language and the aurality of their language, to see their poetry on the page, and to make poetry do the work it needs to do so that outsiders can hear, can understand.
>
> The remarkable Rohingya poet Mayyu Ali says in an interview with editor James Byrne that concludes this collection, a collection I consider a most important document of creative utterance: 'Writing for Rohingya people is activism. For me, a Rohingya, and a victim of the slow-burning genocide in Myanmar, imagism is far removed from activism.' And in this is the absolute truth of these poems – they must speak out, because they are from a crisis that must be addressed right now. Nonetheless, a powerful imagism of life-awareness, of what is being denied an entire people as well as every individual, speaks constantly and powerfully under every expression of the reality. The beauty of the land and forest that are being denied a people, the beauty of the people's cultural expression and their rights to their own history as well as a shared history, are denied, and these poems refuse this denial – these poems claim the beauty back.
>
> This collection is a call to readers to listen and help, to bring hope. It's an affirmation of a strong community who know who they are. The energy and zest of language, of being able to speak at an angle from life itself, enhances their lives. I hope that it helps bring optimism and material improvement to the lives of the Rohingya, and that they can return safely to their home and be treated as a people with the rights of all other people. There is brilliance in here![5]

---

5 James Byrne and Shehzar Doja (eds) *I Am a Rohingya: Poetry from the Camps and Beyond* (Arc Publications, 2019), Preface.

PART ONE

The relationship between issues of ambiguity in creating and reading literary texts, and making use of those texts in environmental and 'rights' activism, can seem incongruous, and frequently even adversarial, but in this section I try to reconcile matters of clarity in commitment with evasiveness in textual slippage. The chapter begins with a poem of unambiguous pro-environment activist intent that, nonetheless, carries its own 'internal' ambiguities. This section considers the nature and implications of such apparent contradictions. From considerations of ambiguities which refuse 'definition' and lead us to 'push beyond ambiguity' in an attempt to maintain clarity of purpose, and the generative slippages of understanding/misreading, we read text outside the investments of institutions (academic/schooling/government etc); we encounter the question of how we use these texts for activist purposes. Considering the making of adaptations and versions out of Hölderlin's poetry, and inflecting through Ivan Illich's 'Deschooling Society', I write, 'I want textual analysis to lead to an articulation of defiance against forces of exclusion and oppression. The university might well have an official policy of supporting cultural, gender, ethnic and even political diversity, but it will never support a position that resists the administrative bedrock upon which it is based.' Concluding the section is 'The truth should be in the blurb', in which I argue that documents of support (blurbs, encomiums, reference letters etc) should operate as an extension of textual activism and be documents of responsibility. I say: 'All of the documents-of-support I have written over the last twenty-five years for others actually fit into a narrative of justice, environmentalism and anti-aesthetics, even when the work itself might seem far from these concerns.' In this, one exchanges/interacts with the text – a sharing rather than a comment from an often (mis)perceived position of 'authority'.

Part one

How does the activist cope with ambiguity?

This poem is more than likely unambiguous in its message, but is made up of many linguistic ambiguities and probably quite a few ambiguities of meaning:

The Bulldozer Poem[1]

Bulldozers rend flesh. Bulldozers make devils
of good people. Bulldozers are compelled to do
as they are told. Bulldozers grimace when they

tear the earth's skin – from earth they came.
Bulldozers are made by people who *also* want new
mobile phones to play games on, *and* to feed families.

Bulldozers are observers of phenomena – decisions
are taken out of their hands. They are full of perceptions.
They will hear our pleas and struggle against their masters.

Bulldozers slice & dice, bulldozers tenderise, bulldozers
reshape the sandpit, make *grrrriiing* noises, kids' motorskills.
Bulldozers slice the snake in half so it chases its own tail,

writing in front of its face. Bulldozers are vigorous
percussionists, sounding the snap and boom of hollows
caving in, feathers of the cockatoos a whisper in the roar.

Bulldozers deny the existence of Aether, though they know
deep down in their pistons, deep in their levers, that all
is spheres and heavens and voices of ancestors worry

at their peace. Bulldozers recognise final causes, and embrace
outcomes that put them out of work. There's always more
scrub to delete, surely … surely? O *continuous tracked tractor*,

O *S* and *U* blades, each to his orders, his skillset. Communal
as D9 Dozers (whose buckets uplift to asteroids waiting
to be quarried). O bulldozer! your history! O those Holt tractors

working the paddocks, O the first slow tanks crushing
the battlefield. The interconnectedness of Being. Philosopher!
O your Makers – Cummings and Caterpillar – O great *Cat*

---

1 This poem can be used for environmental protection activist purposes without acknowledgement. I have also used it in my poetry book *On the Outskirts* (University of Queensland Press, 2019) and in ˈtɛmp(ə)rərɪnəs (with Russell West-Pavlov). Its further replication here seems relevant.

Beyond ambiguity

> we grew up in their thrall whether we knew it or not – playing
> sports where the woodlands grew, where you rode in after
> the great trees had been removed. You innovate and flatten.
>
> We must know your worldliness – working with companies
> to make a world of endless horizons. It's a team effort, excoriating
> an eco-system. Not even you can tackle an old-growth tall tree alone.
>
> But we know your power, your pedigree, your sheer bloody
> mindedness. Sorry, forgive us, we should keep this civil, O dozer!
> In you is a cosmology – we have yelled the names of bandicoots
>
> and possums, of kangaroos and echidnas, of honeyeaters
> and the day-sleeping tawny frogmouth you kill in its silence.
> And now we stand before you, supplicant and yet resistant,
>
> asking you to hear us over your war-cry, over your work
> ethic being played for all it's worth. Hear us, hear *me* –
> don't laugh at our bathos, take us seriously, forgive
>
> our inarticulateness, our scrabbling for words as you crush
> us, the world as we know it, the hands that fed you, that made you.
> Listen not to those officials who have taken advantage
>
> of their position, who have turned their offices to hate
> the world and smile, kissing the tiny hands of babies
> that you can barely hear as your engines roar with power.
>
> But you don't see the exquisite colour of the world, bulldozer –
> green is your irritant. We understand, bulldozer, we do –
> it is fear that compels you, rippling through eternity,
>   embracing the inorganics of modernity.

Ambiguity in a poem can be the generator of a desire to reconsider, to alter, to question. Activist poetry – specifically poetry that seeks to halt environmental damage – is about clearly delineated outcomes, and yet if the poem doesn't enrich the reader in intellectual, spiritual, artistic and/or emotional ways, its impact is necessarily diluted or lost. It's not that the activist poem needs to be 'more than statement', but rather that, in being poetry, it will necessarily be many things at once – many versions of itself, at least some of which will be beyond the poet's understanding.

Language itself generates meanings, and its meanings change over time. Sound, visual references, shape and words themselves will bring different meanings to different people at different times in different places. And this is good and necessary, and in recognising this, activist poets are acknowledging the intimacy with which they are connected to what it is they are trying to protect, to save. Even if we feel that 'nature' should exist outside the human, we still need to understand how we do or don't connect with this.

Ambiguity in a poem generates ways of considering this without setting rules. Can a figurative poem be directly activist? Or does a poem need to be more rather than less polemical to show its integrity regarding change? Can we create an activist poem that has characteristics of metaphor and polemic, and fuse them into something dynamic, ambiguous, indirect, yet still intense and capable of encouraging people to reconsider a situation? Not to tell people what to do, but to encourage them to investigate an issue in diverse ways, to find that language compels us towards liberation and a just position regarding the natural world and our relationship to it? The self as a mirror to the biosphere.

Maybe we can write a rhetorical lyric, we can say – we can rant – but let the poem open those proverbial 'doors of perception' of which we are not even aware when we write. The awareness often comes later. Interestingly, the poet Louis MacNeice (whose politics and ethics were very different from my own, which is fine!), wrote in his *Collected Poems* 'If I had been writing a didactic poem proper, it would have been my job to qualify or eliminate these overstatements and inconsistencies.'[2] First, the idea of writing a purely 'didactic' poem seems odd to me personally, though I can be didactic. But a poem through the act of being a poem undermines its own certainties, and the constraint that form (open or closed) imposes on a reading necessarily bends as much as directs what is being said. It's just not that conclusive, surely?

My purpose is not to define versions of ambiguity (Empson's 'Seven Types' or, for example, to cite *The New Princeton Encyclopedia of Poetry and Poetics*:[3] 'Beardsley, Kooij, and Rimmon make a case for restricting the term "ambiguity" to utterances whose multiple interpretations are mutually exclusive and thus lead to indecisiveness of meaning' (p. 41). Rather I wish to acknowledge ambiguity's essential nature in the poem. In writing an activist poem, we need knowledge of polysemy and of ambiguity – this being, to quote Empson, 'any verbal nuance, however slight, which gives room for alternative reactions to the same piece of language' (p. 40 in the *Princeton*). It is essential to know that whatever we declare as a wrong or a right is actually open to reinterpretation and to misinterpretation. We need to move beyond rhetoric, beyond linguistics and critical discourse, and go to the essence of crisis and work with language under that pressure. The misreading of a text should be the guide, the generator, rather than the specifics of what we want to convey.

A poem is ineffective as an activist moment if we have not understood that meaning is never stable. However, this is not a model, and there is no such thing as an activist poem per se – a poem responding to, for example, an ecological crisis can never be generic as though each crisis is part of a greater ecological crisis; its co-ordinates and variables are specific, if interlinked. So we are creating sequences of interconnected poems that are nonetheless 'case'-specific, or maybe undoing cases.

---

2 Louis MacNeice, *Collected Poems* (Wake Forest University Press, 2013, p. 791).
3 *The New Princeton Encyclopedia of Poetry and Poetics*, edited by Alex Preminger and T. V. F. Brogan (Princeton University Press, Princeton, 1993).

Beyond ambiguity

But are we really talking about variations of 'didactic poetry'? Are we creating an opposition, or maybe a compatible contrary to 'ambiguous poetry'? Of course not. Didactic poetry, like all poetry, can be ambiguous. When I talk of an 'activist poem', I am talking about something that will inevitably be ambiguous in varying degrees, but to a lesser or great degree didactic. Yet even with 'didactic' poetry – a poetry of 'teaching and learning' – what constitutes such qualities is elusive. Back to the *Princeton*: 'Aware of such proliferating contexts, we try to focus here chiefly (but not exclusively) on poetry which clearly *intends* "useful teaching," embodying Horace's "instruction *and* delight" in the genre of "didactic poems"' (p. 292). Well, if I am being didactic in my activist poems, I am doing so to inform as extension of witness, and I do hope to bring positive change, but I am certainly not interested in 'delight', unless it be 'delight' in the agency and intactness of the 'natural world'.

Late in the *Princeton* entry, we read: 'In sum, modern didacticism assumed protean forms that could no longer be forced into the genre classifications of the Augustans' (p. 294). And this would accord with the contemporary possibilities for activist poems that are necessarily ambiguous. The condition of our presence on the earth is no more ambiguous than that of any other life-form, but our relationship with the earth has become increasingly ambiguous. The very act of typing this, of speaking this in a modern performance space, is creating a relationship with the life of the planet itself, a relationship that is at best ambiguous, and at worst, hypocritical. Poems of activism have to be informed by this knowledge – and if not in the writing (as we'd hope), certainly in the experiencing. Activist poems augment and maybe extend direct action, but they rarely operate alone – they perform best in atmospheres of protest, of refusal to comply with the damage being done.

My opinions, attitudes, ethics and politics are not remotely ambiguous. I am a vegan anarchist pacifist, and believe in a non-violent and gradual evolution of the state into smaller communal fragments of consensus and dialogue. I call this 'international regionalism'. It is not isolationist, but it is respectful of difference, geography, culturality and a mutuality of autonomy. On the other hand, though my poems can often be very direct accusations and certainly witnessings, with direct opinion coming through loud and clear, overall I'd say I write an ambiguous poetry.

The act of poetry itself doesn't necessarily have to introduce ambiguity, as much traditional ritualistic song seems to show, but wherever there is figurative language, there is slippage, and even the fixed points of a song alter over time, in the ongoing process of reinterpretation. It is too easy to become anthropological in reading poems as ritual, especially within traditional contexts, which is to colonise symbol and metaphor, to reinvent similes. Poetry, by and large, contains at least aspects of ambiguity because it is repeated – whether through mnemonics and memory, or the passing down of written/inscribed texts. Ambiguity increases as time passes and the originating moment of the poem-song-text is 'lost'.

Ambiguity is more 'threatening' to state-corporate-military control than even didacticism. If the power structures can't comprehend something, they either ignore it or destroy it. A lot of poetry of protest survives because it simply isn't 'got' (understood). Which doesn't mean it is ineffective – often, it means it is highly effective. Meaning is fluid if the form of the poem is relatively stable. And form suggests a kind of conservatism, an inherited recognisable model that operates as an acceptable template. Even the word 'poem' is a kind of state permission to perform a literary act – we all know that 'poetry' is at the core of not only many religious texts but also official expressions of state. Here I mean those poems written for coronations, inaugurations, military victories, celebration of a new building.

On the other hand, poems are also written to express anti-war, republican, anti-state and other oppositions to the status quo. The poem can contain the radical and the conservative and it's this ambiguity in form, in genre, in process and identification, that makes poetry such a valuable mode of radical expression.

In 2015 the state government of New South Wales in Australia published a booklet for schools on how to identify and suppress radicalism in students. Supposedly a 'response' to the radicalisation of Australian youth by operatives of the Islamic State and other violent fundamentalist Islamic groups, the government used the crisis of violence to seek to control other forms of oppositional behaviour by defining them as violent threats to the ordinary Australian citizen.

One case study used in this booklet for schools involved a hypothetical student who became a forest-camp anti-logging protester. We follow the narrative of her 'radicalisation' through assault charges in resisting police and loggers, through to her 'seeing the light' and joining a moderate 'official' ecological group. This narrative is more than an appalling propaganda exercise; it is an overt use of the state-run education system to control an individual's relationship to the state.

Ecological protests are very rarely cases of 'attack', but almost always cases of 'defence'. Loggers and the police most often attack the protesters trying to save ancient woodland from being destroyed by the state and its capitalist overlords. An act of sabotage against logging machinery is very different from police charging down protesters with horses and batons. I know, because I have seen these things at first hand. To align acts of public terror with acts of ecological protection is not only to confuse the issues, but to exploit violent acts of terrorism in order to control other aspects of social and political freedom.

To my mind, poetry must wrest control of language back from these oppressors and propagandists, and undo the state and business control of learning. Poetry is a means of teaching freedom of thought and expression, as well a vehicle for free expression. Ambiguity allows us to write in invisible ink on one hand, beyond detection, yet also to speak loudly and boldly at once. This is not a paradox – it is the very nature of poetry itself, and always has been.

So who is speaking, who is the state to blame for the voice of the poem, for what it does and doesn't say, for what it enacts or 'incites'? What of the ambiguity of the self, ambiguity of the unified self, ambiguity of (personal) pronouns, ambiguity of responsibility, ambiguity of audience, ambiguity of identity and identification? In writing activist poems, in trying to prevent the destruction of habitat, there is a need to be very conscious of the poem's voice – how much of our 'selves' is in there.

Why does this matter? Well, primarily it's a question of integrity and a willingness to be held accountable for what you are 'saying'. But it's also a question of authenticity and reliability – is the poem's voice to be trusted? Can a poem that talks of the destruction of forest be effective if it is full of wrong data? – if the details don't match the situation? Isn't this ambiguity? Isn't this figurative? Can we, for example, say in a poem something about a type of bird or animal that isn't actually present in the forest that we are trying to protect? Is the 'talismanic', protective nature of the poem impaired by what seems 'misinformation'? An experienced teacher of poetry might reply, Well, it's a poem, not a scientific report, what does it matter? What is at stake in the poem are a mood, a suggestion, a conceit, and a deeper point of affect.

That's all true, and I think data isn't vital to making a poem create a mood – after all, we can read a Shelley poem at an Australian forest protest and it can have a powerful effect on an audience, can inspire them to further action through a correlative of affect and mood; but it won't have the same effect as a poem written by, say, an Aboriginal Australian poet who has a profound knowledge of the environment about which he or she is writing. Why is this? Because inherent and specific knowledges of a place extend that place into the audience's psyches. A sharing of presence takes place.

I always try to include correct and informed data in my activist poems, though that data often creates images and impressions that move far away from the 'science' of locale or situation. There are many levels of awareness occurring in any poem, and I like my poems to allow these breadths of expression.

Poems are complex sites, especially when they seem to be at their most obvious. And this complexity allows us to perform many roles of self and non-self in the space of a poem. The activist poem is always going to be about the place, the subject one is trying to protect or advocate for, but sometimes 'I' is too potent a force to exhibit in the poem, and a move away from the lyrical I is far more effective. How close or how distant the self is in a poem can change the poem's reception and potency in all sorts of ways.

In writing poems of protection and protest in recent environmental actions, I have made use of the 'ambiguous' and evasive figure of Sweeney.

Sweeney the Barn Owl Opens His Eyes Wide in Broad Daylight

Sweeney looks down at the people coming out of the hospital –
they have seen him, he knows it in his bones. Yes, now their eyes
search his eyes and the shock of light reaches as far inside

as the flames that drove him out of the tall tree on the hillside.
Where can I rest? he asks them. The Main Roads are cutting down
all the old-growth wandoos and salmon gums and York gums,

slicing through their anniversaries with a righteousness
that will truck no argument. These living heritage buildings
we conduct our lives in and around, *our* places of eating and worship.

Sweeney shuts his eyes on them, high up in the gum that clings
to the edge of the car-park. Tonight he will fly south-east, aiming
to reach the great trees still remaining on the York-Quairading

Road before they are brought down, before red-tailed phascogale
and Carnaby's black cockatoo and rainbow bee-eater are forced
to find somewhere else to feed and nest and hide from owl, or *vanish* –

and in the matutinal revelation that abbreviates his waking hours,
upside down in a tree-killer's world, Sweeney will hoot at their stupidity,
a klaxon-call just before the crash that will wipe us all out.[4]

On the other hand, where something has directly affected the well-being of my own son – also protesting – I am personal and direct: a parent speaking to parents, to children, as we all are:

Accounts – to the Premier of Western Australia

I hold you accountable for the trauma our thirteen-year-old
is going through as habitat for the birds he loves is destroyed.

I hold you accountable for the emphysema of the biosphere,
that gasp you add to our last gasps, deoxygenated, stranded by the road.

I hold you accountable for the zoo of death, for the ark scuttled
and going down with all hands on board, for survivors shot on the surface.

I hold you accountable for helping boil the planet in its own oil,
for encasing it in bitumen dredged from the pits of hell.

I hold you accountable for making science a convenience store
in which well-fed bullies stuff their baskets without paying.

I hold you accountable for cruelty and torture, for casualties
you don't acknowledge, for ignoring alternatives to feed your vanity.

I hold you accountable for treating life as a game in which winner
takes all, a psychology of childhood instilled by abusive adults.

---

4 See John Kinsella, *The Wound* (Arc Publications, 2019).

And, extending responses to an imposing and malign State, I take a late nineteenth-century poem by the 'Goldfields poet' 'Willy Willy: The Boulder Bard', which ironises both the ode's form and a place very far away from the ode's origins and conventions, and reconfigures the ode as a critique of the State in its impact on the local, and as a broader generic entity of oppression, control and absurdity. So, starting with the late nineteenth-century piece of ironic versifying that is a declaration of both extremity and difference, but also of a weird camaraderie of connection in this 'isolation' (of course, there is irony in its being an expression of alienation on stolen indigenous land which, for the local people, had been anything but a 'hell'):

'Ode to Westralia'

Land of Forrests, fleas and flies,
Blighted hopes and blighted eyes,
Art thou hell in earth's disguise,
        Westralia?

Art thou some volcanic blast
By volcanoes spurned, outcast?
Art unfinished – made the last
        Westralia?

Wert thou once the chosen land
Where Adam broke God's one command?
That He in wrath changed thee to sand,
        Westralia!

Land of politicians silly,
Home of wind and willy-willy,
Land of blanket, tent and billy,
        Westralia.

Home of brokers, bummers, clerks,
Nest of sharpers, mining sharks,
Dried up lakes and desert parks,
        Westralia!

Land of humpies, brothels, inns,
Old bag huts and empty tins,
Land of blackest, grievous sins
        Westralia.[5]

My response comes in the context of oppression, dispossession, environmental destruction and some people's desire to deny the truths of these issues. The

---

[5] In *The Fremantle Press Anthology of Western Australian Poetry*, edited by John Kinsella and Tracy Ryan, (Fremantle Press, 2017, p. 107).

question to ask, maybe, is whether or not it's more or less ambiguous than the 'original' (in itself a somewhat faint and distant simulacrum and parody of the Pindarian Ode)? The politics and ethics at work are obviously different, but it's worth wondering where ambiguity and didacticism fade in and out of perspective. Does humour in the first enhance or intensify ambiguity; do my version's brutal confrontations with what I consider a sad reality manifest ambiguities in its exponential metatexts (the form of the ode itself, the 'Ode to Westralia', Plato, the trajectories of rhetoric and Latin poetry, 'popular culture' references, environmentalism, Victoriana, contemporary political discourse etc)? Both are metatextual poems, of course, but the first is speaking with those in the know, those in the goldfields who share the experience of the 'outback'. Mine is a direct confrontation with authority. But both are anti-authoritarian. Here's mine:

A New Ode to Westralia: Anthem for All Future Sporting Events

The state is killing our souls
The state has murdered the people – some they murder over and over
The state has deployed vicious antibodies to kill the good cells
    and let the infection thrive
The state has equated work with destruction and manipulated the outcome –
    remember, the state has no love for unions.
The state deployed its shock troops who watched on as poems were yelled
    at them, their commander marshalling attitude, saying: how can we
    shut this one up? Poets of the world, take notice. They will close
    you down the moment you break free of your anthologies,
    your safety in pages of literary journals, the comforts
    of award nights.
The state shapes itself out of the dust rising from underforest
    which is its soul exposed to a caustic, toxic atmosphere
    made by so many other such actions of malice – the shape
    is cartoonish to start with, then like a Hollywood effect
    then just terrifying ectoplasm feeding on sap and blood and grit.
The state chips and mulches because it has heard rumours of Plato's
    theory of forms and thinks it needs a new translation full of local
    business inflection, full of their own brand of 'civilisation'.
The state has no intention of letting traditional owners maintain traditional
    places of worship of culture of belonging – it's always been about
    the twin poles of denial and deletion.
The state has reservoirs of species names and the odd pressed sample
    of a flower they wish only to remain as a Latin name and a collectible,
    gathering in worth, which is the essence of market economics,
    rolling on through the bushland with gung-ho in-your-face finality.
The state wants you to gasp as the tall tree cracks and is brought down fast,
    the pair of tawny frogmouths lifting to nowhere, dazzled by daylight.

And finally, the seemingly unambiguous address to a chainsaw – extension of the state. It takes us back to the Bulldozer poem with which I began, in which 'modernity's' complex and shifting array of ambiguities is operating at full tilt to create a desire for liberation, for the natural over the machine choice. In the Bulldozer poem, modernity is associated with inorganics and destruction – the bulldozer will become redundant if the destruction is halted:

> it is fear that compels you, rippling through eternity,
>   embracing the inorganics of modernity.

And in the same way, the Chainsaw poem does the same, but differently – modernity represented as loss, not gain for the planet and, ultimately, for humanity. The Chainsaw poem was written back in the early 2000s, so the Bulldozer poem echoes that poem, the personified object ironising the human failure to empathise with other living things. In 'Chainsaw', the machine becomes an extension of the human, almost organic – this irony is at play in both poems.

Chainsaw

The seared flesh of wood, cut
to a polish, deceives: the rip and tear
of the chain, its rapid cycling
a covering up of raw savagery.
It is not just machine. In the blur
of its action, in its guttural roar,
it hides the malice of organics.
Cybernetic, empirical, absolutist.
The separation of Church and State,
conspiracies against the environmental
lobby, enforcement of fear, are at the core
of its modus operandi. The cut of softwood
is deceptive, hardwood dramatic: just
before dark on a chill evening
the sparks rain out – dirty wood,
hollowed by termites, their digested
sand deposits, capillaried highways
imploded: the chainsaw effect.
It is not subtle. It is not ambient.
It is trans nothing. A clogged airfilter
has it sucking up more juice –
it gargles, floods, chokes
into silence. Sawdust dresses boots,
jeans, the field. Gradually
the paddock is cleared, the wood
stacked in cords along the lounge-room wall.
A darkness kicks back and the cutout
bar jerks into place, a distant chainsaw
dissipates. Further on, some seconds later,
another does the same. They follow

> the onset of darkness, a relay of severing,
> a ragged harmonics stretching back
> to its beginning – gung-ho,
> blazon, overconfident. Hubristic
> to the final cut, last drop of fuel.

In the face of global habitat-destruction, it would seem the time for radical solutions to the problem. But radical solutions, and pragmatic outcomes that are non-violent and that damage nothing in their implementation, are difficult to achieve.

The work of a radical feminist such as Shulamith Firestone's *The Dialectic of Sex*[6] might identify a problem in the biology of reproduction limiting women's freedom and ensuring the damaging infrastructure of patriarchy, but her solution of cybernetic laboratory reproduction and gestation is a destructive process in terms of technology's impact on the planet, aside from being a denial of free will. Firestone says, 'The division of labour would be ended by the elimination of labour altogether (through cybernetics). The tyranny of the biological family would be broken.' This may be true, but a tyranny of further environmental exploitation to facilitate such cybernetics, even if they could be considered an answer to this inequality and oppression, would be the result. The scale of biological machinery required would come at a cost to the biosphere.

So, solutions to radical problems require radically non-invasive answers. It should be noted that writing out of her time (the late 1960s), a radical correction seemed an answer. Those males giving up ownership of the family (Engels)[7] and sharing the role of child-rearing have at least made a step in the right direction. In this context, let us consider the activist power of Anne Sexton's poem 'Unknown Girl in the Maternity Ward' and its lines regarding the responsibility of life itself falling entirely on the young woman who has just given birth in the absence of the baby's father, and the social pressures on that circumstance:[8]

> Down the hall the baskets start back. My arms
> fit you like a sleeve, they hold
> catkins of your willows, the wild bee farms
> of your nerves, each muscle and fold
> of your first days. Your old man's face disarms
> the nurses. But the doctors return to scold
> me. I speak. It is you my silence harms.
> I should have known; I should have told

---

6   Shulamith Firestone, *The Dialectic of Sex* (The Women's Press, 1979). www.marxists.org/subject/women/authors/firestone-shulamith/dialectic-sex.htm.

7   As noted by Firestone: 'Engels did observe that the original division of labour was between man and woman for the purposes of child-breeding; that within the family the husband was the owner, the wife the means of production, the children the labour; and that reproduction of the human species was an important economic system distinct from the means of production.'

8   First published in Anne Sexton, *From Bedlam and Part Way Back* (Houghton Mifflin, 1960).

> them something to write down. My voice alarms
> my throat. 'Name of father – none.' I hold
> you and name you bastard in my arms.

Now, without change in societal attitudes, and without a shift away from patriarchal oppressions, this poem can't truly work as an activist tool (whatever the poet's intentions), but in conjunction with 'on-the-ground' activisms, it can. The poem's ambiguities open pathways to numerous overlapping intercultural and cross-gendering conversations. We can read the poem many ways, and those many ways are an advantage when combined with direct action. Very often, presenting the 'condition' of a wrong is adequate to prompt a movement towards change, especially when operating on a collective, communal level.

Radical notions don't necessarily provide radical solutions to problems. If more damage is done, then that's no answer. The Marxist who correctly identifies labour as a source of inequality does not solve the problem by technologising at the cost of the planet, shutting the biosphere down to bring a temporary equality. Equality and fairness come through ecological consciousness and respecting natural environments – we need them, and our integrity absolutely requires such justice. In the activist moment, in the poetry of dialogue with place and environment, we might as poets be part of this, with minimal damage as consequence.

Resisting the compliant text[9]

Texts are 'taught' in order to illustrate versions or contestations of human presence, to slot things into place, and to offer a methodology for close-reading the world via the text as thing-in-itself. In doing so, the teacher of literary texts may actually pave the way to compliance while often believing they are doing the opposite. Unless a text causes agitation, and that agitation is expressed in oppositional terms, a person's university years might be years of apparent freethinking, even 'radicalism', but only insofar as they allow 'steam to be let off' before the student becomes The Citizen, becomes a factor inside the designs of corporations and the state.

Universities play it both ways – fundamentally conservative (funding rules the roost – knowledge is a commodity), and yet encouraging 'enquiring minds'. In many ways, universities and other institutions of learning could be seen to manage outbreaks of 'radical' thought *for* the state, rather than prove to be hotbeds of agitation against the state. There have been stunning exceptions over history, of course, but so often these have actually arisen from subversive readings of texts, readings in which the teacher is left far behind. Texts aren't what they tell us they are; they're what we *will* them to be.

---

9 Sections of this text pertaining to Hölderlin appear in ˈtɛmp(ə)rərɪnəs (with Russell West-Pavlov).

So what am I asking for? Close readings that reveal our own conservatisms and failures to act, no matter how conscientious we think we are. If we are part of universities, our activism is going to be curtailed. It shouldn't be!

If we study a text like Montherlant's *Les Jeunes Filles*, doors should be opened to resisting misogyny, because the work itself is misogynistic. If we read Wilfred Owen's anti-war poems, we should act against war because the poems show war's horrors. Two activisms – one unintended (we think) and one intended? But the reality is, though these texts might contribute to a world-view, and the teacher might encourage that world-view, they become pictures in a personal puzzle, and a personal decoding of the world's injustices.

What doesn't happen, and can't ultimately happen (at present – I hope this can change) in a university ecology, is that teacher and students take their readings to a level of shared, communal resistance. Textual awarenesses made in a university need to be shared with the broader community – there should be no separation between 'town and gown' (as they call it in Cambridge). Such acts of *genuine* textual-knowledge sharing would be likely to undermine the very institutions of which the readers are part. Good.

As a pacifist, I come to this argument from a very particular position. I want to see non-violent resistance, always. I want textual analysis to lead to an articulation of defiance against forces of exclusion and oppression. The university might well have an official policy of supporting cultural, gender, ethnic, and even political diversity, but it will never support a position that resists the administrative bedrock upon which it is based.

As I also come from an anarchist position, I believe universities should operate as accumulations of smaller communities, in which rights (and I categorically include animal rights in this) are absolute, and difference is pivotal and desirable. Disagreement is the essence of understanding, though only functioning within a discourse of mutual respect. In this manner, the refugee and the 'citizen', the religious and secular, the 'radical' and 'conservative', can co-exist, and maybe even grow through each other's input and presence. Exclusion is not enlightenment.

We are living in times of right-wing extremes. But when we are talking of nation-states, and also city-states and certainly empires, manifestations of right-wing oppression are basically what 'history' is made of/consists of, with few exceptions. What has come as a shock to the political left and ethical left (these are not necessarily one and the same thing!) around the world is the brazen effrontery with which the tenets of *party right-wingism* have emerged as individualised discourse within the community. In the age of social media this should come as no surprise. Apparent freedom of (sourcing and sharing) information (be it 'false' or 'true' or *inbetween*) necessarily engenders a freedom to share opinions in a way never before achievable outside the village, the family.

But this 'freedom' of information is frequently used as a way of policing and controlling other people's viewpoints and liberties. Many of us have provided our own self-surveillance, made ourselves accessible to the forces of the neoliberal right on a person-to-person basis, while also offering ourselves through participation in information technology to the corporate state. We might bring more 'knowledge' to the reading of a text, but we are increasingly reading a text with many others who will exploit and manipulate us, looking over our shoulder. They are not helping investigation and (re)consideration of the text for generative and just purposes, but as a kind of market survey to increase their sales, their control, their exclusions. In allowing this (and if we have a mobile phone or use a credit card we are part of this surveillance), the most 'radical' reader of a text becomes compliant – agitation becomes an emoticon, not a generative force for positive change.

So, I make a proposition, though it will take me a while to get to it ...

As we sit in our classroom group to discuss a particular text, it's likely we do so having already read and thought about it, considered its contexts of creation and the author's (probable or possible) intentions. We can create a comparative literary discussion around it, bringing in other texts from other geographies and culturalities, and we can create a complex matrix of allusions, digressions, even misprisions and disruptions. Some of us will infuriate others in the group with a rupture of the very language itself, giving destabilised readings, leading to a breakdown of cause and effect. All of this is possible in the classroom.

But what I suggest is that we perforce (and most often unwittingly) treat texts as inevitable acts of compliance, no matter how radical they might seem. Consider, for example, a poem written by a radical figure who is known to resist racism, environmental destruction, capitalism, militarism and bigotry in all its forms. We might well be (hopefully ...) reading because we want to resist the oppressions of the states and the right-wing tendencies of international communities – we are using the classroom for generative purposes and teaching methodologies, ways of processing information, of building arguments and applying them to life inside/outside the classroom. We are relearning the tools of classical rhetoric for modern, radical environmental purposes.

However, what are we really doing? We are identifying a resistant text that is probably already doing the work it is intended to do within an over-determined media-focussed world. We are agreeing with it. Rather, surely even where we 'agree', we should contest and rewrite. We should take it further, question its own terms of engagement and expression. Once a text is stable (i.e. 'readable'), its effectiveness as advocacy or resistance is lessened. A text needs to weave its way around analysis, to 'outrun' it, to continue to grow and not be pinned down. By 'learning' it, we are reducing it to non-activism and compliance – we have muted it, at least in that environment of presentation (not necessarily elsewhere).

So what can we do with it as teachers, as students – as people in community and dialogue around the text (I have never differentiated between teachers and students)? Well ... We *rewrite*, we rework, we recontextualise, we make pertinent to the where-we-are, and the why-we-are, and how our presence affects others, creates absences. This is why no literature-studies course can be separated off from the creative. Literary writing is and should be creative writing. They are one and the same. The text we are studying is not only best understood by rewriting it, writing variations on it, but also by allowing it to live in the present, in the topography of 'here', and then sending it out into broader community to act as non-compliant, agitating presence. 'There' comes alive in the 'here' by departing the familiar, by making 'strange' (ostranenie).

I'll give a personal example. I have been working on versions of Friedrich Hölderlin's poems for years – ever since visiting his 'tower' in Tübingen during the horrific war in the Balkans. I wrote a sequence of poems critiquing global politics while considering the 'nature' of place, of the lyric, of the memorialised poet. I do not have access to the subtleties of his German, and I rely on translations into English by other writers, including my partner and academic friends.

But I follow the German as much as I can, and I bring to the process a deep immersion in poetry and poetics, and in the poet 'himself'. I feel I understand in ways that many native speakers of German might not – this may not be true, but I like to feel it's possible by way of personal vision, incentive and even compulsion.

I *do* bring to the process a life of radical activism and radical reading. In writing 'fantasias' and 'variations' and 'versions' of Hölderlin's poems, I might not 'translate' what he says literally, but I reach into the process of poetry and bring something else to the surface. And, of course, I have other agendas – anti-nationalist (particularly interesting and somewhat ironic in the context of Hölderlin's Germanist agenda focalised through classical Greece), environmentalism (Hölderlin's honed and specific observations of nature that are embodied in his texts), and a pantheistic view of existence (Hölderlin's synthesis of nature and theology is maybe more disruptive than readers allow?). Further, I see the 'late' poems of his 'madness' (which I contest) as some of his most brilliant and non-compliant, though they are sold by critics (and translators) as having been written almost hebephrenically.[10]

So as an example of perhaps a less compliant *reading* of text, I want to take a Hölderlin text into a German university classroom (of students who, necessarily, also understand English, but if not, other such 'exercises' or 'examples' could be enacted – this is not a case of language exclusion or exclusivity!), and use it as a tool of agitation, of non-compliance.

The first thing I will do is ask the students to rewrite the poem individually or collectively, and *then* discuss it and how it might relate to the crisis of liberty, respect and generosity of which we are all now part.

---

10 See R. Hodge and V. Mishra's *Dark Side of the Dream: Australian Literature and the Postolonial Mind* (Allen & Unwin, 1991), and their quoting Gregory Bateson to argue for an opposition between paranoid readings and the hebephrenic.

I have recently been working with Hölderlin's brilliant Pindar translations (they are beyond brilliant!) of 'fragments' with commentaries of from 1805, and reversioning seems relevant to this discussion (I imagine them accompanied by song, dance: choric elements). Michael Hamburger's English translations are in themselves reversionings (if still quite 'direct') of Hölderlin's reversioning, but I am taking the process *exponentially* further. Versions mutate into other versions, and so on. Hölderlin, in his Dionysian intensities, made a pantheistic theology of Hellenistic presence within his 'now', within his radicalising poetry as a place for the extraordinary to declare itself. Hölderlin's love for Susette and their inability to be together have a cascading effect in terms of fusing nature and *occurrence* from this Dionysian universe, *and* love, into a theology of unrestraint, of non-compliance, which will inevitably break down as the whole cannot remained unified. But in this is the possibility of a more direct, and even politically and ethically specific, activism!

I have taken a Hölderlin-Pindar fragment and commentary and produced – by way of creating a non-compliant, agitating text – this reversioning:

After Hölderlin's Pindar Extravaganza When He Was Supposedly Past It: 'Vom Dolphin'

And so, the river dolphins ingest the gifts of human toxins,
small whitehorses nudging their baffled corpses.

>   When I hear a stranger – jogging along the path by the river – call out, 'See the dolphins!' and later, the sun askew through musty clouds, another ask, 'Have you seen the river-dolphins today?' I know the death of river-dolphins is immense to the humans who mark their lives by appearances and disappearances. Whether or not joggers connect their human-actions to the sudden decline river-dolphin numbers, I don't know. 'Nature' is a health-variable in riverside café discussions of river-health, and the very smell of water on a hot day is subject for debate.
>   Waves *do* occur in the river when storms clamp down on the coastal plain – dark-frothed white horses, the stained waters breeching the dolphins' trust.[11]

The poem, as I have remade it, is concerned with the death of dolphins in the Swan River, Perth, Western Australia – deaths caused by human-made pollutants. The poem is about the relationship between humans and the river, about nature being fetishised in a capitalist environment. The subtext is the dispossession of Whadjuk Noongar people from the river and riverland, which was their homeland for tens of thousands of years (and remains so, of course, though under the state's mediation and control). That's not declared openly, but it's in my text as far as I am concerned and, with any comparative literary study, would probably be evident. Yet being evident is not enough – I want it to stimulate response and action, a remaking, and consequently new, localised activist

---

11 See my *The Wound*.

poetic text. What are *your* concerns? You'll need to dismantle and reversion the text yourselves!

To have sympathy with (othered) people who have lost their homes, who have had their homes taken from them, who have been born without homes, or have been made homeless, we need to understand acts of isolation and separation. Hölderlin expresses this isolation and separation *intensely* across his poetry. Michael Hamburger in his introduction to *Friedrich Holderlin: Poems and Fragments*, notes, 'In his tragic odes, as in his novel, Hölderlin's pantheism, his desire to be one with the cosmos, continually comes up against his awareness not only of the differences between human and non-human nature, but of the isolation into which human beings are precipitated by their consciousness.'[12]

Hölderlin's growing personal sense of 'outsider' status increasingly alienated him from his time, and in looking back to the Hellenistic world *or* to a more illuminated future, he 'distanced' himself from a cultural, artistic and intellectual discourse that he felt had little (or less than he desired) room for him (and his 'visionariness'). Hamburger is good in talking about aspects of this, but is wrong in labelling an alienation of feeling and its loss as reasons for a kind of poetic collapse (with Hölderlin's 'treatment' in Tübingen). I don't think this is what happened either outside or inside the poems, and though *seemingly* relatively 'sterile', Hölderlin's late poems, for me, are intense containment-fields of feeling for nature and 'the world' that are maps not of a hebephrenia, but of a restraint that is so tense it snaps with every line. Close creative re-readings of these poems can yield intense activist fruit.

Hamburger writes:

> The voice of the heart – words that also occur in one of Hölderlin's odes – was more than a sentimental trope in a poet who believed that the capacity to feel is a prerequisite even for religious dedication. It was the loss of that capacity – after the loss of the one woman [Susette] he had loved religiously – that marks the poems written not by Hölderlin but by the person he became when his sufferings had broken him. Whether or not we call that condition 'catatonic stupor' – or 'schizophrenia', to use the later term – has little bearing on his poetry. (p. 36)

I find this an outrageous declaration – Hölderlin was the same person and the same poet before and after his 'collapse'. True, it matters not what we call this 'collapse', but the suggestion that he became another person is deeply offensive on so many levels. Hölderlin's post-'collapse' poems, few as they might have been, and 'occasional' as they might have been, are still remarkable poems, and still communing with his 'ideal' of the poet and poetry. They are still prophetic if we know how to hear their 'prophecies'. They are the work of a poet who has decided the 'team' of poets doesn't want him; that the sport of poetry (for it can be!) might not recognise (adequately) a 'player', but that this doesn't mean the knowledge, skills and vision of that player have been lost.

---

12   Michael Hamburger, *Friedrich Holderlin: Poems and Fragments* (Anvil Press, 2004), p. 28.

Hölderlin's signing of his name as 'Scardanelli' during this 'late poem period' is still part of a process of his looking 'forward', even if through a nothingness and eternity of the present. Of one of Hölderlin's 'Der Sommer' poems (Wenn dann vorbei ...), Hamburger notes, 'The fictitious date and the signature 'Scardanelli' are typical of Hölderlin's escape from both time and identity at this period. He would also call himself 'Buonarroti' or 'Scaliger Rosa' (p. 811). Hamburger notes that after 1806 (and his 'personality change'), Hölderlin would not accept visitors using his 'real' name; that he would only recognise the 'pseudonyms' he selected for himself, and would call people 'Your Majesty' etc I would add that rather than an act of 'escape' and a failure to face a lost and damaged past, this was, at least in part, a conscious ploy by the poet to destabilise a textual present – a critique of the discourse around 'time' and 'identity'. (Hamburger notes regarding the *Odes* that they range across time and space).[13] This poem, with his signing-off in that way, remains visionary, and the self is displaced within nature (not ignored, not a matter of indifference because the poem is written to please a 'visitor' – in fact, the 'false' signature is evidence of the importance of identity and its slippages).

Here is my *distraction* of that poem:

After Hölderlin's 'Der Sommer' – 'Wenn dann vorbei'

The vanishing of back-when's spring-flowers,
Summer's *now*, entwining the year.
And, as through the valley, Toodyay Brook –
The ranges at full stretch to hold it back.
Paddocks are exhausted but glassy-bright
With day, arching towards twilight;
And so the year hangs 'round, a summer's
Day for men as impressions might fade with nature.

May 24th
1778.   Scardanelli

The activist key is in the word 'exhausted', which agitates around the nature of colonised and mono-*agriculturalised* landscape.

---

13 'Hamburger has the following in parenthesis in his note to the remarkable 'late' poem 'Wenn aus der Ferne': 'All the reports of his decades in the Tübingen tower confirm that the one thing that enraged him repeatedly was to be reminded of anything whatever to do with his former life and person, but especially the name of Hölderlin, so that, when presented with a copy of his first book of poems, he said that the poems were genuine, but the name was false. Yet even here was a contradiction, incompatible with the medical diagnoses, in that he remained capable of signing all the letters to his mother with the forbidden name of Hölderlin' (p. 808). One can't help think of the musician-composer Syd Barrett and the claim he suffered from mental illness and his sister insisting he didn't. And the comparisons to the brilliant and different Barrett bear fruit in other ways, too – something I intended to explore in a future essay comparing the two in terms of creativity and 'crisis'.

I am trying to make a very serious point about how and why we read literary texts in a time of crisis (ongoing crisis!). The proposal is that we read and rewrite; that we refuse to comply with the model that would have scholarly criticism separate from creativity; that we disrupt and agitate texts to make them of the moment, to give them life to adjust to each topographical and cultural variant that is in evidence. To me, this is an act of respect, of community. To me, it seems we make our universities into zones of positive change and inclusiveness by stepping out and interacting with broader communities.

I say all of this in the context of having taught literary texts for many years in various universities around the world, and also in the context of having made proto-steps towards trying to create an alternative 'university' in which 'marks', 'examinations', 'assessment' and hierarchies of knowledge would be overturned and replaced with a communal system of recognition and 'progress'. This was (and is) known as 'The School of Environmental Poetics and Creativity'.[14]

I am interested in altering the terms of discussion on the nature of relationships between texts and those making use of them, and creating them. A text is a living entity and should be treated as existing contingently and contiguously within and with a vulnerable ecology that is under threat, a biosphere that is collapsing due in no small part to human behaviours – especially corporate and state exploitations of the fragile, remaining 'natural' habitats. No text, *whatever* it is, can be read outside this context of damage.

I believe that Ivan Illich's recommendation of 'deschooling' is only a beginning, and that we need to go further in how we interact with habitat and knowledge within all communities, and redistribute learning into fragmented spatialities that are less impacting on environment. All places of learning should be arranged around energy sources as sustainable as possible (be they solar, wind-power, or the use of natural light-sources etc). All learning should involve rehabilitation of flora and fauna (small campuses with revegetation programmes, bird nesting programmes, reintroduction of native animal species etc). And these learning zones should be spread throughout communities so that they become part of the general discourse of presence.

Illich wrote at the beginning of his revolutionary work, *Deschooling Society*:

1. Why We Must Disestablish School

Many students, especially those who are poor, intuitively know what the schools do for them. They school them to confuse process and substance. Once these become blurred, a new logic is assumed: the more treatment there is, the better are the results; or, escalation leads to success. The pupil is thereby 'schooled' to confuse teaching with learning, grade advancement with education, a diploma with competence, and fluency with the ability to say something new. His imagination is 'schooled' to accept service in place of value.[15]

---

14 See Kinsella, *Activist Poetics*, Chapter 13, pp. 176–183.
15 Ivan Illich, *Deschooling Society* (Harper and Row, 1971), www.davidtinapple.com/illich/1970_deschooling.html.

And thus begins one of the most remarkable documents of de-investing the text of learning ever written. Illich also noted:

> The paradox of the schools is evident: increased expenditure escalates their destructiveness at home and abroad. This paradox must be made a public issue. It is now generally accepted that the physical environment will soon be destroyed by biochemical pollution unless we reverse current trends in the production of physical goods. It should also be recognized that social and personal life is threatened equally by HEW pollution, the inevitable by-product of obligatory and competitive consumption of welfare.
>
> The escalation of the schools is as destructive as the escalation of weapons but less visibly so.[16]

He *knew*. We should *know*. Illich unpicked the hypocrisies and euphemisms of educational practice, now reaching its apogee in ecological studies (and ecopoetics) wherein the mobile-phone user, university technological infrastructurism, car-driving poet or ecologist, speaks out on behalf of the planet while contributing overtly to the planet's destruction. Tools for liberation? We know that can't be the case.

Writing in Mexico in 1970, Illich was able to observe:

> Many people are just awakening to the inexorable destruction which present production trends imply for the environment, but individuals have only very limited power to change these trends. The manipulation of men and women begun in school has also reached a point of no return, and most people are still unaware of it. They still encourage school reform, as Henry Ford II proposes less poisonous automobiles.[17]

As with Rachel Carson's epiphanic *Silent Spring* (1962), we decry the pesticides, but keep eating food treated with them, walk the parks where weeds have been eliminated by herbicides, say nothing as our universities use more poisons in gardens, bathrooms, corridors and offices than Illich might have imagined, or even Carson imagined, only five or six decades ago. We have more 'knowledge', more texts critiquing our condition, and yet we grow more and more implicated in the collective destruction. The writers and critics of texts learn, critique, pontificate, and yet, in reality, exclude themselves from the evidence. *Rewrite* the texts, learn, implicate yourself, change! *Change change change!* Knowledge is irrelevant if it is theory without praxis.

And one more quote from Illich:

> I believe that a desirable future depends on our deliberately choosing a life of action over a life of consumption, on our engendering a life style which will enable us to be spontaneous, independent, yet related to each other, rather than maintaining a life style which only allows us to make and unmake, produce and

16 Ibid.
17 Ibid.

consume – a style of life which is merely a way station on the road to the depletion and pollution of the environment. The future depends more upon our choice of institutions which support a life of action than on our developing new ideologies and technologies.[18]

He sees it all. However, as a priest of the church (despite the complexities and contradictions in his relationship with his church), Illich was also complicit in institutionalism – being *aware* isn't the answer, action is. And maybe Illich's activism went as far as it could go; maybe it could have gone further? One must abandon and break down institutions and create open and organic spaces, and spatialities, of learning, which have an intimate and highly sensitised 'awareness' of the levels of place with and within which they operate.

Further, participating in, say, the exploitation of animals (from slaughterhouses to the keeping of pets as human distractions or emotional lightning-rods, as opposed to, say, looking after animals to save them from slaughter or to give them a home away from abuse and destruction: e.g. 'rescue-animals'), is a concomitant concession to the control of institutions. And that's to say nothing of the torture and abuse of animals in university research programmes. Vivisection is not learning, is not knowledge; it is a crime against life.

If we are going to liberate the teaching and reading and writing of texts, to free the 'university' from the constraints of cultural and political imperialism, from corporate greed, from racism and ecological indifference and destructiveness, we need to be holistic in our approach. Our approach needs to be entirely non-violent, non-aggressive but revolutionary, taking all concerns of gender, spiritual, cultural and ethnic diversity and liberty into consideration, with non-human life as a major focus as well.

And so, I will sign off with another Hölderlin version, written in the context of an environmental 'campaign'.[19] During this action, a protest camp was established on site, and numerous people from many 'different walks of life' were physically involved in trying to stop machines from destroying the bushland, animal life and bird life. The site became a place of horrific learning about greed, rapacity, corruption, and also about nature's intricacies and magnificence. I found it significant how many academics became involved (there was even an environmental anti-development advocacy group of university professors) as well as students, but also alternative learners, and a serious awareness of Aboriginal knowledges of place, through the presence of Whadjuk Elders. The *land* itself as university – the real university of the planet, where all knowledge is present *if* we are willing to try and learn from those who know, and read the text of the land.

---

18 Ibid.
19 The word 'campaign' is barely adequate – it was a full-blown protective action to stop the destruction of rare bushland in Perth, Western Australia, from being destroyed through gratuitous and rapacious development by the conservative Barnett Liberal-National Party government and their partners in private industry.

As part of my many poems and writings of this act of resistance, this act of nurturing what is left of the bushland, of rehabilitating the 'wound' inflicted by developers and government before they were driven off (a rare 'victory' for the environmental movement), I wrote:

After Hölderlin's 'Der Winkel von Hahrdt'[20]

The bush is gone, but wheelbarrows
are arriving to staunch the wound – woodchips
of shattered trees, verdure's fragments
of ghost, market-failure's dissed commodity.
These causes that stem out of night,
canticles to dawns that are never
quite the same – but out of an enclave of hope,
where charismatic selves imagine a future of comforting
growth, belief is marked out, communicated.

And this, I hope reinforces my proposal, the points I am desperate to make. In solidarity!

The truth should be in blurbs, encomiums, references, letters of support and launch speeches etc.

I call documents of reference and approval 'support (of) heteroglossia'[21] because, though an opinion is being asked for and given to support a person or text (a *textuality*), something of the refereed's opinions needs to be considered and/or discussed in the support document, bringing at least a whisper or echo into dialogue with the referee, within the narrative of someone's life (and those 'being' around it in the context).

---

20 For an interesting 'quiet conversation' (Russell's words) regarding his reading of my 'Winkel' translation-version, see Russell West-Pavlov, *German as Contact Zone: Towards a Quantum Theory of Translation from the Global South* (Narr-Francke-Attempto, 2018), pp. 190–192. Zones and maybe *zonality* (my inflection in terms of *this* manifestation of accrual) is a conceptualisation of space characteristic to both our practices, 'independently' (as much as these things in discourse can ever be), but also a shared notion as expressed in a variety of intersecting and diverging ways in Kinsella and West-Pavlov, ˈtɛmp(ə)rərinəs.

21 Yes, Bakhtin's 1934 'Discourse in the Novel'... of course, but with diversions that become evident as this text unfurls. For convenience, as this is one of my re-applications, not a critical application per se, we could make use of the Oxford 'Quick' Reference just as a point of reference: 'The existence of conflicting discourses within any field of linguistic activity, such as a national language, a novel, or a specific conversation. The term appears in translations of the writings of the Russian linguistic and literary theorist Mikhail Bakhtin (1895–1975), as an equivalent for his Russian term *raznorechie* ('differentspeechness'). In Bakhtin's works, this term addresses linguistic variety as an aspect of social conflict, as in tensions between central and marginal uses of the same national language; these may be echoed in, for example, the differences between the narrative voice and the voices of the characters in a novel. *Adjectives*: heteroglot, heteroglossic...' (www.oxfordreference.com/view/10.1093/oi/authority.20110803095934670).

So, a statement of support becomes a conversation, even if a seemingly lop-sided one, in which *choice* to use a text of support (a 'blurb') may be exercised – and often is, especially by commercial publishers with a different view from their authors as to what best 'gets a book out there' or 'the message across'. Or, with regard to those who request and receive references for, say, an advertised employment position, the process of a follow-up request/conversation for a promised reference/blurb. There are ongoing and complex conversations around a support text beyond the text-writer's support of a specific (con)*textuality*.

But often references for employment are confidential documents, which would suggest there's no broader collaborative aspect (between all parties involved in the process); in fact, such interaction with the refereed would constitute a violation of the trust of confidential uncompromised response. This is true, and always to be upheld and respected if one enters into such an agreement with a host over being a referee, but in order to have knowledge of the applicant I believe an immersion in that person's texts and indeed public-embodied utterances, their textuality, is an equally ethical if not more ethical obligation. A collaboration between referee and refereed seems essential, to me.

As a referee, to comment cursorily on a person/text is to damn with faint praise or lack necessary subtlety – and I am not talking about being 'succinct' here. Even when being supportive, other agendas can lurk behind even positive brief comments. I resist these categorisations and see support document writing as a critical-creative artform that is demanding in its technical requirements, its imaginative liberties and ethical rigours.

I don't write support documents and comments if I don't mean them. But if I am asked to provide a comment or commentary on a work or for an individual or a community (of whatever form it takes), and I believe in what the work or person or people stand for, and how they articulate their position, I will do so unreservedly. In this, I would say that such 'writings' are among the most legitimate critical work one can do. It's not a matter of praise, but of pinpointing the salient, of highlighting the strengths and the worth of a 'subject'.

The many different contexts for such 'praise', and, indeed, commentary that has nothing to do with praise, necessitate many different formal constraints and expectations. And in the case of blurbs and encomiums, publishers and authors often want to cut back to fit a space, and in this a whole new set of dialogic ethics come into play. What is often not assumed or appreciated or even thought about is how the writer who writes many support documents makes choices about what is written about, how it is written about, and how it fits into a broader commentary on the world.

All of the documents-of-support I have written over the last twenty-five years actually fit into a narrative of justice, environmentalism and anti-aesthetics, even when the referenced work itself might seem far from these concerns. This is not to say one bends the work to suit a greater purpose, but rather to acknowledge that one draws it to a critical and ethical purpose that justifies the act of acceding to a request. One assumes those asking 'for the favour' (I never see it as such, but as sharing, but it is often expressed – kindly and respectfully – this way) realise this, or if it's a random attempt to get an imprimatur, that they knoweth-of-whom they ask. If not, inevitably the request will be rejected.

Different writers, different communities with different needs, are bound together in a narrative of *publicly given support* that relies on the public voice and presence of the blurber or referee or validator. Then there's the assumptions about how those for whom the support is 'aimed' will receive this support: is the writer of the support document considered an 'authority' (and how is this in itself assessed, and more importantly *why* is it assessed – something that always bothers me), and thus 'valid(ated)', or is there slippage between what they stand for and what they are supporting?

Every time I write a support document, I do so with these questions in mind. The marginalia and even glossolalia that comes as an aside to the reified comments and observations, the approvals and the highlightings, are every bit as important in their codes and distractions as the primary document. From writing so many support documents for others, I developed a politics-poetics of encounter and support that builds a picture of connection even when the material is sometimes outside my experience, and tangential to why I have been asked to 'help'. My voice is a tangent for the *difference* to well-up and truly depart from, or, maybe more accurately, define itself against. So, in such cases, it's not what I do (in life, professionally – most often in my 'public capacity') specifically, but what is recognised by me as valid and useful and generative. I don't have to be the *same* to approve, so I can approve if I see point in doing so.

And it's often in this kind of slippage that generative moments develop and that engagements go beyond the work itself, often resulting in literal collaboration at a later time. What kind of contact have we made? That's why I see such acts of support as being deeply truthful in this ecology of contact: they become exchanges between interested minds, who respect something the 'other' does. And an agreement to interact has been made, and for that to be made public or, in the case of references, public at least among a few making a decision as to the 'worth' of a candidate. We don't know everything about those we support, but we should know their work as well as we can – which is why I often write long references (essay-length on occasion) and sometimes long blurbs (usually edited back by author or publisher), which are literally *reviews*, because I try to look at the works concerned with a critical distance. And as I tend to write interconnected reviews and essays, I write interconnected documents of support (always within the zone of respect for integrity and privacy and confidentiality): discrete and yet sharing liminal space of the public-private, of confidence and the broader public of language, of ethics, of cause and effect. Some will be short, some long, but they will need to be the length I feel fits the purpose of the pronouncement. And integrity comes wanting the document to be more than something 'tossed off' in the moment to meet an obligation; I want *it* to be an engagement, a declaration of shared responsibility, and also carry the sense of specific and personalised approval.

Most relevant, and maybe most interestingly, is the issue of comments on 'personal' and 'social' qualities of an applicant when reference[22] writing: being asked how an individual will fit into a prescribed community (often a construct of administration), or, rather, how one thinks they will fit. This is dubious territory, and may or may not accord with the comments on work published and, say, skills in teaching a class. I do not reference someone I don't feel I can support in all aspects of a job, but sometimes I question the criteria they are expected to fill, and I offer different ways of interpreting their skills and what *they* have to offer. Often I have found that institutions need to adapt to a candidate's textuality more than vice versa.

To avoid privileging modes of 'being' (of living one's life, of expressing one's views, of conversing with others) in a reference over 'better' and 'worse' qualities is to be *the arbiter* I philosophically resist. I only answer for what I know. Strangely, one might write a reference about an academic applicant for an institution one finds objectionable, and often the 'authority' that is required is the authority embedded in the more objectionable 'official' nature of the position one is writing from. This needs to be identified and deconstructed. In such cases, as referee, one admits a culpability.

If the platform of one's perceived authority is, say, a professorship, the *event* that gives you authority is a combination of that imprimatur and your publication record, of a position within a stratifying hierarchy that has lauded some and inevitably oppressed and rejected many. That event synthesis is to be used as conduit for the event of the applicant to become the event of the job and new position. This transference of authority is flawed and retrograde, and participants inevitably know this, but 'have to make a living' and so on. As an anarchist vegan pacifist, recommending from positions that I feel are dubious in their faux authority and usurpations of validation of what counts as knowledge and what is ignored, I try to build into all my references critiques of authority and position, whilst fully supporting the qualities of scholarship, writing and humanity that I see in the applicant.

This, to me, is what makes the references more than formulaic acts of duty – it makes them engagements and encounters, opportunities to support but also offer a critique of process and give the applicant, should they be successful, room to be the voices they need to be. Obviously, I feel they are voices who will bring positive change and push against institutional repression, or I wouldn't support them in the first place!

---

22 A 'reference' says things specifically about a text or candidate, but implies much more in what is not said. No reference is a set of data – it is an interlocutor, a moment of exchange that shifts as space and time shift. What it refers to is necessarily the self of the referee, and the perception by the referee of the referent in their semantic-'personal' relationship. This is always unstable as qualification in text is unstable. What is being referred to breaks down into many component parts, in which each object as it relates to its word introduces further instability. Maybe 'mediated reference theory' (Gottlob Frege et al.) is useful and relevant here. https://iep.utm.edu/frege/.

Blurbs and encomiums for books are different in many ways (and similar in others), of course. Mostly I am supporting poets as a poet, or writers as a writer. The politics I come out of may or may not be of direct interest to the person making the request for support, but blurbs I am pleased with, which often become review essays, are those where the requester knows exactly why they're asking and are wanting more than 'a name' [fill name in here].

The zone in which I find most room to manoeuvre and take up all the issues of a text – in what is written and how it is presented – is the launch speech. To send a book into the world is a responsibility to the author/s, audience, and future readers and hearers of the text. A launch speech can set a pattern of reading a text, and it can be lost to the moment. Both outcomes are relevant. I need to clarify here that I am not allotting 'genre' distinction to these modes of writing, as that's an entrapment I think can and should be avoided – they are creative ethical utterances of support that can also be deeply honed critical tools intended to offer generative improvement to a range of justice issues. I do not support for entertainment's sake, or simply to approve another step in societal machinic ladders of state and enterprise (commercial publishers where they care more for product than author and/or reader). Rather, I offer support where relevant and useful from whatever 'position' in textual discourse I might hold, to each and every person, community and text I believe able – and mostly better able than myself – to work as a corrective to the wrongs of oppressive state capitalism and its arms of enforcement.

Even from within the system (often places of learning), a good teacher or researcher can make a better social and ecological environment. That will sometimes also mean losing the position 'gained', and I referee/reference people I feel will likely make the just choice if confronted with such choices. So, when a university asks for a comment on the moral and character attributes (or pretend not to ask but do in fact ask in subtle ways), what I am actually giving them in my references, as I am in a launch speech for a book, are the materials that can also undo the very status quo and aesthetic qualities expected by the audience (be it the 'selection committee' or the readership of a book at a launch who are being encouraged to purchase or engage with an author and their text).

So, is it a case of someone launching a new book speaking to a demographically expected – even assumed – audience, in sync or partially at least in sync with what you expect the subject is hoping for? Is the subject-requester's desire for the outcome that best suits their 'needs' an extension of your support or merely an act of approval and verification? Partly all these, but none of this is adequate. On the part of the subject-requester (sometimes it might be the author, sometimes their representative – agent, publisher etc), it's a willingness to make themselves vulnerable as an act of trust, and it's also an act of hope in that the 'referee'-speaker-launcher will speak in a way that the subject-requester thinks of themselves, or might hope for themselves.

When one is personally close or familiar with the subject-requester, it fits a pre-existing dialogue, interaction, which has its own patterns, but sometimes it's more generic and more outside the personal; in such cases, it follows the traces of public utterance, of knowledge gleaned via reading texts of the subject, of public and private comments, of possible intersections with one's own practice. But intersection is the wrong word, and, as I point out often, I am increasingly thinking in terms of a nexus in which there are points of concentrated overlap or connection – nodal points drawing on ambiguity to create a post-ambiguous sharing and even gelling – and less 'warm' areas still caught up in the echoes of these points of overlap and meshing. A space of concordance forms or emulates an idea of intertextual communalism. References and encomiums come strongly out of these, drawing on all the threads of knowing and awareness that create a community of intimacy of text and idea, and of responsibility and loyalty but within a maybe even stronger commitment to positions of public reliability and trust. The referee needs to trust themselves to do the right thing, and to know the audience has reason not to distrust them. Ironically, in creating such 'support (of) heteroglossia' documentation, more than at any time in one's own writing, there is an emphasis on drawing attention, of being trusted, of sharing: the referee becomes 'responsible' for the outcomes of the support they have proffered, which are actually and ultimately unpredictable once the text leaves the space of writing and goes 'public'. There is the chaos of reception and accountability of misreading as much as reading as one wishes one be read. So, there's a risk, not of supporting something that one hasn't understood, but of being read against the grain of how one has read/understood (the text, the person, the community).

Inevitably, a quote given to support one text is then used in different contexts later to support other later work, as if what you've said as supporter/referee/blurber includes all future diversions and possibilities. This sometimes fits, but often it doesn't. But it *is* part of the responsibility – the potential for re-contextualising – to be covered in/by what one writes. In other words, the support statement needs to be intact and meta-textual and accept also that it will be understood by some as being somewhat porous and re-contextualisable. It is simple enough to state purpose clearly, to say how something may or may not be used, and to elaborate enough to cope with displacements. But they still have to be understood as potentials if not inevitable: the *immanence* of the support document!

A blurb used out of context deconstructs the condition of its re-representation, even its misrepresentation. It acts as its own critic in a dialogue of futurity because futurity is necessarily a flawed usage of the past – it can't build confidently because it has too many variables at work. How something you say is understood 'down the track' will inevitability be different. Be conscious of this issue, be conscious of the space you write out of and the spaces your words might project into, carried by others' work that you have, in a given time and place, supported.

Core considerations for me when writing at request for a specific circumstance (different from context, but connected), include issues of privacy and confidentiality, diversity and fairness, the general audience and the specific environment of reception. Caution and understatement or wild enthusiasm? A tone 'suitable' for the position/location from which one is being asked to speak, and a consciousness of the 'target audience', or, as I prefer, the 'ambience' best suited to the aspect of community being focussed on. Locus to loci.

Historically speaking, pre-telegraphic communications in the form of letters of recommendation being carried by the hopeful invested with the authority of signatories, were referrals of trust relying on the knowledge of a given party by another known to the party being approached. That relay of trust can have ill-consequences for the referee if the refereed contradicts the qualities recommended, but nonetheless, these communiques are interactive vehicles in which the referee presumably has some knowledge of both parties (refereed and recipient) in some capacity at least. In other words, one resolves to cede some space of self into a shared legitimacy and has to accept there maybe consequences. But spatial and temporal issues of distance (letters carried by foot, horse, sea ...) might mean a different person arriving from the one who departed! This is not to okay misuse of documents of support, but to say one has to be aware it's possible this might happen. Trust is a complex issue in the cases of increasing degrees of separation.

Waiting to leave Italy, S. T. Coleridge takes letters of recommendation from the American painter-poet Washington Allston (written in Italy – so no great time or distance in this one) to try and gain access and support – of likely multiplicitous and fracturing forms – from painter and Professor of Painting at the Florentine Academy, Pietro Benvenuti, with *adverse* results:

Tuesday, June 17, 1806.

My dear Allston, – No want of affection has occasioned my silence. Day after day I expected Mr. Wallis. Benvenuti received me with almost insulting coldness, not even asking me to sit down; neither could I, by any enquiry, find that he ever returned my call, and even in answer to a very polite note enquiring for letters, sent a verbal message, that there was one, and that I might call for it. However, within the last seven or eight days he has called and made his *amende honourable*; he says he forgot the name of my inn, and called at two or three in vain. Whoo! I did not tell him that within five days I sent him a note in which the inn was mentioned, and that he sent me a message in consequence, and yet never called for ten days afterwards. However, yester-evening the truth came out. He had been bored by letters of recommendation, and till he received a letter from Mr. — looked upon me as a bore – which, however, he might and ought to have got rid of in a more gentlemanly manner. Nothing more was necessary than the day after my arrival to have sent his card by his servant. But I forgive him from my heart. It should, however, be a lesson to Mr. Wallis, to whom, and for whom, he gives letters of recommendation ...[23]

S. T. Coleridge

---

23 www.gutenberg.org/files/44554/44554-h/44554-h.htm.

Is this a comment on the quality of the recommendations, the way in which they were delivered, the look of the bearer, the attitude the recipient truly held towards the referee? And so on.

The issue of illustration here is that the reference is always unstable depending on contexts that will inevitably shift and collapse. Whether the proffered letter comes as an act of bolstering or affirmation, or as an article that the writer genuinely believes will lead to an interaction of benefit to the party they support or both parties (whom they might also support), the act of trust is implicit. For me, writing words of support for another is an extension of my own interaction with the world, and also an exchange-act, a mutual aid in articulating a community of presence.

I was asked to write a blurb for a book by an author I greatly respect, but who, I think, feels I have quite different views on a particular issue that is defining for him (and, indeed, humanity). In truth, I feel we share the same ground, but our viewpoints are inflected in different ways. We both want the same end result, but because I am entirely anti-state and anti-centralisation and anti-consolidation-of-power even as a resistance to power[24] and he is not, something will always lack in my documents of support – something he is looking for that I can't provide. But that doesn't mean I won't contribute documents of support if relevant in cases where a requester still wants my support while having even strong disagreements with my viewpoint: if I believe in the integrity of them and their work, I *do* offer my support.

So what's the difference between, say, a supportive statement, or indeed a negative one, under an article in an online newspaper, and writing a blurb, reference, letter of support, launching a book etc? The difference is the *personal* request, that collaborative communalising engendered by the specifics of request. And that's where the ethics of appropriateness and 'tone' come into play – writing to suit is not a bending of one's ethics, it's finding a space in one's ethics where the nodal points within a Venn diagram *diagram* out further, or indeed, intersect. Or becomes a nexus of difference with points/nodes of aggregation.

But there are many failed points in the nexus of connectivity and expectation – the references that don't work or don't add enough, or the reference that could never work because the recipients were never going to take on board the applicant, or the bearer. When writing a job reference, a lot of

---

24 For me, power triggers power and thus vacuums created by the removal of oppression bring oppressive apparatuses in their place unless we disregard that apparatus of all states as an answer. States bring oppression in order to conserve their existence, whereas networks of interacting but self-defining communities have more chance of resisting the machinery of oppression, the distancing between every person and culpability. It's an argument of nuance in the face of a need for immediacy. I support the immediacy, but believe in cause and effect and nuance has to be part of immediacy. I have had the same issues with Extinction Rebellion, which I inherently support, but I believe their actions too often lack nuanced thinking, and that they avoid more difficult broader issues that are deeply relevant (e.g. veganism) in their manifesto-making.

research is needed (and raw materials are often provided to the referee by the applicant), and decisions need to be made about angles and focal points. By agreeing to act as referee, one is committing to an act of trust, but often your name is put forward and the location (the institution, so often) requests your reference, which is often on the basis of 'closed' or 'open' in terms of the applicant being able to see what you wrote or not. I find this appalling and believe an applicant should always see what has been written about them and actually have the right to see it before it is submitted. People who write references out of professional obligation and not out of commitment would do better by the applicant to refuse (politely) if they feel they can't fully support what amounts to a case of the subject being a *vulnerable party*. Nobody likes to be in a position of having to ask, and as I see all institutions guided by gatekeeping and rules of 'quality' being in varying degrees oppressive – though those I proffer references to are ones I consider within the range of better work choices than state-corporate-capitalism readily offers, serving only its own interests – I try to do so primarily and ultimately with the well-being of the applicant in mind. However, I also have the well-being of other people trapped within those institutions in mind, so always answer precisely with how I feel that applicant will or won't 'fit in' with the community being discussed. This is not a value judgement, it's an offering of viewpoint and no more.

I find the same with writing blurbs for, say, a poetry book. I am talking of what I see as the worth of the book, but also offering portals for many different viewpoints into the text. I do not want or expect a reader to see a text as I see it, but they might share an enthusiasm for ways of seeing and points of contact. I try to succinctly offer a view of contour lines that might be followed, but not a map in itself because a map, especially a printed map as opposed to a rough sketch, is too prescriptive and carries the tones of occupation, dispossession and colonisation for me, with the experience I come out of.

We attach a name to a blurb and its ilk. That name attaches (or, sadly, latches on) to gender, class, social position, public actions, and issues of privacy in terms of how available the recommending party makes themselves, or is thought to make themselves. How I identify is more relevant in my blurbing and referencing than any other spaces I speak out of or through. The fact that I am identified as being of a particular gender and ethnicity is often bemusing to me, but I also know that not acknowledging that in being identified as such it carries either privileging (likely) or denial of privilege (less likely), is also relevant. I don't want to be any part of the masculinity that bullied me into being a writer of subversive texts, but I am. I don't wish to be any part of ableist discourse. I don't want to be any part of the colonial apparatus, but I am. I resist and am inside. In being asked for a reference this is usually known, and names bring identification both stable and unstable. I have been 'controversial' in ways I am comfortable with, and also in ways I find deeply personally distressing. Even for many of those who find what I do interesting, I come with baggage. But what's the self-declaring in talking about writing of the qualities of others' work, and even their 'personalities' (a diabolical thing, really)? Well, it's the vacuum of obligation in this – one has to be willing to be held accountable and up for scrutiny, to agree to a level (slight or more and much more) of exposure. As one identified as male, I become like the flânuer moving through the streets taking all in and offering comment, a role I reject. Doreen Massey in *Space, Place and Gender* observes so acutely:

> could a woman experience modernity, defined in this way, at all?
> ... one of the key figures embodying this definition of modernity is the *flâneur*, the stroller in the crowd, observing but not observed. But the *flâneur* is irretrievably male. As Wolff (1985) has argued, the *flâneuse* was an impossibility. In part this is so because 'respectable' women simply could not wander around the streets and parks alone. (This was for reasons of socially constructed 'propriety', but for those 'non-respectable' women who did roam the public spaces movement would still be effectively restricted by the threat of male violence.) In part, the notion of a *flâneuse* is impossible because of the one-way-ness and the directionality of the gaze. *Flâneurs* observed others; they were not observed themselves. And for reasons which link together the debate on perspective and spatial organization of painting, and most women's exclusion from the public sphere, the modern gaze belonged (belongs?) to men.[25]

I become like *it* but I reject *it*, and try to renegotiate the reference/blurb as an act of collaboration, of observing but being observed. Confidentiality, to me, is the ultimate form of accountability, and I believe those who ask of me should be able to trust in me if I accept their request to participate in their public-private utterances. This is how communities outside the state but in the context of state control manage to define themselves, to breakdown that state control. If I am writing a reference for someone who identifies as 'they' or 'he' or 'she', or uses another identifier or dispenses with a pronoun altogether, that becomes part of my dynamic of engagement re my privilege and position in terms of reception. My own 'issues' of self and identity are both relevant and also asides, as the weight of conversation in writing the blurb/reference shifts from my *self* to their *self*. The act of writing support becomes a support for difference, temporarily scaffolded by who one is writing it. The scaffold can then fall away and was only ever a very temporary moment – almost an allusion, but one built in honesty and trust. No residue of the referee need remain and collaborations are only steps to other collaborations. We are temporary in the permanence of just outcomes.

Letters of support that come out of reading and commenting on work-in-progress are of particular interest to me because they are an act of reading and textual engagement *in medias res*, so to speak. One is often being shown work that is unpublished, or that has been journal-published but will become part of a projected larger book-length work. We are seeing working parts and ideas and 'pieces' that are to be part of a greater whole, and (often financial)

---

25 Doreen Massey, *Space, Place and Gender* (Polity, 1994, reprinted 2007), p. 234.

support is being sought to facilitate space for the writing of this work. Space is often hard to find for writers, and very often that need for space is being defined against many constrictions (time off 'regular' work, looking after family and so on, but also specifically gender and societal restrictions that need to be resisted), and as such a letter of support becomes an intervention. Too many works remain unwritten because writing is seen as secondary or even inimical by vast tranches of the state-social machinery, with its worth being measured in contexts of material productivity rather than creative, spiritual, philosophical, social justice and other such 'intangibles'. I write letters of support for works I can see will shift things in ways that will act as correctives against injustices, but also fit into the creative jigsaw, the meshwork of interactions of creative purpose – I see a work that is a potential node, a focal point for conversation about the interstices between language and being. It's an existential and ontological issue, and often if not always cultural, but it's also material in its implications for the creator looking for support. Great ideas that are suppressed, or disregarded, because society doesn't recognise they deserve 'space', struggle to be allowed full expression. If the internet allows mass distribution for creative (and all) ideas, the space to create them to their fullest is always difficult to find under the pressures of life.

So, I get to be in a privileged position of responsibility and get to see many remarkable works at their genesis and at vulnerable points where they may or may not find the space needed to reach that *full expression*. I recently read a remarkable as yet unpublished suite of poems by Western Australian poet Lucy Dougan which needed support to be developed and reach its audience. I imagine the poet asked for other letters of support, but I did not know about this (and usually never know of other referees), so, as always, I wrote out of my knowledge of her work as a whole and on the basis of the new work. It was superb, and this is what I wrote (reproduced with permission) as a critical engagement with the actual poetry – and I consider this statement as much part of my critical work as any critical commentary:

To Whom it May Concern

I wish unreservedly to add my voice of support for Lucy Dougan's remarkable poetry as a whole, and especially for her new book-vision, *Monster Field*. Dougan has long been a poet concerned with the 'immediate' – what surrounds us physically and conceptually at any given moment – but also deeply concerned, as she notes herself, with a need to 'articulate a part of the visible world that is not always perceived'. In poems that meticulously build a sense of causality as it issues from encounter, and intensity of perception, she creates a unique vision of 'being'.

Lucy Dougan's new work is revelatory. In a process of cross-pollination, aesthetics switch back and forth with relationships and personal change, creating a sense that something significant is to be searched for, needs to be found but won't necessarily reveal itself. In the sense that Paul Nash's 'Monster Field', noting felled ancient trees in a field (of reality, of the artwork, of vision) is a decisive moment of seeing, of being in and part of what is seen, and yet can be missed or not seen in future passings, so too Dougan's poems *encounter*; they intimate decisive personal and aesthetic shifts, even change, and yet such moments might or might not come again. In dealing with paradoxes of certainty and uncertainty in perception, we get a distinct sense of the material (a blanket, a painting ...); we can envisage it, and yet we know to 'look' further and more intensely because in order to understand purpose of being, we require something more.

These are poems of survival in that objects become symbols of resistance to mortality, and to a crisis of spirit, but also transform (in the Ovidean sense of metamorphosis) into something 'new' – not necessarily 'different', but something we can re-encounter and consequently reconsider in a different light. Home, for example, is emptied, and yet filled with representations of what was, but these representations, seen anew (and anew again and again), escape categorisation, leave the archive, and become active suggestions for newness, for departure.

There is beguiling sophistication in these new works and this vision for a new book-length manuscript, that is exciting, genuinely original, and also constantly on the precipice of trauma. After all, the founding vision is the loss of an ancient forest. The conversation between visual art and the poem is active, and Dougan has a deeply formed sense of aesthetics – but the self is changing as it perceives, and it needs to be receptive to the unseen in the familiar. As shown in Dougan's highly regarded book *The Guardians*, a poem is tactile resistance to vulnerability, bodily and emotionally, and an assertion not only of one's own existence (reader ... writer), but of material connection with the external world.

In her poems of interiors and exteriors, of the familiar and quotidian, of controlled considerations of 'the immediate', Dougan is building a vision of meaningful survival, of continuance fused with change. This can be challenging, sometimes upsetting and even quietly traumatic (Dougan never *shouts* in her poems), but is also deeply affirming about the relevant need for 'discovery', for growing with life and allowing insight to increase with encounter.

Lucy Dougan is one of our finest poets, and is already making a remarkable contribution to contemporary English-language poetry and poetics. This new work is ground-breaking, challenging, aesthetically risk-taking, and deeply affirming. It deserves support in every possible way.

Sincerely,
John Kinsella

I have also been the recipient of blurbs, references and launch speeches, and have always appreciated these acts of trust and the exchanges around them. Some have been sent anonymously, often I have seen them, and in the case of book encomiums and launch speeches, have always received copies. I take these gifts as acts of sharing, collaboration and solidarity, and they enter into my personal and writing self. I hope they have given back to their givers as well. Such generous acts are decisive in what they say, and how they say it in the contexts of 'being on the spot', and as expressions of goodwill, at the same time requiring absolute commitment to one's own take on the text and textuality, and also in giving some of their creative and ethical energy to another.

People outside such exchanges might see them as a kind of personal (at least) quid pro quo of friendship or professional acquaintance, but I have rarely ever found it to be simply that. Courtesy and generosity are very different things. I would not approach someone I knew would only be socially courteous, but would ask someone I emphatically trust to be who they are. People are not asked to be what we want them to be, but who they are. This is the interesting aspect of stepping outside the *do unto others* scenario, and separating the writing of a reference from the being a recipient of one. It's not a formula, and when it becomes one, to my mind it defeats the purpose and is also self-defeating.

Further, sometimes one is asked to write a blurb by a publisher for a text with which the publisher/editor feels you might, as a fellow writer, have a sense of connection – you might never have read the author before, or might have only encountered, say, a few poems in journals. I have found these don't often progress, but sometimes they do in dramatic and revelatory ways – one encounters a voice that demands attention and reconsideration of personal knowledges of writing. To have not heard and appreciated a voice is a reflection of one's own limitations of receptivity and reading practice.

Sometimes you are invited into a cultural space that is not your own, but you pass by near enough to offer some observations that may or may not be useful. I cherish such moments and learn from them. Sometimes one gets to comment from within the paradox of presence that is damaging, from within the colonial experience as part of an attempt to undo that damage, or try to. In such circumstances, they are not requests for support documents, but invitations, offerings to speak, to acknowledge one's own failure to speak in the best way possible, to comprehend. The person who grows in this is the blurber. In fact, no matter the dynamic, I feel I have always been the person to get most from writing blurbs – not the recipients. I am grateful to them all for offering me the opportunity to interact with them, their texts, their communities.

What I do know is that the privilege of collaboration is never an accession and never an excuse for appropriation – that by sharing one doesn't take or own anything. Collaboration doesn't have to be a giving or taking, but literally an act of respectful conversation that maintains and respects difference.

I have been interested, for something else I am working on, or thinking about, to read references sent from American college figures to W. E. B. Dubois, and to see their formalities. These are institutional references that come out of the structuring of the white state via places of learning that are likely (at the time) prejudicial, and yet the referees are seeking to be supportive through recommendation. *Oberlin College. Letter of recommendation from Oberlin College to W. E. B. Du Bois, January 28, 1932*,[26] which is positive if brief, notes that the

---

26 *Oberlin College. Letter of recommendation from Oberlin College to W. E. B. Du Bois, January 28, 1932* (W. E. B. Du Bois Papers (MS 312). Special Collections and University Archives, University of Massachusetts Amherst Libraries).

student being recommended to Du Bois (Joseph S. Himes, Jnr) is 'colored' and each category of the reference form is minimally dealt with.

A reading of this reference in the context of its writing, the context of its destination, and the context of its reception, is telling in so many ways, but my point here is to say that a positive reference out of likely institutionalised racism[27] trying to be 'positive' and 'supportive', and in the context of many references being issued (likely) for many different students with many different job ambitions, lifts above the constraint. In a way, the lifting of the reference performs the act of decontextualising in retrieval and citing that I am attempting to critique here, and I acknowledge that the discourse of life as is, and life as constructed within ongoing oppression of institutionalised bigotry (racist, ableist, sexist, wealth-orientated etc.) in the United States, does not benefit from this observation. But I celebrate the success of the refereed against the prescription, the format and text of the reference (whatever the actual intention of its writer/s).

Under the rubric of 'General scholarship', Joseph S. Himes, Jnr, is described as 'Very Good. Phi Beta Kappa (elected in his junior year)' and under 'General appearance' as 'Pleasing and neat. Is almost blind, but is very skilful at getting about.' Then follows 'Personal qualifications': 'An attractive personality. Alert and ambitious. Well poised. Has a keen mind. Dependable. Cooperated well.' This reference is stunning in many ways, but maybe the 'Cooperated well' is the loophole in the reference – not as a sign to its intended audience as a warning, but as a statement of the institution's control over its subject, and subjects. It may be generic, it may have appeared on many other students' references whatever their background, but regardless, it is a sign of 'compliance' within that particular establishment. What message did it carry to Du Bois, though? He must have been very familiar with the patterns of expression and how to read them. The student, who will become one of the United States' prominent scholars and citizens, comes from a highly regarded academic family. He is outstanding in so many ways. He is working against the system to improve the system. This student will change American scholarship.[28]

And since he majored in sociology (to become one of the great sociologists), I would guess 'the student' was outwitting that 'cooperation' in order to move through it, and that 'cooperation' is both specific and relative ...? That's reading a reference in a different place and a different time, but also thinking about Du Bois' writings of the time, and actions and the displacement of reception in the here and now for me in 'wheatbelt' Western Australia, and the problems such reading generates. What matters is the agency of the refereed, not the referee, and not the commentator (in this case, me). The dynamic that

---

27 As a friend has pointed out, this of course needs to be closely contextualised against other such letters during the period for both students of colour and white students. It is worth looking at this article, which focusses on the 1920s (so a slightly earlier period): *'This Scholarly and Colored Alumna:' Anna Julia Cooper's Troubled Relationship with Oberlin College* by Katherine Shilton [OC 2003] www2.oberlin.edu/external/EOG/History322/AnnaJuliaCooper/AnnaJuliaCooper.htm.

28 See www.blackpast.org/african-american-history/himes-joseph-sandy-jr-1908-1992/.

ensued when Du Bois read it is its own trajectory, and not mine to assume. There are many conversations in and around this reference socially, scholastically and politically taking place, to which we might or might not historically and biographically have access. This is part of the impact of a reference, and the context of its making and reception. This is pivotal.

What I am concerned about is the formulation of such references, and the persuasions the formulaic categories are designed to engender even when they are seemingly 'positive', and maybe were entirely intended as positive. They can have positive outcomes, but are they intended, encouraged or are they indifferent? It would seem this was far from indifferent, but it's hard to read much in the brevity. Would an essay-length review have worked any better? Probably not – those making employment decisions inevitably read many references, and readers and assessors want to *get though them*. Brevity is powerful. But it can also operate as a screen. For me, a referee or a blurber, if they take on the task, need to *commit*. But maybe that's the difference between official obligation and a desire to support. These points can, of course, coincide as a nodal point, and maybe they did here, but not always.

Am I reading against the grain? I *am* reading outside biography, but I am also reading with the idea of the 'neutral party' (who can't be such) coming to information and making decisions from their own knowledge-base/experience. Maybe, but when I write a reference within categories I try to signify a subversion of those categories so as not to constrain readings of the refereed – I want them to speak louder than my words which are necessarily *opinion* and mediated by all that makes 'me'.

One is always dealing with vested interests outside the party or parties one is supporting – publishers, universities, the people who have the job vacancy they want filled, and, in the case of writing, prospective audience/s. Issues of personal compromise are weighed up against better prospects of the person concerned (and the causes they represent). Derrida used to say that he had to stop writing book blurbs because so many people asked him, it necessarily reduced the effectiveness of his sign/signature of support to the realms of the rubber stamp – useless and irrelevant. I see his point, but ultimately disagree. To refuse for these reasons is to sign out of a community.

On the other hand, it allows a blanket fairness – the person you would support is treated the same as the person you wouldn't. But it's a negative level playing field and also privileges the self as authority whose final word is no word. His position was unique in its perceived value of/for approval, in its bargaining power within the supposedly less-than-material world of ideas – sadly, what he recognised (and disliked) was its 'value', its trade-ability, its worth as imprimatur, and that devalued the idea, the sign and his own voice. He was trying to protect his integrity and to leave as few traces of compromise as possible. But he *did* continue to give support to many in so many other ways. He would write his support in personal handwritten inscriptions in books, speak well of someone privately or in public. His approval was still out there, but maybe not on the back of books at request. I don't see it this way, but I get it. In

Disclosed Poetics I touched on Derrida's comments in the Preface,[29] and I think they are subtextually relevant here.

It's also worth considering that the text we put our name to might not be the text that stays attached to our names. Or the text itself might be altered. There's a criminality that intrudes, hacks, misrepresents, shifts accountability, defies checks, shifts confirmation to 'mirror sites', and alters who we are, disembodying the subject and the object, the referee and the refereed, and, ultimately, the sign and signified. This is beyond writing documents of support that deconstruct their own porousness and 'adaptability', it is being aware of ill-intent and manipulation of words we put out there intended to attach to another text or person. Resistance to this takes the support document into meta-critical activism that is fraught with contradictions over ownership and rights of access. 'Theft' is theft.

But where the text in the capitalist state has an inherent relationship to copyright, ownership and property, the blurb of encomium ultimately doesn't. It will be quoted freely because it has been offered freely – it is not a thing in itself, but an extension, an appendage. It is a commentary in which its side of the conversation is 'property' in common, and as such, a form of non-property or even anti-property.

This aspect of such writing greatly appeals to me, even when it's in bed with the possessive publishing dynamic: the act of sharing (anti-theft, anti-criminality) may be a peculiar kind of collaboration, even a one-sided one, but it is an act of sharing without the expectation of reward. To me, in such contexts, it becomes the ultimate expression of umbrella anarchism, of co-existing with the survey to disrupt the survey in the longer run. Eventually, even by state declarations, texts escape copyright (the Emily Dickinson dash vs. regularised punctuation issue and a university's copyright renewal is an interesting attempt at some form of 'exemption' for control of profit in 'idea' and material reward from sales) and joins the blurb in freedom. Often 'prefaces' and 'introductions' are copyrighted and part of the publishing contract deal, but requested words of support (and references) are not. Launch speeches are 'owned' by their makers and speakers, though may be 'given' for general use by publisher, writer/s or others. Or they may have further life as articles (then permissions to quote from books launched might come into play, a weird irony and counter-freedom) in the launcher's own book or scholarly-creative-public contexts, which creates further nodal departures with affecting (and consequential) echoes.

'References' of support for community from within community are integral to the 'self-awareness' of that community, but probably need to be porous enough

---

29 '[T]o the observation of Derrida that "Prefaces, along with fore-words, introductions, preludes, preliminaries, preambles, prologues, and prolegomena, have always been written, it seems, in view of their own self-effacement" through to his question via routes, marks, and erasure: "But does a preface exist?" [Jacques Derrida, *Dissemination* (Chicago University Press, trans. 1981, p. 9], we might be rightfully suspicious of the integrity of the prefatory comment, its allusion to a whole, its "residue" that will inform and tyrannise our reading of the "main" data, inscription' (Kinsella, *Disclosed Poetics*, p. 70).

for some shared space and interactions with commentary from other communities. Support is necessarily internal and external – interactive.

There is no saviour role in highlighting a text or its authorial qualities – it is a role of privilege in which the highlighter or 'referee' must show self-awareness of position and responsibility in order to protect the integrity of the 'process'. Is this a form of the vanity of the supporter, the approver? And if it is, can it develop such that it *becomes*[30] communal, collaborative. If it is otherwise, it's a form of self-flattery at the expense of what one is supporting, and consequently patronising and hypocritical. The person being refereed is always more significant that the referee, the blurb more significant than the blurb writer. And thus is a gift and a joy,[31] providing growth for the referee.

Now I find myself thinking of medical referrals and institutional expectations 'triggering' a process of investigation or scrutiny – the negative referral for further action, the positive to bring reward and/or improvement; the overlap and gap depending on who the parties are, who they aggrieved party is, who is on the defensive. Is it a big leap to thinking of the weaponising characteristics of university culture as it smokescreens hidden unethical research with ethics committees and praise from 'outside' (especially government and 'industry') to sanction the status quo? Citations (from citizens and organisations) used to validate the modus operandi. Self-awarding to bolster. Awards and commendations. Prize culture. And the judiciary (promoted by other mechanisms) 'reference' of punishment in calling up, demanding presence of testimony, 'subpoena ad testificandum'.

How much is the reference writing I am talking about in all its manifestations an act of testimony, and can it ever be a true act of witness?

And as we slip further into the implications of 'support documentation', of the ephemera of life that can have such positive and negative consequences, I arrive at 'guidelines for references', online forms that autopopulate and won't let you 'progress' without filling out – 'this field needs to be completed' or 'this is a required field'. These needs to be filled in before advancing to the next (often hidden) page – field of the page, field of action, taking the field – the mechanism of the state and the corporate state learning from 'each other'. There's also the increasing need to self-witness, attest and self-reference, which gives an out from 'self-promotion' because it is an institutional requirement – we too easily cede agency to gain the comfort of instruction, of contractual or 'heavily encouraged' (leaned on) behavioural necessity. Research and teaching approval comes through acts of self-referencing and garnering and gathering testimonial, too often, as well as being subjected to 'blind judgement' in terms of 'surveys' (student surveys over 'quality' of a teaching course). For me, putting my name to a qualitative and deep-textual interaction as 'blurb' is far

---

30 Just a touch of *D & G* (the collaborative work I wrote via fax with Urs Jaeggi in the mid-1990s).
31 Need I say Derrida – you've got the drift of this chapter now?

more honest and genuine as critical discourse than most if not all mentioned in this paragraph.

One can rarely second-guess the precise nature of bigotry should it arise, and the negative environments of reception in 'official' zones, though it's often possible one is writing a support document against the flow – that is, writing against the patterns of prescription that have arisen from historic oppressions. It is always at least worth considering that receptivity is going to be subject to a potential array of bigotries against both the 'candidate' and the referee.

Obviously, this all depends on context and what one is recommending for, and to whom; but in 'blind' processes, you can't know what you're 'up against'. A support text necessarily needs to deconstruct its own position of writing and reception in this light. Even in 'friendly' political environments, the mere act of referring occurs within a 'peer' hierarchising – that contradiction in terms – and thus a power differential. A 'left'-leaning poet recommending to presumed 'left'-leaning assessors, for example, doesn't mean power isn't in play – of course it is. Empathy in choice-making, in selecting over others, in trying to lift visibility of a text or candidate above the plimsoll line of reception, immediately brings the power differential into play. So we attempt to write against this, we recommend not at the expense of others or an ethical position, but in conversation with it. Collaboration isn't conspiracy in this, collaboration isn't 'siding up', it's dialogue from a declared position. Of course, the 'receivers', the audience, of both declared and undeclared (clash of interests declared, reading against the grain) demographics, are in constantly shifting relationships with the source texts. This is the very nature of textuality.

In a way, comments sections of news outlets and response to other public declarations (online and, say, on-air or print letters pages etc) become a kind of blurbing or anti-blurbing; and this anti-blurb dissing becomes the 'critical distance', and the *approval* becomes the 'like', when in fact neither is one nor the other. Critical validity is not a case of negative comment, though it might entail this, *nor* blanket approval; it is always a dialogue with a text, with cause and effect.

So it is with references and blurbs. 'Vox pop', and especially comments sections, are frequently edited, selected, merged and interrupted by and with 'moderation' and censorship of proffered opinion. In order to protect the rights of authors and others in the community, such moderation changes the nature of commentary – a narrow band, but not always a safe band. In the space of the confidential report, there is no moderation outside what the recipients do or don't take on board. This censorship demands 'standards', and in most official applications they exist, but they are applied with necessary inconsistency. Again, an awareness of this in the writing is essential.

'Legacy' issues arise from the 'permanent record'. Be it on the university files, or on the back of a book, or in a deleted comment retrieved from the Wayback Machine,[32] we are configured as referees for a future that will have varying

---

32 https://archive.org/web.

degrees of privacy and a shifting relationship of public and private. Those who make decisions on the basis of a candidate's work should do so on that basis alone, ultimately, and what a 'peer' thinks is a very small part of it, if any part of it at all. My opinion may be ultimately irrelevant, but the need for support texts makes it at least partially and temporarily 'relevant'. An intersecting of time and place, of circumstances that engenders an artificial and temporary node. The need to fit when there should be no need, is a conundrum I can only reconcile by thinking of this as a *tangential* act of collaboration – a dialogue in which one has a role of interpretation and transfer.

I have obvious problems with 'peer review' (how does one select a peer, or who 'authorises' those who will read, say, letters of support?), and anonymity in this bothers me because if one is not held accountable for a decision, it is not necessarily the decision one would have made if 'vulnerable' to witness. On the other hand, it is often argued that such openness leaves a decision-maker *vulnerable* to persuasion and corruption. The more transparent a process, the less likely it will be corrupt, surely?

Regardless, transparency of dialogue and (as an) interlocutor is the key to all my practice, and not just with writing blurbs and references and the like. For me, this is at the core of my critical work and as a writer – and especially as a poet – to be at a variegating interface with and between the public and private, between different zones of textuality. There is always an ambiguity in the relationship behind *what* one is supporting and *how* one is actually doing this. The infinite complexity the relationships (multidirectional) between referee and refereed *and* the audience/s both are attempting to speak to/with and all the textualities therein, means there is no stable model of critical analysis to position ourselves around in any of our roles of reading the textuality of support documentation and documenting.

To consider as a critically valid dynamic a 'support (of) heteroglossia' seems essential to me. But to consider it in all its integrity we must surely look *beyond ambiguity* and into the infinite variety of possible readings, into where the cross- and-counter-textual utterance occurs, where public and private conversations and collaborations blur and consequently consolidate as nodal points. I have never considered *any* document of support I've written for another a 'puff' – and one should be wary of such attempts to invalidate this most emphatic of critical forms if the writer is committed to the text and/or the author/subject/person.

PART TWO

This section is about encounters with non-human life and an articulation of vegan animal-rights activism and mode of living. The 'nature' model of literary making that often comes (to my mind) at the expense of animals is considered, refuted and criticised. Starting with a 'letter to an editor' that's as much critique of a mode of talking about 'nature' texts as it is about a book being reviewed, I write: 'Written with that oozing, sickly fluidity of so much neo-colonial cross-referential "nature writing", which seeks to historicise experience as knowledge from which definite conclusions about the right and wrong of human interaction with nature might be drawn, the article leaves us with the "experience" of encountering the author's encounters and epiphanies.' I then seek to justify other approaches through a vegan animal-rights environmentalism, and consider how important conversation and exchange of information are around this (and, yes, accommodating different approaches). The topic of loving animals and yet not wanting to 'keep animals' is explored in detail; the section finishes by reconsidering my long-term 'anti-pastoral' poetics with a look at the fraughtness between pastoral constructs of a rural 'nation' and the brute reality of such impositions – a consideration of the ongoing colonial exploitation that is supported by literary tropes. We are brought back to the point of ambiguity and its 'consequences' and movements: 'The pastoral is inherently connected with an agriculturalism of progress ... the mechanisation of the means of producing food. As such, in text, it becomes as if a "magic roundabout" that sends spokes and tracks out into ambiguities of literary expression'.

An Unambiguous Response to Helen MacDonald's Article 'The Forbidden Wonder of Birds' Nests and Eggs'

11/9/2017

Dear Editors

I write this in response to Helen MacDonald's article 'The Forbidden Wonder of Birds' Nests and Eggs',[1] which I found one of the most offensive and duplicitous articles about 'nature' I have ever encountered. It epitomised that Western-colonial genre, 'nature writing'. The self-mythologising, self-centred, and anthropocentric cues of the piece aside, it is ultimately a piece of Thanatos-driven (her Eros?) colonialism that needs challenging and showing up for what it is. The internal colonisations of Britain are well attested as a driver for the colonial project of the English, and later the British in general, regarding the rest of the globe, but what is missed so often is the fact that the collector side of the naturalist is one of the key underpinnings of possession and consequent dispossession. The rewriting of the 'observed' and surveyed into a gridwork of imperial control is possibly an unconscious characteristic of the article, but it is demonstrably evident.

The young MacDonald, as described in the older MacDonald's article, might have formed her collection of specimens from the natural world to enhance her own understanding and sense of connection with 'nature', but her present-day uncritical consideration of her drives and needs, and the vatic incorporation of this into her self-mythologising of connectivity with nature, shows an uncritical trajectory and a deep belief in her moral right. Any questionings we encounter are of manners and self, not of the broader impacts of what she is saying on the biosphere. The sense of the self as both part of nature and a controller of nature (for its benefit) is an extension of the romantic project of assimilation: what matters, in the end, is the self, not 'nature'.

Written with that oozing, sickly fluidity of so much neo-colonial cross-referential 'nature writing', which seeks to historicise experience as knowledge from which definite conclusions about the right and wrong of human interaction with nature might be drawn, the article leaves us with the 'experience' of encountering the author's encounters and epiphanies. Such encounters are sold as wisdom and science, and art. We are supposed to learn more about ourselves by learning about her *self* and its relationship to nature, specifically to birds, and their nesting/nests.

We are offered a personal rebelliousness that segues into a desire for class transgression which, rather than destabilising class, reinforces it. An *us* and *them* is created. Most telling in this is her glib usage of the 'national' in terms of the protection of birds, nests and eggs after the Second World War, and the displacement of soldiering, carnage and national identity onto the natural world in literature and film and civilian life in general. The contradiction begins with the 'gloriously eccentric' that is wholly British – as soon as you see the word 'eccentric' deployed you know you have cosy familiarity and contempt working hand in hand, but even more salient is the exclusivity of 'we can laugh at ourselves because we are omnipotent in our knowledge'. The glory of the empire. Excelsior. Breaking the taboo, reaching into the forbidden, is violation imagery as rebellion, when in fact it is compliance with colonial brutality.

1 www.theguardian.com/books/2017/sep/09/helen-macdonald-birds-nests-eggs.

There's something more than subtextually 'Brexit' about sourcing an argument of national character to refute a controlling nationalism, defining attributes of Britishness per nature as opposed to any other take on nature. The issue is further entrenched through the use of the term 'elites', a particular clarion call of the right with regard to a belief in bigoted populism, which is as much a propaganda construct as any reality. MacDonald's nervous anxiety about her 'failure' to intrude in the way she now sees as regrettable is like the dissembling surrounding the bigotry that is actually core to Brexit discussions. It goes against the grain to relinquish moral control, to leave the birds' nests to their own devices. To gain control over the right of intrusion, of judgement, to guide and shape nature, to understand through invasive 'science', are essentially being sold as a natural right, a natural justice.

The only unselfconscious part of this mellifluous piece of control writing is the somewhat vicarious connection MacDonald makes between herself and those 'factory workers' and 'poachers' and nest-robbers who wander the outskirts on land they don't own, and their points of contact with nature. They probably won't tell her what they're doing now because she represents 'authority'/control? She looks at their less privileged positions wistfully? Desiring what she doesn't have? This is class elitism of the most repugnant kind. Their (*now* they are the 'other' for MacDonald?) interaction with nature is legitimised (as, essentially, *natural*), though for one who doesn't recognise the ownership of property (as I don't), the deployment of the idea that a more equitable relationship to nature is formed by those who pillage and kill and don't have property, as opposed to those who do, seems a form of class system protectionism.

In fact, classification is at the root of MacDonald's argument – the identification of individual birds and families of birds, to file within a system of shared understanding. That shared understanding is a colonial one, and in the same way that she can now see her home as being within her – as mobile as Western privilege allows, a privilege built out of dispossessing entire peoples and plundering habitats to build the picture of interconnection and belonging, where every difference finds its way into the imperialising nomenclature – she can see 'nature' as being available. So, one is more *connected* by stealing birds' eggs, raiding their nests? And it's worse than this; the vicarious desire to have been informed by direct pillage wafts around her self-ideation: the regret that she wasn't born of a different generation when she could have got away with such invasiveness, could have been one of the proto-colonialists rather than one who lives in the aura of its rewards.

MacDonald's article invites people to respect those who are not in, say, a Cambridge elite, to go out and take a bird's egg. Maybe a single egg from a nest? Really, what's the damage. I mean, if you have triplets in hospital and someone takes one and places it in a collection, embalmed, what does it really do to the order of humanity? Who will miss it, really? She has written 'A Modest Proposal' without the satire. So, the unhatched bird speaks through its shell out of the incubator to the human child of the incubator? The symmetry of it all – the natural way of it all?

My anger isn't just the outrage of a vegan anarchist pacifist animal rights and environmental activist, or any other descriptors we might want to throw in that will tilt objections towards bathos – O the power of language, eh. Rather, it comes through being one who lives in a land colonised by the British (and the Irish, and in my case, Irish driven out of Ireland by the British!), a land still in an ongoing colonial state-of-being, where Aboriginal people are still struggling for their rights and their land. It is an anger come of being subjected to a nation that holds allegiance to the Crown of England, where the collecting of specimens by European, especially British, naturalists in the eighteen and nineteenth centuries set a pattern in place that included people, and was as violent as any act of war.

What MacDonald is talking about is warfare against nature – a 'just war', a war we have to have to secure our place in nature, rendering the nest a repository of human feelings, of extending the human into the most private of realms. The nest is not hers. We too, living at Jam Tree Gully in the Western Australian 'wheatbelt', watch birds and record their activities every day we are here. But we do not mess with nests, nor see it as our right to. Nor do we seek to control the birds, outside restoring habitat. We try to interfere as little as possible with their lives, and we still learn about them and ourselves in approaching it like this. We are no less 'connected' for such an approach, and, in fact, given our invasive presence as living on Noongar land without proper means of restitution in place, we might consider ourselves especially lucky. The control of birds, and all animals, for imperial-colonising personal and collective subjectivity, to perpetuate an ongoing mysticism of Enlightenment, is simply a case of possessing and dispossessing, of control. It is not admirable that birds have to make do with cigarette butts to make nests, but a statement about capital and intrusion by human profit-drives.

The condescension behind those on the 'edges' of the naturalists' control-desires, the 'real' people of the land ('tooth and claw'?), and those factory workers who surely need the tactile engagement of raiding birds' nests, is the utterance of privilege, which MacDonald's deployment of 'beautiful' (to quote many a response) language shows with every paragraph.

Sorry, mate, but even out here, you know, where the absentee landlords of Britain profited from the abuse of *country*, a few 'eccentrics' (how marvellous) among them, even those who go around blasting everything to shit with their high-powered rifles, know the wrong they are doing, and do it because it's wrong. Death is control, and they want control over death. Often they can tell you what they're shooting, and give a defence for it, but the blood-rites celebrations are self-justification and refusal to be challenged. Do they collect? I don't know, maybe, maybe not. But death is death, and we all know what that is in this space where efforts to 'decolonise' are met with a cascading colonialism of British literature sold as 'authentic' and at the core of the language itself.

We weep too. We weep for the capturing, the training, the collecting, the building of your knowledge bases upon which you can find who you are, *your* identity. MacDonald is wistful for a form of abuse, for a molesting of the natural world. How insulting is it to imply that the less well-off (than her? her readers?) gain by interfering with nature, with abusing it. That they are part of nature and understand it all the more for the interference in it? The appropriation of a synecdoche with country is characteristic of so much imperial borrowing, syncretism of indigenous spirituality and law stolen in collective efforts. And this from peoples who now refuse refugees and migrants when they are a nation built on the exploitation of the world for their own leisured or profitable movement/traversal – as is modern Australia – is repulsive.

For in opposing control over people's interface with the natural world, MacDonald is either overtly or inadvertently suggesting a naturalism of rapacity; that a balance will be made if it is left to those who are 'out there'. Well, your Australian experiment shows otherwise. And the liberty is actually a form of deep nationalism, a nationalism of creature and person, of land and rights, of the Western self. How we 'belong' to a place is *connected* to the respect we show place, and place includes all who inhabit it. The temporary visitor, the newly arrived migrant, the person whose family have been there for generations, all have the ability to respect place, to treat it fairly and justly.

Abusing the nests of birds to satisfy the collector's need or curiosity, to display the pickings and to make of it some kind of pantheism or scientific wish-fulfilment, is obscene. As we read translated from another colonial language (or other colonial languages) with its fair share of literary-science dissemblers (as cited by Stendhal): 'Language was given to people to hide their thoughts', and this abuse of language is a propaganda designed to whitewash the abuse of nature, including humanity itself.

Sincerely,
John Kinsella

How do poems come out of conversations?

How do poems come out of conversations, and become conversations in themselves – *generative* exchanges? Well, one has to start a conversation first. And here's a fragment of my first 'explanation' to Humphrey Crick:[2] I have been recording birds and other 'wildlife' in my poetry, along with climate (literally – rainfall, heat, winds etc) since the late 1970s, and sadly my poetry is like a map of environmental catastrophe. Poetry as record, which I guess might segue with your keeping 'scientific records' and data regarding climate change and loss.

Humphrey responded (in part) with: 'I started work on climate change when, back in the late 1990s, as a researcher at the British Trust for Ornithology I had started a process whereby we started to report back on all the huge volumes of data that our volunteers sent back on the nesting of birds. The Nest Record Scheme receives something like 30,000–40,000 records of individual nests each year and, up until that point, had not really reported back on trends. When the result came off the computer (a big old 1980s movie-type one with large whirling tapes) it gradually dawned on me that there was a glaringly obvious set of trends in laying dates across a majority of species towards earlier laying. Nobody had seen this pattern before'.[3]

I sent poems that largely related concerns about the movement away (south, to the cooler zones) of birds at 'our' place (it is Ballardong Noongar land stolen by colonists), and the arrival of other species (mostly from further inland where it is driest) that we'd not seen or rarely seen before, and Humphrey sent articles on bird response to human-induced climate change at Jam Tree Gully.

---

2 Humphrey Crick: life-long bird-watcher; Red-throated Bee-eaters in Nigeria; pesticide side-effects in Scotland and Zimbabwe; demography and climate-change at the British Trust for Ornithology; ecological networks in Natural England; Cambridge Conservation Forum Chair. https://magmapoetry.com/archive/magma-72/.

3 Private correspondence for *Magma* Climate Issue 72 (email 22/05/18).

Beyond ambiguity

The poem 'Refugia', included in the *Climate* issue of *Magma*, comes out of our final exchange of data and metaphor ... Humphrey's email included a link to a paper referring to 'information we have to how that species in Britain have been redistributing northwards – and they have been' and also this:

> We have been able to demonstrate that there are places where species are able to hang on – refugia – where they appear less affected by climate change and where the climate doesn't change as fast as the surrounding areas. We found these areas by (a) looking at where species population changes are less affected by general weather patterns than other areas and (b) by looking for places where we expect species to hold on, and finding that indeed they do. Such refugia tend to be in more topographically varied areas where species can 'move round to the cooler side of the hill' etc because there is a larger range of microclimates. We found that species loss was 22% less for plants and 9% less for insects – even though our ability to really localise the data was quite crude.

In constructing my poem 'Refugia', I wanted to make it both a 'response' to the research, and also *subjectively* interactive with the research because all living things are subjective, and not just data (as I am sure Humphrey would agree). In other words, the poem is an exchange rather than a response, a fluctuating barometer to the research that takes in moral and ethical issues of how we respond to and even discuss human-induced climate change and its effect on life (bird life in particular).

Along with the poem as 'exchange' or 'dialogue', I sent this message: 'Just to explain the paradox of the poem 'Refugia' – yes, we need to do all we can to create such *refugia*, but we need to do all we can to *prevent* having to increasingly create such refugia. This is stating the obvious, but a poem can do that and be indirect in its analysis and critiques as well and hopefully elicit questions or maybe anxieties and disruptions that weren't so evident.

A 'critique' and an affirmation (of refugia) all in one poem, I hope. That's the way I see things – no simple answers outside stopping the abuse of the planet. And in an earlier email to Humphrey I had said: These are actions of conservation *and* prevention (remedial action linked with preventative action – loss should not mean an inevitability of further loss) – to me, art is worthless if it doesn't do something. Birds and their habitats need saving. And ours, too ... they somewhat overlap!

Refugia

> 'Such refugia tend to be in more topographically varied areas where species can "move round to the cooler side of the hill" etc because there is a larger range of microclimates.'

(Humphrey Crick)

We are used to searching for the coolest
part of the garden, the house, even the bed.

It's a hot topicality we take in our packs
back to the fens, where there's always potential

for a pitiless deep fire that will drive us from hearth
and home. Who keeps to the places they know

and love, never dislodged? Those of us managing
to stay ahead of the *increase*, lifting higher up the hill,

or one step ahead – away from the afternoon sun,
perched or huddled under a rocky ledge,

altering our orientation as the deathrays mark
the calendar? Or in some Schlaraffenland, climbing

beyond a summit, making celestial the cairn
or survey peg. In the steps up the graph, I trip over

the longhorns and the lacewings, imitating
their movements in diverse places, watching

and counting, as if I've a right to petition
familiarity. This stroll across the campus

of realpolitik and pragmatics as costly as a chill
caught up in the rare snow on Bluff Knoll[4]

in the Southwest Australian Stirling Ranges –
a photo op for some, for others 'nature's fridge'

for a beer, and for others a ghost to hide behind
as Africa records its highest temperature in Algeria.

Each peak we pond hop – such voyages of exploration!
And the birds we follow no longer able to drag our weight.

On being an ethical vegan for thirty-three or so years …

I live in a vegan family situation. I have been a vegan for over thirty-three years and my partner – poet and novelist Tracy Ryan – has been a vegan for over a quarter of a century; our sixteen-year-old son Tim was conceived and born a vegan, and remains one. If you ever doubt it's his choice, ask him – he's eloquent on his veganism, and has angles on it that we don't, neither Tracy nor I

---

4 For the Noongar people, Bular Mial ('Bluff Knoll') is culturally highly significant and they prefer people not to climb it; but whenever it snows (a rare event), photos are inevitably taken by climbers offensively cavorting in the conditions.

having been born vegans. Tracy has always had a deep interest in nutrition, and raising children vegan has been a deeply informed life-act – done with respect for their rights as well as animal rights. We don't use animal products in any way we are aware of. Rather than seeing our food, clothes, shoes and working materials as animal-product 'alternatives', they are our norms.

Over the decades we have seen and heard it all when it comes to the arguments and attacks on veganism. Really, people find their own way through such things as they do if they hold any committed ethical position that is about principle and not style. One of the first that vegans encounter is the specious argument about denying children before a certain age a choice in the matter, that veganism is forced on them. It's such an obvious reply: aren't you forcing your carnivorism (or more accurately, omnivorism) on *your* children? They are also not given a choice – people make decisions for their children before they are empowered (informed enough) to make decisions for themselves. It is possible to have a balanced vegan diet, and even back in the mid-1980s, vegan sources of B12 and other more complex nutritional requirements were available.

But the point of this argument is not about the *fors* and *againsts*, because these are well attested, and even the most slipshod research-skills will reveal what is and isn't the case. Rather, this is an account of long-term veganism in the context of the recent increase in vegan consciousness,[5] and availability of vegan foods. Actually, vegan food has always been available, of course, just in raw and rudimentary and unrefined ways – what we are talking about in the 'now' is the widespread replacement of mass slaughterhouse products with non-slaughterhouse products that 'equate' and move from being 'faux' meat (protein), or ersatz, to food definitions and realities in their own terms. That's what has industry scared and reactive. Personally, I have a problem with all industrialisations and capital processes of market – the fetishisation of products that increase wealth rather than answer needs – but it is this 'mass' that so upsets animal-exploitation agri-industrialism. Little of it is cultural, outside profit-making. Arguments about what's best for the planet are placed far down the list of priorities, as the fossil-fuel desire shows.

There are exceptions, and cultural beliefs do need to be respected. When I began being a vegan, I was outwardly proselytising; now I am only so in my writing and via how I live. I have learnt that respecting others' journeys is the only way that long-term change comes. That's an argument re all ethical issues, and it could be argued that all killing must be stopped immediately or we simply appease our own consciences at the expense of being concerned about our own behaviours – many mass murders have taken place as people let their nation's military go about its business outside their personal scrutiny, as that

---

5 A consciousness in the broader 'public mind' largely driven by increased availability of vegan 'goods' – but this is also a reflection of a sizeable vegan demographic and the efforts of vegan activists and organisations working for labelling and promotion of those 'goods' as well as increasing scrutiny of animal-testing regimes, factory farming, and the relationship between meat production and climate change (etc.).

scrutiny is confronting to undertake. Ethical positions are not 'cults'; cults are the control of others to remove their capacity for personal choice – but it is a paradox to see veganism called a cult by meat-eaters who have been part of an industrial slaughter-cult all their lives. Cultism isn't small, always; most often it's huge, just huge and has the state to back it.

Ironically, I come from a background of fishing and hunting. I was obsessed with guns when I was a child and a teenager – I wanted to become an army officer. My turning away from these values was conscious and specific – by my late teens and early twenties, I was a committed vegan, anarchist and pacifist. I found my way there via the paradox of loving animals (I always have) and exploiting them (to my mind). My poetry was tracking my concern, so my poetry helped in the decision-making – that old argument of poetic language expressing the inexpressible. When I wrote of casting aside the gun, of leaving animals be, it was because I had – but also to articulate and mark it. To give a sign in word as well as thought and action. A pact, a long-term agreement written out for myself. A constant reminder of how and why I'd got to that point of change.

This was not easily the case – as an alcoholic in former days, I was aggressive, often in trouble, and confrontational. After seventeen years of alcohol and substance addiction I 'got sober' in 1995 and have remained so ever since so I could better hold the values I believed in. It wasn't an easy journey, but one in which I knew I had to reduce my own hypocrisies. And that's it; that's where a lot of misunderstanding manifests between vegans and non-vegans – it's not a holier-than-thou situation, but a move towards being less impacting, less damaging, and more respectful of life. I've actually known vegans quite violent (towards people), and I have rejected their positions because of this unresolved hypocrisy, but this has been rare. And even in these cases, in time if they stayed vegan (they often didn't), they moved away from their own anger and aggression and lived a life more in tune with their values. I say this because veganism is both an ethical position, and a position that eventually calls on a variety of consistencies with regard to how we treat *people*, who are, after all, *animals too*.

A lot of older vegans will talk about the 1980s as being a time of Nutmeat, avocadoes and bananas, of boiling pulses to make protein patties to add to the steamed veggies, of reading labels carefully because there wasn't the vegan certification process (or 'market' for that to be insisted on) back then. Sure, it is nice to be able to go out and eat more 'cheffed' foods from supermarkets and in restaurants, but it's not the be-all and end-all, and you still weigh up issues such as processing, origins and cultivation methods, and air-miles on products.

If we fall into dependence on mass food production processes, then ultimately we will damage animals in other ways. A classic example is that of palm oil – so essential to many processed vegan foods (as indeed non-vegan). The destruction of habitat to increase palm-oil production eventually led to an ethical response and a call for palm oil that's non-exploitative (of people and ecologies) – a regulation. People survive the best way they can, and as with so many raw food materials, they are sourced in less-wealthy zones to feed wealthier areas – capitalist exploitation works fast to adjust to new markets.

So any veganism not in tune with these issues quickly becomes an appeasement of one's own conscience while hiding from the potential for damaging impacts. The response has to be holistic – vegan food producers need to work with non-vegans and different cultural realities to ensure transitions that don't damage in other ways. This is not wisdom from on high; it's just decades of seeing faddism and change, of people calling themselves vegan when they don't closely consider what's in a 'product', or deploying the terms as a social definition while allowing themselves 'exceptions to the rule', or, say, eating honey (an animal product!), or whatever exception they find to the 'rule'.

The point is, 'vegan' means something, and of course be whatever you are, but let's allow a term to represent a value we can share and understand. Play with language by all means (that's what writers do), but not with the ethics of commitment. Mobile phones, whose raw materials destroy whole communities and habitats (I am not equating these per se) in their extraction and manufacture, are an example of a contradiction with the new spreading of the message of veganism – we have to find a way through to a commonality of understanding cause and effect. It's a big and complex picture that tussles with the obvious fact that an animal hurt or killed is an animal hurt or killed.

Veganism intersects with many cultural attitudes, and diverges from many others, across the globe, but mutual respect is, in my experience, an unassailable value. I have never tried to force anyone to eat vegan, yet attempts have been made to shame me into not eating vegan, in order not to offend my hosts. I have never compromised my ethical position, but I have gone to great effort to explain my position and my desire not to offend a host.

That was early on – now I carefully have discussions before, say, sharing an eating space with those who have invited me about how and why I eat (and don't eat) what I do. An intercultural conversation needs to be had. Confronting? Surely, in a pluralistic society we have these conversations to ensure respectful co-awareness all the time? If not, then we probably should. I have no problem in being forward about who and what I am – in fact, I see saying so as a sign of respect for my hosts. An unambiguous position that always needs to be sensitised to the ambiguities of the human condition, and also to the different equally unambiguous nature of cultural beliefs and attitudes. In itself, difference is not ambiguity, but we reconfigure it as an 'answer' regarding why we need to respect difference.

The bottom line in all this, for me, for my family, is animal rights. We live among animals but keep none – they are part of the world around us and we wish to have no control over them. We deal with 'pests' in non-invasive and non-damaging ways, and we work towards a consistency of respectful interaction. That's to do with seeing no hierarchies of control, no speciesist superiority. Then you get the unthought-out attack-mode on saying such a thing (seriously): Are you saying if a lion was attacking your baby, you'd do nothing? Well, of course I would … What do you expect? Would I be cruel and seek to hurt and exploit the lion? No. Anyway!

Living in the UK in the late 1990s, we – as a family – were invited to appear on the television programme Susan Brooks's Family Recipes. We went up to Manchester from Cambridge, and the chefs, Susan and her daughter, prepared us a vegan meal on set, and we sampled it and discussed what it was like being a vegan family. It was a fascinating experience because of the warm attitude to how we lived, coming from a 'regular' cooking programme.

Britain has long been more in tune with vegan living (the terms comes from post-War Britain), but in the 1990s it was still very 'minority'. If we were not part of the dissenting opinion, we were still giving a minority report. At the same time I spoke to the *Vegan* magazine about being a poet and a vegan, and how it informed my writing practice. There was a context. And it was broad in its conception – if you wanted medical research without vivisection or abuse of animals, you could support the Dr Hadwen Trust!

Such contexts are still being created in Australia – the aggressive response from some people to veganism accords with a macho public culture that seeks to manipulate markets to defend old colonial land-usage and the machinery of animal pastoralism. In this, I am not commenting on individuals nor even communities, but on the machine of capitalism and its empowered defenders. A stunning (I use no words carelessly, I think) example is the providing of no vegan food options in prison to an imprisoned vegan activist – this is control, this is oppression, and this is the state protecting its ongoing colonial interests. There is a disconnect between (in part or primarily) 'traditional hunter-gatherer' societies and the mass-consumer export–import underpinnings of colonial capitalism. It is the latter that concerns me because I have been part of it – it is to that I speak.

There's a new generation of vegan activists in Australia who have quickly been turned into public enemies – they are targeted by media, police and government, and seen as interfering with what amounts to an ongoing sell of Australian values. And we know the recent governmental history of that trope! As a poet, I've tried to speak through poetry in support of these activists, while also recognising that I come from a very different space through being older and longer-term in my activism.

I live in rural Australia, and co-exist with farmers and people who eat and use animals. Not in the house I share, and not on the Noongar boodja land where I live, and which I acknowledge is not 'mine'. But nearby. They know who we are and how we live, and we offer an alternative. Animals find refuge if they look for it. It's their place, too. The conversation is ongoing, persistent, and there's no compromise in our position, but it's also respectful of other people's humanity, their free will and their journeys. They are not us and we are not them. I will stand in front of a bulldozer to save bush, and I will live next to a bulldozer driver.

People act in ways they know how to act; each of us can only offer one another examples of alternatives. That's how real change comes; that's how fewer and fewer animals will suffer. In the long run, but in this crisis mode of biospheric collapse, the reason there are more and more vegans is that the time has come to act. And people are acting. Others will too, because they see a need and want to, not because they are told to. Bullying happens in many directions at once.

If I see a problem with the New Veganism it's a possible connection with presentation and social monitoring. Social media try to direct, but also dilute the commitment of person to person, person to animal, person to real place where animals live. Veganism doesn't need 'influencers' – though if anything stops animals being exploited, it's a good thing. But as we – Tracy, Tim and I – see each animal as an individual with their own intact rights, as we see people, so we see the collective, the community, the herd, the hive, the loner, the gregarious ... all these 'types' ... we also see the interconnected fate of the biosphere.

Technology that promotes veganism which consumes the planet is, for us, an irresolvable contradiction. A lot of thinking needs to be done around this – and modes of presentation and discussion need to be considered as well. The slaughterhouse is obvious and hidden; it is literal and a metaphor that can become real for all life in sudden ways.

Just a positive to finish with. I have crossed Australia many times (though not recently) by train, as I avoid flying in Australia (to lessen eco-damage impact), and I have done so with much pre-prepared vegan food. But the train caterers were always willing to make 'bespoke' food for me, to supplement my food stash. The door to a broader veganism in 'Western' societies has actually long been open – and if Western capitalism could learn from many non-capitalist, non-Western cultures around the world, not only would they find much precedent sometimes on a very large scale, but also much communal goodwill around the choice of what we eat, and why we do or don't eat it.

And to reiterate my support for the new generation of vegan activists looking to intervene in non-violent ways to stop the pastoral-factory exploitation of animals, I wrote this poem, which appeared through PETA (People for the Ethical Treatment of Animals): I am not on social media, but they took it into that realm, the realm of style, influence, but also loss and consumer endgame if people are not wary.

I am here now

> for the young vegan activists saving animals from slaughter

I am here now
because a young human
interrupted my journey to the slaughtering,
hoisted me over their shoulders
and carried me towards animation.

I am here now
my eyes dilating fast
to take in this extension
to life – and the blood of my kin
is a river never divided.

I am here now
because an intervention
drew out the length of my days;

the things I have learnt we have taken –
we breathe the same air as our dead.

I am here now
because the young humans
are rising peacefully from their screens
to step into the killing zones,
to bend down and lift us back to the light.

No pets but surrounded by animals – proximity sensors and warnings

We don't, as a family, or as individuals living together, keep 'pets', so as not to directly control animals and/or subject them to human needs and uses. Much is written about the calmative and therapeutic and developmental benefits to children of keeping pets, but I feel that is a construct at the expense of an animal's rights, and the loss of animal rights is an occlusion of human rights as well. For me, animals and humans should very often share similar rights, and sometimes the same rights.

People might generally agree with this in terms of a right not to experience cruelty and pain. However, I take this much further, into the realm of real liberty and psychological freedoms. Where we live, in a fragment of degraded bushland in the largely cleared Western Australian wheatbelt, our son Tim is surrounded by 'wildlife' and has, likely as a consequence, developed non-intrusive respectful interactions with animals, birds and insects – he has developed acute sensors to the proximity of all living things, including plants, but especially non-human animal life.

This does not mean that we *live among* as a kind of animal-behaviouralist witnessing to acquire knowledge for reflecting back on our human condition, or even as an understanding of animal behaviour in itself. Rather, it is a means of sharing space in the least intrusive way while still being aware of our own impact, yet also our own vulnerabilities. From such acts of respect a sharing can arise, and familiarity creates a language of presence that is 'living', and non-denominational, non-speciesist.

Immersion in a vulnerable habitat, for observation of vulnerable animal species, might ultimately serve *itself* more than who/what it is trying to protect (not always – this argument is not absolutist, but a possible interpretation ... things are constantly in flux with regard to actuality and perception), as in, say, the case of the butterfly lover who spends so much time in the field and loves, as Nabokov did, butterflies beyond conception, and yet could not only net and kill and display them, always hoping to capture a new species, but infuse his writings with them as key symbol and more. In such cases, the animal becomes the servant of textual control. In the same way, we might think of the many poems dedicated to pets in which the clearly 'loved' pet does poly-duty as real-life entity and proliferating symbol or linguistic device. Maybe there are exceptions, such as Thomas Hardy's remarkable 'Last Words to a Dumb Friend' with lines such as:

> Never another pet for me!
> Let your place all vacant be;
> Better blankness day by day
> Than companion torn away.

and:

> Housemate, I can think you still
> Bounding to the window-sill

But even here, where pet is perceived as equal in worth to its 'master', it is still occupying the space of the animal within the house; it is still doing what we expect in the manner of descriptors of 'cat' (or 'dog'): 'bounding'. The companion is soothing. But this is not to doubt Hardy's sincerity, as the poet/pet-owner also says:

> Strange it is this speechless thing,
> Subject to our mastering,
> Subject for his life and food
> To our gift, and time, and mood;
> Timid pensioner of us Powers,
> His existence ruled by ours,

and:

> As a prisoner, flight debarred,
> Exercising in a yard,
> Still retain I, troubled, shaken,
> Mean estate, by him forsaken;

The poet possibly suggests he is incarcerated in the loss as much as the pet was in the 'master'-pet dynamic, and is prime beneficiary of the relationship. He is now, for all his wide domain, limited to the space of his pet's former life. In another Hardy poem, we have a dog digging on its mistress's grave ('Ah, Are You Digging On My Grave' with the ironic twist that it's not from love or pining but from finding a place to hide a bone – soft ground!6). Note I use the word 'owner' not because of how the 'master' or 'mistress' necessarily perceives their relationship to their pet, but how the law in these circumstances would see it.

And keeping to the Westminster colonialism, we might try Elizabeth Barrett Browning's 'Flush or Faunus' (her oft-kidnapped and ransomed spaniel), who finds

---

6 Mistress, I dug upon your grave
   To bury a bone, in case
   I should be hungry near this spot
   When passing on my daily trot.
   I am sorry, but I quite forgot
   It was your resting-place.

a way through to the quiddity of love via the pet: 'Who, by low creatures, leads to heights of love' wherein primal necessity, love, wildness, meet a kind of warped colonial-centre domesticity. A collapsing metaphor of a rotten imperialism? There's an interesting item on the PETA website entitled 'You Can't be Feminist and Buy Dogs', which links to a cascading intersectionality of discourse built out of the contradictions of control and deprivation.[7] Human rights are animal rights. Human rights are not constants, though they have certain inviolables across cultural difference, and animal rights if we sync them with human rights will undergo the same variations. That's a human legal perspective that has little to do with the animals themselves, and all the metaphors we can compile won't liberate animals from the constraints we directly or indirectly impose on them.

The butterfly is the wild animal that can be made a temporary pet – not temporary in its life-span but temporary in the interest or satisfaction it can give the human with its considerably longer lifespan, then conserved in death if pinned to a display board. Vladimir Nabokov's childhood collection of butterflies (in its display boxes, labelled 0 was left behind in Russia when he left after the Bolshevik revolution, but bits of it are still to be found. Nabokov made textual pets of exactness and precision (especially in his drawings), which serve as a collapsing metaphor in the movement from child collector to adult obsessive. He was later obsessed with butterfly genitalia.[8]

As a child with many pets, I would sometimes keep butterflies in an aquarium – caught, let sit with little room for flight among the flowers in the aquarium, I would watch the monarchs and painted ladies live their short lives. Sometimes it was caterpillars through chrysalis to emergence in the tank, then free. I didn't 'play' with them, but made observations which I recorded in a journal. Pets and science, and where one began and the other ended. Their names were species names, and I watched them constantly. When I released a butterfly, careful of its wings (the risk of *damage*/hurt is so easy), it was with my hands – intimacy and empathy? The butterflies cycled in my room towards their deaths surrounded by model tanks and planes and toy soldiers and books. When all else was devastated, Australian soldiers after a battle in the First World War managed to save a major butterfly collection.[9] Filmmaker Sam Hobbs, great-grandson of Lieutenant General Sir Joseph Talbot Hobbs, in partnership with the Western Australian Museum, created a documentary film telling a poignant true story. The film reveals how, in 1918, on the eve of the Villers-Bretonneux offensive, under the command of Lieutenant General Sir Joseph Talbot Hobbs and Major General Harold Edward 'Pompey' Elliott, Australian troops rescued French Lepidopterist Eugene Boullet's priceless collection of butterflies.

In researching the identity – the 'naming' – of a small native mammal I saw recently where we live, I was appalled to come across 'local' graduate student

---

7   www.peta.org/features/you-cant-be-feminist-and-buy-dogs/.
8   See *Nabokov's Butterflies*, edited by Brian Boyd (Allen Lane, 2000), p. 11.
9   http://museum.wa.gov.au/museums/wa-maritime-museum/bayonets-and-butterflies-film-screenings.

research trapping, tracking, marking and 'environmentalising' native fauna, by which I mean purporting to work for the animals' benefit, which no doubt most do believe because of the propaganda generated by 'education-institutional' processes. The expressed love of animals extends to creating a research totemics that often pays lip service to traditional custodial knowledges, but can run the risk of being more about one's own professional progress. It is easier to 'save' ('protect', 'conserve') your speciality – your research *topic* (the signified) – when you are prepared to sacrifice the agency of an individual animal for the 'greater good'. When this happens, it isn't about life; it's about notions of order – 'habitat' as substitute for colonial mechanisms, for the educational and scientific organisations in which life is product. So many of the graduates from such courses will work for mining companies whose love of life goes as far as finding the most efficient way through red-tape.

We keep no pets. We don't believe any animals should be subject to that kind of human control of 'ownership'. This is not to say that we don't think there can't be forms of *symbiosis* between animal and human, because there can, and nothing is prescriptive, and the exception to any pattern is inbuilt in the chaos. But to 'own' an animal is an act of body and mind control, and reflects issues of power, subjectivity and displacement as much as it does 'natural affinity'.

It would seem ironic that to weave one's way out of the impasse of the field study, out of the confirmable data, out of the peer approval process of observation and comparison, we might find more defence of an animal's rights in metaphor than in scientific evidence accrued to 'better conserve'. And by metaphor, I mean the space between animal linguistics and human linguistics – not utterances and signs we can mutually recognise, but in the frisson of proximity. Proximity[10] is about co-existence with tenuousness, not about control and ownership. There might be threat – we live where there are inevitably 'poisonous snakes' moving through in the ever-widening warmer part of the year – but we are aware, and can co-exist. Awareness, caution, distance. When we cut grass, we leave some uncut patches for animal life (in all its forms) because though these are introduced pasture grasses that have 'weeded', they are now part of an adaptive habitat. We don't blame feral animals for colonial destruction, but recognise human culpability. Where we are, so many feral cats began as house cats.

Non-human life is a constant where we live and is part of our living. Animals and plants. It is dry and damaged and getting more so, though we plant and plant and try to protect habitat. But observation isn't about visiting a nature reserve or going into an area that's to be mined; it's living among animals. Recently, while grass-cutting (shire obligations along with firebreaks – we cut, never spray, as less damaging to all life, including the biosphere as an entity), I knocked an arm-thick fallen branch – long since termite-eaten and become one with the ground, high wild oats grown up around it year after year, cut down

---

10 For this context of 'proximity' see Kinsella, *Spatial Relations*, Vol. 2, p. 111. For variations on related concepts of 'proximity' see Kinsella and West-Pavlov, *'temp(ə)rərməs*, and also Kinsella, *Polysituatedness*.

when dry. As I bumped it a mammal emerged. It was the size of maybe three field mice, was shortish but fat-tailed, big ears, and moved oddly. I watched it closely as it moved from grass tuft to grass tuft, then let it be.

At first – before working through various identification guides with our son, Tim, who originally suggested what it in fact turned out to be – I thought it might be an ash-grey native mouse, but that didn't quite fit. Eventually, I made a positive identification as a short-tailed dunnart – I haven't seen one in the wheatbelt since I was a kid, though they are more common in some places than others. They favour the semi-degraded peripheral area of open and sheltered ground I found it on – I hesitate to use the expression 'edge effect', but if not literally it works effectively within the metaphor of co-habitation across partially enforced ecotones, and ones that were created over longer periods of time. Colonisation is about rapid conversion – the human impact on place is always part of human presence, but the colonial-collector-scientist vanguard of occupation is about preparation for rapid change, for assertive and coercive impact. The colonial presence is about consequence to serve the centres of power from which colonists are deployed, so often believing they have an agency they don't. So, the fat-tailed dunnart is here.

This year there have been multiple nest failures around our house, and no doubt many more out across the granites and patches of York gum and jam tree that constitute the hillside of 'Jam Tree Gully', our own construct of surveillance, for all our removal of internal fences. This former horse and sheep property, in which no animals are kept, and kangaroos and echidnas move from the public reserve land through where we locate. The nest failures have come about this year because of the introduced laughing kookaburra – we observe it observe, but don't interfere. Two years ago, the native pied butcherbird worked its way through songbird nests, feeding on nestlings with methodical intent.

Recently, at a Hills pub, a man described by his lawyer as a 'bushie' ripped the head off a kookaburra that was trying to take the man's food – a bird well-known to patrons, and one considered part of the construct of the place. The pet that wasn't a pet; but the act of brutality was defended as 'getting rid of a pest' – the introduced bird whose death the lawyer claimed would have been lauded not long ago. I don't need to deconstruct this. As I have pointed out again and again, you get gatherings of feral animal killers who claim to defend environment but you never see those same people out stopping the bulldozing of native habitat, and if you do, it's at publicly acknowledged protest sites, not among the tens of thousands of hectares of mining and pastoral land-clearing that takes place every year across Australia. I can tell you, you don't see them. On the other hand, the local shooters love to fight feral animals.

We don't keep pets. Let's work through this, making reference, with his permission, to our son Tim who loves animals beyond all other things. Yesterday he was excited to see a Burton's Snake-Lizard basking in the driveway – pointing out that when we last saw one, it was still being called Burton's Legless Lizard.[11]

---

11 Note proper name caps!

Tim didn't disturb it, but with his keen eye did observe it, and every detail was taken in, as well as the figurative language of associations and proximity.

I was a little bemused recently to read a study of a native animal in which the student scientist – as is not uncommon – gave the animal she was researching a 'personal' name. A pet name? To name an animal personally (as opposed to its species naming) can be an act of respect and protection, of acknowledgement of an analogous agency – the productive anthropomorphics of respect that may or may not be mutual but is accorded from the human end, the respect expected of us in morality and law towards other humans, extended to animals as a kind of 'protection'. Of course, such naming can be a temporary sign of affection, or it can be objectification – it's not a simple equation.

But to name when one has trapped an animal, glued a transmitter to it, painted it with glow paint to make it easier to track, and so on, surely risks a glib kind of objectification, even if the ultimate aim is to collect data for species conservation. The named individual is used for the greater good? There's no animal choice or rights in that.

Having said this, when we see an animal here at Jam Tree Gully on a regular basis, we differentiate it for our own sakes – and it is for our sakes … a positioning of where we might sit here and how we might sit – by giving names. This is something come about through Tim not having pets yet wanting a special but non-intrusive familiarity with the animals that surrounded his days.

The magpie that followed me around for a day, even wanting to enter the house and watching me through windows and so on, checking out the mating and nesting territory, Tim asked me to name because it makes him feel a respectful connection to an individual rather than a species, or to life in general. The magpie was called Brent and we see it often. We named it for our benefit, not its own, so we could differentiate when talking between ourselves. And maybe it's also because our son has always liked to give names to animals we see regularly as a kind of non-pet soothing of connection – 'the boy with his dog' sans owning a dog. Familiarity without possession. Maybe.

We did not intrude on 'Brent' – the magpie's – life other than being colonially here, the ultimate intrusion, but one in which we paradoxically live refusing its tenets. Part of that refusal is to abuse the 'wildlife' by damaging more of its habitat – rather, we try to repair, understand the many different overlapping animal territories here, and move around them, and through them cautiously.

Establishing a Proximity

Magpie lands close – almost eye-to-eye –
to avianise me to sum up whether or not we might co-exist,
family beside family, to find a safe zone within perspective,
a nesting place close to human habitation, working facial recognition.

Hours of up-close interaction – followings, conversation, scrutiny.
And the rest of his group arrives to check us out in consultation. I can guess

they don't use words like 'tribe' or 'parliament' to self-describe but have *other*
words more attuned to their local condition, their specific vocality.

The *male* I liaise with is setting-up and surveying and in negotiation
(*welcome!*), but there's group-talk I'm not privy to – a robust discussion
over acts of imposing magpie qualities to human features, the tendency to
avianise
the friendly, the seemingly *empathetic*. Even so, I insist I *connect* – it *is* the case.

But this comparing of magpie life to human life, of human life to magpie life,
leaves the afternoon open to three-dimensional paths: collusion, understanding,
withdrawal, escape. There are immediate social and familial obligations
that must take precedence. All those trigger-words let go in our intense

tête-à-tête, our finding common ground, close to the ground airspacing –
yes, we can do this, can accommodate, respect and appreciate, *liaise*.
And we say, *Rather than how it looks* – those skills of description –
We can envisage ... a beak smoothing feathers, a hand wiping a brow,

the skin texture of our legs, quick claws, quick nails, adjustable gait
a sense of humour, acute hearing, decisiveness. All outside the bar-coding
of *who* and *what*, our non-product selves mulling over experience, tilting
heads and eyeing off the space, the logistics falling into place.

Such clarity beyond vanishing points. And this the material
of spiritual and literal transcriptions from our versions of faith.
Know magpies have terms for phenomena that more than equate, and *know*
they are aware how they can be ripped-off and turned into software

that has nothing to say for *them*. And so, this rite de passage,
this shadow to shadow rights-issue that is no colour by number,
that is a worn path reconsidered, a lifted wing and a lifted hand.
To make pact to make language the devices can't parse. No, it's being

in dialogue – contending and discerning and learning. Beak by mouth,
face to face. Crux of syrinx and throat, signing through metaphor.

And Tim gets the naming act from his early days when we got back from the opossums and pileated woodpeckers of his babyhood in Ohio, to stay with extended family under Walwalinj in York and the 'family dog' being a big feature of his life there. This old kelpie sheepdog was named Shep and yes, was *much loved*, originally saved by my brother because as a lame animal in a working dog world, it would have been shot – my brother must have been Australia's only vegan shearer back then ... So we have the scenario of the saved animal who becomes 'family'.

The pet of necessity? Yes, of course, but it's because of animal usage in the first place, and if the fetishisation of the animal as extension of the human could lessen, especially in colonial-industrial constructs, such dynamics would need less to exist. Pet-keeping is a complex equation. The animal as extension of the human goes from the guide dog to the empathy animal to the drug search and policing dog. At some point all will be considered necessary to have a bond beyond mere human usage to elevate the animal above utility – of course. There are degrees, and it's certainly not my right to judge these degrees or claim to understand them – I have seen such bonds between animals, and, indeed when I was a child and had many pets and was responsible for the 'keeping' of many animals, I certainly felt this to be the case.

Yet the false proximity of those animals, who would not have stayed – other than the dogs, one of 'my' many parrots, and vague interactions with a cat – if they had not been constrained in some way, developed a Stockholm-syndrome-like affection and need on their part, and a desperate act of transference on mine (I was a bullied kid at school) and self-affirmation (I was caring and appealing to them – a just person). It fitted a pattern, as pet-keeping does. This is not an attack on people who love their 'pets'; it is a committed challenge to the formalising of interactions between people as owners and 'pets' as property. Chips in pets? Registration? Pedigrees? Constructing breeds? Speaks for itself. Or as Gary L. Francione writes in *Introduction to Animal Rights: Your Child or the Dog*:

> The status of animals as property renders meaningless our claim that we can reject the status of animals as things. We treat animals as the moral equivalent of inanimate objects with no morally significant interests or rights. We bring billions of animals into existence annually simply for the purpose of killing them. Animals have market prices. Dogs and cats are sold in pet stores like compact discs; financial markets trade in futures for pork bellies and cattle. Any interest that an animal has is nothing more than an economic commodity that may be bought and sold when it is in the economic interest of the property owner. That is what it means to be property.[12]

The unwanted 'pet' is usually one without worth to its owner, or one that costs more for upkeep than it gives in satisfaction, comfort, 'empathy', companionship or even work (cattle and sheep dogs, drug dogs etc). Degraded property. The just human will try to recoup life for that animal, provide refuge, but if the process is genuine and not a quid pro quo, they should expect no rewards for doing so. The dog with a difficult personality doesn't suddenly have to find a more amenable personality to be acceptable. No amount of animal psychologising can repair the damage done by cruelty. These animals don't need the status of pets; they need lives. Loving homes may be homes that too often expect some kind of return for their largesse.

I am a huge fan of the writings of Ursula K. Le Guin. She blogged about (and *behalf of?*) her cat. Her cat. Her pet cat. It's a complex array of separating animals and humans, of owning and not owning (conceptually), of role-playing.

---

12 Gary L. Francione, *Introduction to Animal Rights: Your Child or the Dog* (Temple University Press, 2000), p. 79.

I will quote her here about cruelty (a cat with a mouse situation), because for me the irony is that pet-keeping is often a form of cruelty not intending to be that.

> I want to say clearly that I do not believe any animal is capable of being cruel. Cruelty implies consciousness of another's pain and the intent to cause it. Cruelty is a human specialty, which human beings continue to practice, and perfect, and institutionalize, though we seldom boast about it. We prefer to disown it, calling it 'inhumanity,' ascribing it to animals. ... Wild cat and wild mouse have a clear, highly developed, well-understood connection – predator and prey. But Pard's and his ancestors' relationship with human beings has interfered with his instincts, confusing that fierce clarity, half taming it, leaving him and his prey in an unsatisfactory, unhappy place.[13]

True and not true by definition of Le Guin's own role in Pard's life. Of course, she was aware of all readings – this was a subtle and brilliant thinker at work. But there's a need for Pard's presence, clearly, and it's a settled paradox I can't settle with. And cruelty? The 'hunting instinct' of any creature, 'interfered with' or not, shifts definitions of cruelty. Animal rights and human rights dialoguing over difficult conceptual terrain.

So our children – other than vicariously through interacting with others who did – did not keep pets. One of children wanted to keep them, we later became aware, one doesn't and never has (he has made clear). Tim is clear in his attitudes to animals – a vegan all his life, he lives to 'see' and 'hear' and 'sense' animals, especially birds, in proximity. He has lost nothing of the empathy humans seem to want, even need, from animals to placate the human-superiority lies of power, and is fascinated by mutual aid as opposed to a competitive anthropocentrics. He has had serendipitous interactions with animals that become figurative, and offer ontological purpose, and even answers.

The behavioural aspects are interesting insofar as a 'natural' tendency to non-violence is the result of seeing animals live 'tooth and claw', as opposed to say the Ted Hughes parsing of animal violence into an extended metaphor of human sexuality, relationships and indeed interaction with the animal world. In doing this Hughes is being speciesist, as the animals that exemplify human qualities of aggression and even 'passion' in this view are always those that are carnivorous and have 'sharp' teeth or claws. Communities that live a hunter-gatherer lifestyle traditionally, then utilise their traditional ways in modernity-colonial affected and inflicted contexts, inevitably call on complex totemic relationships to animals that are entirely figuratively different from such 'tooth and claw' constructions of 'human savagery'.

The *savagery* comes in the consumer subjectivised 'relationship' of human as product consumer in a Western state-corporate power structure (inevitably militarised), and not in the 'othered' and *primitivised* (by colonial corporate-states) traditional societies and their continuations and adaptations. The racist and

---

13 https://longreads.com/2017/09/12/ursula-k-le-guin-literary-legend-and-cat-blogger/.

colonial 'heart of darkness' is a product of savagery-desiring, like breeding dogs that can tear people to pieces, like using Cetaceans in anti-mine warfare, and in the massive *science of abuse* inherent in adapting every component of animals to human usage and profit. That's savagery, and that's a theft of animal rights to serve human greed. Savagery is *capital*. Pets are so easily capital. Owners are savage, not pets, who have no choice because choice is always denied them.

It seems to me that the need humans have for the non-human animal as companion can be so overwhelming that people cut themselves off from other humans and spend time with 'their animals' because they feel better understood and even more respected and secure than they do among humans.[14] But it's still an issue of control – animals can make choices to be with humans, but I feel that all space needs to exist for an animal to make this decision with as little 'persuasion' as possible. Proximity brings familiarity.

Speciesist arguments built out of extensive observation and testing are those I least trust when it comes to individual human-animal bonds. If you watch a gravel ant 'colony' function over a number of years, you become aware that a massive collective intelligence works alongside the intelligences of each individual ant. How does one have a distant yet necessarily interactive relationship with such a colony? Sounds absurd, but we have to here in our home. After a long dry spell, we had a summer storm, and gravel ants rapidly diverted their foraging trails and started building new tunnel structures down around the house. We couldn't co-exist with them in this capacity. As always (I hope!), I found a non-damaging way of communicating with them, using orange spray (non-toxic), and upturning areas of ground on their new foraging trails (when the trails were quiet in the cooler evening); I persisted at this for two weeks and they moved back to their old zone about sixty metres away. Interaction, communication and mutual understanding. They've not been back around the house other than on their usage of trails foraging.

I mention these ants because our son Tim has been watching and learning from that colony for a decade. He knows everything observable about it, and has drawn many metaphors – literally – from it. It's part of his language of comparison, shared presence, and a linchpin of discussing all the 'theres' he sees with the 'here' of Jam Tree Gully. He has not captured or interfered with the ants, and, indeed, walks with an awareness of their possible presence. When I was a

---

14   Whitman's 'Song of Myself, 32' – 'I think I could turn and live with animals' – has a bizarre irony insofar as his own sense of human self-absorbs all life, including animal, and seems to claim to outdo it all! In becoming 'one' with the stallion, the rider-human-self claims to elevate the used animal to the status of 'pleasure'. This sexualising is its own liberty. The final lines: 'I but use you a minute, then I resign you, stallion,/Why do I need your paces when I myself out-gallop them?/Even as I stand or sit passing faster than you.' (https://poets.org/poem/song-myself-32)

By way of contrast, consider Sylvia Plath's poem 'Whiteness I Remember', in which the horse 'Sam' has agency and control over its rider (Plath), and is not an extension of the human spirit/body but an extension of his own 'off-white' (ness), self-determining against the 'reins' – 'The world subdued to his run of it'.

child, I insisted I needed an ant colony kit, which I stocked, kept, and watched perish in time. Science as cruelty. I wouldn't have called my farmed ants pets, neither probably would anyone else, though I am sure the queen got a name. Maybe The Queen. And I would have had Workers and Soldiers. Generics with a touch of the familiar. Naming as an enactment of control, of ordering. Of knowledge, data. That's learning?

I had that ant colony in my bedroom. Proximity. Outside, I had a pet sheep, pet kangaroo, pet ducks, pet dog (family pet and I didn't feed or clean up after it), pet quail, pet parrots, pet budgies, pet guinea pigs, and my brother had a herpetarium full of Western Skinks, bobtails, and even bearded dragons down the back inside the silver walls of an old above-ground swimming pool. Not even the dragons could scale its walls. My brother loved those reptiles, and they had a relatively large open space, and were often 'rescued' from bush that was being bulldozed for developments or land-clearing for farming. He knew each reptile and had them for years – he fed them, and obsessed over them. Yet he wouldn't do that now. Neither would I. And neither would our son, Tim.

What have we done at 'Jam Tree Gully'? We have tried to provide an open-air refuge where animals have choice to come and go. Birds fly in and out, some are resident, some appear for nesting, others pass through. They have their patterns, though climate change and further land assaults around us are changing those patterns. We observe and record and lament and, other than trying to repair habitat, don't interfere. Is our expectation of them being here, coming here, part

Figure 1 The author aged 11 in his younger brother's herpetarium holding a bearded dragon with another bearded dragon sunning itself on a chunk of wood.

of a pet-desiring? I don't think so – rather, life and signs of life as purpose. And when they go, sadly, they are often shot or hurt by the increasing land developments around the region. The clearing hasn't stopped. But the most obvious layer of choice remains to them, and that's life. They lose choice in our presence, and our proximity is always impacting, but it can also seek to repair intactness.

Dream pastoral inversions: re-approaching pastoral fraughtness through questions of Australian rurality

Now the dream is a picture-puzzle of this sort, and our predecessors in the field of dream interpretation have made the mistake of judging the rebus as an artistic composition. As such it appears nonsensical and worthless.[15]

Sigmund Freud

mum's partner was in a rollover last night after leaving jam tree gully ... he was run off a gravel road and the ute with mower on the back (he'd just been doing our top paddocks between the trees) caught a culvert as he pulled over to avoid a collision and the ute went through a fence and rolled. the person who caused it didn't stop but fortunately someone found him a short while later (and it's a very isolated gravel road so he was lucky!) and he is now in hospital down in the city – tracy is driving my mum down now. he's okay, but lot of staples in head etc etc.[16]

email to Russ

Inside the pastoral is no field trip but rather entails separations from a rurality that have been and remain invasive, biospherically damaging, and degrading to so many people outside the land-food-capital interface. We are intended to fear the power of farmers – the non-unionised collective of property owning or land controlling (tilling) – because they hold *food* over us. Mass agriculture is sold as the panacea against mass starvation. Increasing populations have to be fed, obviously, but the use of (multinational) agrichemicals and genetically modified crops often act as a 'saviour' commentary in sync with profiteering in the context of 'Global South' 'rapidly increasing' populations, significantly enhancing Global North capital's ability to manipulate fear/anxiety across 'demographics' and to concentrate its wealth and control. The case of the 'unwanted' GM cows in Australia's south-easternmost state, Victoria, adds a further dimension;[17] from Dolly the Sheep via a mammary-gland cell, and certainly in medical research, the animal of science is also the animal of food that privileges and prioritises human bodies. Big Pharma agriculture is the dream rebus of horror – the words of largesse and gifting combine with images of the well-managed *locus*

---

15 Sigmund Freud, *The Interpretation of Dreams*, https://en.wikisource.org/w/index.php?title=The_Interpretation_of_Dreams/Chapter_6&oldid=3954821.
16 email to Russ, 2018.
17 Michael Slezak and Penny Timms, 'Mutants or Miracles?' *ABC News*, 15 March 2020, www.abc.net.au/news/2020-03-14/genetically-modified-cows-no-horns-in-australia/12018078?nw=0.

amoenus, at every 'spot' redressed by seed patents, heavy-industry machinery, satnavs and apps developed in the counter-contextuality of the decolonised 'ideas' spaces still being manipulated by colonial capital. As industrial agriculture retains its footing and profitability and only collapses under present virus conditions where labour cannot be accessed, a more sustenance-based (and in dialogue with habitat) agriculture is completely devastated by sickness.[18]

Emerging from these nodal points of 'pastoral' referentiality, necessity and desire make for a seemingly nonsensical rebus that can form poems of devastating clarity. 'Western' pastoral poetry essentially arises from aesthetically configuring (for entertaining a privileged audience) herding and grazing (by those who serve) on land, if not held in common, often bordering on the cordon sanitaire if not beyond. And, if on a rich patriarch's land, that land still having a certain amount of threat and wildness to embody the patriarch's sense of the chthonic, of hunting prowess, of control 'over the forces of nature'. And if that sounds a little like the black-and-white movies of the Rank Studios or Hollywood of the 1930s–1950s, then think again: the big white houses of colonial land grants are still central in many Western Australian wheatbelt districts, and if family connections have changed (many have not), the symbol of the (restored) house remains, uncannily.

Modernising pastoral begins with the rise of (ancient) Rome as an obscenely militant, self-automating superpower, and not with the 'early modern' period – and is certainly set by the late eighteenth century and might be seen as a subtext, even, of the French Revolution. Post-1968, the struggle over the compulsion to increase profits *while* retaining 'traditional' farming rights and protecting land-usage patterns by farmers in France (prior to the Yellow Jackets' cross-communal consumer-driven anti-wealth and pro-energy usage contradictions) was one of the greatest and most virulent sources of social agitation. A pastoral protectionism on one level, but of a pastoral that tried to reconcile private property ownership with 'tradition', and anti-control by big business, but with tariff protection and market sureties. The pastoral life is a construct of freedom and profit, of openness and behind the closed doors of the barns where the research takes place: it is the window in the side of a cow on a university property in a city pretending to be a farm, then being sold off for housing. It is the breath of fresh air from a country-rural ride with a dose of Roundup spray drift; it is the class action that follows in America, not Australia. It is writing a poem against Monsanto and being legally silenced.

The dream of the pastoral is the advertising campaign – Barthes by proxy; of course I am thinking specifically of 'The Rhetoric of the Image' (1964)[19] – in which the denoted is the list of 'benefits' the farm and its literary correlatives

---

18 Ebola is another concern for the Global North because the virus can spread out of designated areas of small agriculture and small and communal landholdings and can also impair supply of gathering and harvesting (cocoa) in ways directly damaging to Global North capital.
19 https://pages.ucsd.edu/~bgoldfarb/cocu108/data/texts/barthes_rhetoric_of.pdf.

(insert name of poet and name of poem of agri-mining-industrial-landgrab-colonialism HERE) and the connoted is THE FARM as universal signifier, it being essential in itself, and also overriding other land uses (be it collective, communal, industrial, privatised or familial). THE FARM connotes life, a control of nature, presence and permanence. The farm as concept highlights the competitive aesthetics of traditional familial connections with specific tracts of land, and the 'need' to increase production because in bringing fruition and fertility it will ideally increase human life, seemingly to boost productivity to feed people, but ultimately to maintain profit and if not a labour force in the age of mechanisation and post-mechanisation, then to maintain an audience for products thought up and sold, profited from, by capital. State and business collude in this but are also at loggerheads, and this drives an ongoing pastoralism in the arts. And I am not talking per se of, for instance, Hugo's Normandy or Rimbaud's vagabondage with the possibilities the countryside offered for social disruption (and avoidance – and the cascading racialisms and bigotries that implode in *A Season in Hell*), but a universalism of THE FARM that is utilised as an extension of *The Art of War* in all its cultural variant – that is, extensions of state and capital, of individuals, groups and also families entrenching power in the earth itself (as with mining) and often making it dynastic in the process. So if the farm is the code, it is also its decoding. We buy or are supplied with its produce and are indebted to its clarity of meaning, which are in fact obfuscations of design, research and control. Farms are claims to the past but are about controls of 'future'. They contain many variants of rurality, even the more industrialised farms, but they always rely on the persistence of memory of having to provide, meaning that they are likely to continue to provide, no matter what the ecological, social and health (and animal rights) 'costs' might be. They are implicit and explicit at once. They are of the dream, but 'real', seasonal and controlled, natural and artificial.

In Australia, rural causation of climate damage, land toxicity, extinction through clearing (flora and fauna), and mass fire events that extinguish ancient forests are counteracted or even entirely denied because of the 'necessity' of food production and even a colonial-generational relationship to landholdings. The 'need' for fire to germinate and regenerate is deployed by capital as an excuse to limit economic loss through a reduction in emissions, controls on rapacity. Indigenous knowledges of fire usage are ignored on an official level, though given some acknowledgement on the level of decoration, rather than concede that this is stolen country, which was 'agriculturally' far better managed and lived with before invasion and colonial control. Acts of dispossession of Aboriginal people are absorbed into a patriotic nationalism that is reinforced by rural-town war memorials and an ongoing active myth of the rural that serves Canberra and state parliaments as a lever for large-urban-population needs and fears. They will be fed if the rural is not messed with. As long as someone is out there providing poems that give comfort to this national myth, it will roll on. Les Murray, brilliant a poet as he was, happily filled this role. Judith

Wright didn't, but she was thought to do so by people who didn't actually read her poems closely, and especially not her non-fiction.

In *Feminism & Geography*,[20] Gillian Rose notes (and cites) the historic 'stronger men' dynamic of the 'field trip' and also its 'heroic ethos'. Geographers become stronger men by challenging Nature – 'geographers, like the mythical giant Anteus, derive their strength from contact with the earth. Anteus became stronger each time he was hurled to the ground' – and the real geographer faces wild *Nature* for the sake of knowledge, 'even though it may on occasion mean taking risks, living dangerously' (p. 70). Pastoral poets, *contra* geographers, are in a constant state of field tripping, wandering or hallucinating from the writing zone into the paddocks/fields/gorts etc, seeking an order of words to denote the relationship between wild (or the errant 'wilderness' that becomes a form of open 'untamed' farm) and farm per se, between nature and nurture, between power and surveillance, between eating and singing. This mediation serves the state well – it ensures that lines of supply are kept open and encrypted as topoi, as tropes of presence and the need to 'defend' that crucible of body and mind. The field trip from the city to the farm is entertainment that brings back information to reassure but also allow for adaptation and prescience. The field trip allows the pastoral state to be one step ahead and, arguably, poetry is its propaganda. It is an inherently patriarchal incursion that requires the farmed land to be reconstructed in field notes as a rebus of performative figures and textualising of the land. The next step in this is the poetic boustrophedon, but the irony is in the reading against the Euro-colonial light, right to left, left to right, the furrows turning against themselves, and yet the land marked. Ways out, from grinding the soil with disc plough on disc plough. Chemical ploughing – super-toxic farming (dream that rebus and find the words). Overseeding.

I have often walked vast farming areas alone, and still do. As a child, I always felt vulnerable to the sudden appearance of strangers, though usually only the farmers and their workers that I likely already knew were around. But in vast 'emptiness' scattered with occasional pockets of trees, there was always the prospect of a stranger emerging from the horizon and being able to see your retreat through a low field of wheat, or down a firebreak, along a fence line, into a small stand of trees. I thought about this when out alone. The field seemed a haunted place because the cuts in the ground were always with you. The markers of earth-body that could be transferred to your own body. What are the politics of this, or will it only, for me, remain suggestion, the waking dream of connection rather than incursion?

I began thinking about how I would look, walking the farmlands, to a viewer walking across the salty curves of the earth, and what we might yell at each other to ward each other off. I started yelling poems of farming out to mirages and blurs in the distance from early childhood. One time I had sunstroke. The visitor, always the visitor, looking for a place to hide amid places where the

---

20 Gillian Rose, *Feminism & Geography: The Limits of Geographical Knowledge* (Polity Press, 1993).

Beyond ambiguity

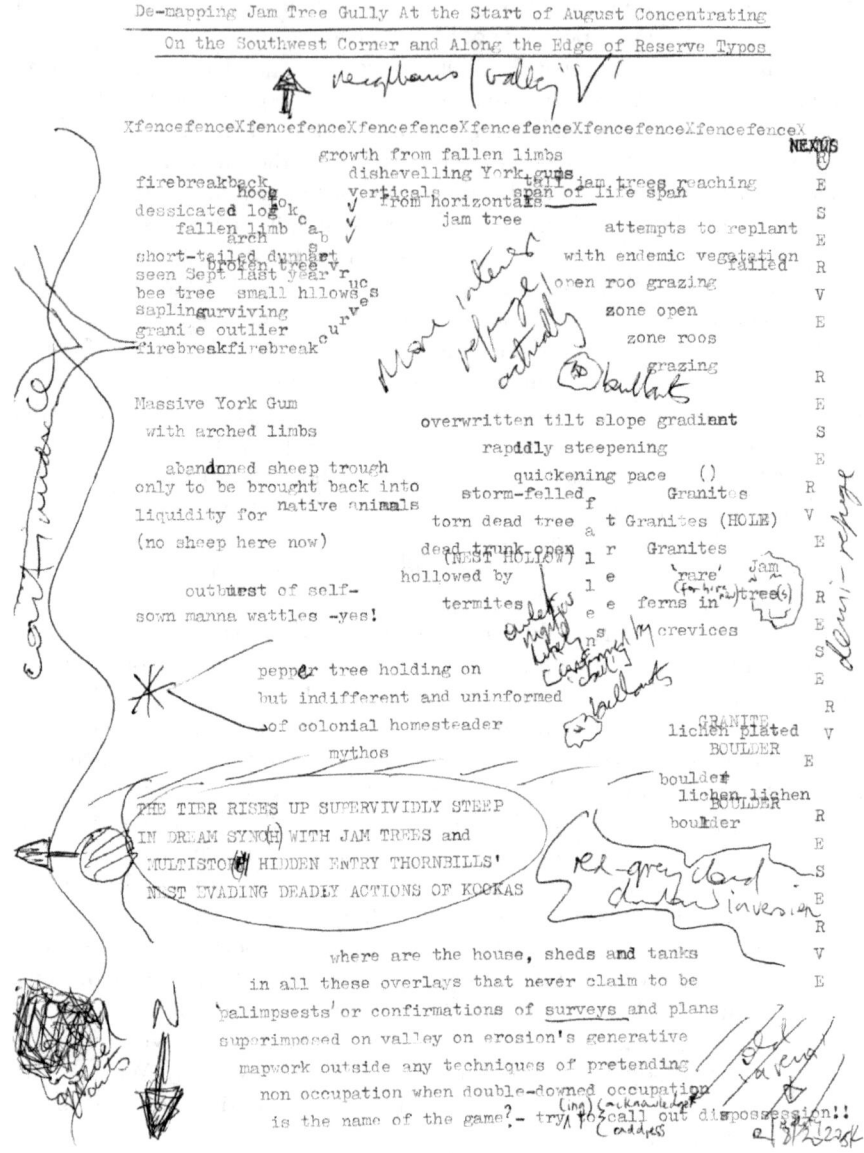

Figure 2 Demapping Jam Tree Gully at the start of August, concentrating on the southwest corner.

vegetation had been stripped away. One day I lay down in an almost dried-off crop of wheat and made a body impression. Then I felt so guilty I got sick trying to lift the broken stalks, raise the fallen heads back to the vertical. As I was saying to someone the other day, 'Vertical Poetry' travels the continents (*viz.*

W. S. Merwin's translations of Roberto Juarroz). It may be urban in its distribution, its location of publishing and sending out, maybe in its making, but its roots will always be non-urban. But it carries the colonial residues, even where what it reaches up or in to is not colonial. The poem as farm that feeds but doesn't mark? I concrete poems so they vanish. I de-map 'rural space' that was once farm, that was and will always be Ballardong Noongar land with usages not open to me. I denote the materials of being here in typewritten words on recycled paper. I scan it and invalidate, and this is the end of any happiness where just acts might bring some happiness to those who have lost happiness. The wish-fulfilment of the pastoral dreaming is self-disgust. A pastoral restoration project? An advert without audience?

When 'Guru' (Mum's partner) was driven off the road and rolled the ute, the mower and whipper snipper were damaged and it affected grass-cutting across two zones. His body was damaged, and our ability to control our relationship with Jam Tree Gully (mower and whipper snipper wrecked – shire-enforced grass-cutting and fire-preparedness necessary) was damaged, too. He was the priority, of course, but we all discussed contingencies in retaining control. To protect the nature here from intrusion (if we don't do it ourselves the shire will spray with herbicides, then fine us – the fine doesn't matter, but the toxins do!). We cut dry grass, but always leave pockets of dry long grass for creatures (sustenance and/or habitat); we pattern safety. Rebus again. The damaged body bled on the damaged machinery, and a farming couple rescued Guru, his blood on the pasture they'd cultivated.

Meanwhile, back where Mum and Guru are, under the ancient mountain of Walwaling with its stories as precise as any science (as Noongar Elder Len Collard points out regarding the deep science of Aboriginal 'dreamtime' stories), Guru is recuperating. The accident altered my poem-making. Always anti-pastoral and counter-pastoral, always a pastoral of bloodstain and accident and incursion, it also became a pastoral of allowing a space for personal compassion and adjusting to local situations and personal-specific needs. So the pastoral got more 'anti', but also more empathetic, I hope. Can that be the case for me? I think it must (be). I rarely sleep and when I dream I dream super-vividly. I unravel the codes as I write, looking out onto my tasks of rurality – not of THE FARM, but of vegetable gardening, firebreaks, tree planting, restorations.

Always the paradox, but a paradox disrupted. This 'compassion' is always there because I like people, even when I disagree with them, and even when they loathe me. Something inherent in life, I like. In *The Silo: A Pastoral Symphony*,[21] almost twenty-five years ago now, in poem after poem I object to the rapacity and the damage wrought across the Western Australian 'wheatbelt' (so called, but I find the human qualities eternally interesting. The human quiddity. And I live – we live – always among people who it would seem mostly

---

21   John Kinsella, *The Silo: A Pastoral Symphony* (FACP, 1995 and Arc Publications, 1997).

oppose what we 'stand for'). That's a fraught situation, but also one necessary to break up the dynamic of field tripping, of taking the plough disc back to town or city space to aestheticise, to connect with components of empire without direct culpability. But many farmers (not all) will clear vegetation from land and lament an increase in drought patterns. Suffering doesn't become less no matter its cause, and compassion is necessary, but so is resistance to clearing and an ongoing intervention in the pastoral poem. Aboriginal poets I have read and heard do not write pastoral poems, even when they are writing of the pastoral – their declared identity and kinship contradict the totality of the machine of agri-culturalism, its theft of country and claims of legitimacy in utility and agency, its claims that it feeds those who need to be fed (all of us, but the disenfranchised are the lightning rod for accusations of rural self-interest).

As such, farmers will always be 'our farmers' in the nation state's propaganda, its harvest- and slaughter-driven raison d'être. In *Poetics of Relation*[22] Édouard Glissant notes: 'The empire is the absolute manifestation of totality. The thought of empire is selective: what it brings to the universal is not the quantity of total-ity that has been realized but a quality that it represents as the Whole' (p. 28).

The Australian version/construction of the 'Western farm' is contemplated as a Whole, even when it is in financial or psychological distress, even when it has been dry for years or scorched by fire events, or the farming people have suffered loss or illness and can't farm and keep the books balanced, are in debt to banks, rely on subsidies and so forth. It remains across the various land titles 'Whole' as a concept. The farm is protected, not those who serve the idea of farm – though too often those serving the farm are caught up in the national and empire myth of farm and serve its purposes, frequently to their own detriment. The agri-corporations, the larger, wealthier landholders – well, it is in their interests to perpetuate the myth of the farm and its wholeness, and of the pasto-ral vision of cooperative rivalry. 'Primary' (industry) is core to this propaganda. The advertising.

So, fraught in all utterances, and the poem has to draw on this and find a way of shifting the song so the empire can have no totality in any form, and will eventually break down. So the pastoral poetry I seek to write is one of land returning to a different functionality and relationship with people, with respect for and in dialogue with knowledge of land grown over vast periods of time. The new poem needs to be very very old in its listening.

The pastoral is inherently connected with an agriculturalism of progress, even if this is traditionally an inversion of progress or even performatively 'anti-progress' – to retain a Golden Age, to keep things as they always were … but, in the country houses, profit will always be the foremost concern, and profit comes with 'progress' and the truth of pastoral exploitation resides in this paradox: the mechanisation of the means of producing food. As such, in text, it becomes a 'magic roundabout' that sends spokes and tracks out into ambiguities

---

22   Édouard Glissant, *Poetics of Relation* [1997], trans. Betsy Wing (University of Michigan Press, 2019).

of literary expression (from memoir to the 'Aga saga' to documenting the tithing starvation of the rural subaltern and other puzzlings of inequality in literary depictions of land–food production relationships – so often, the more sensitivity that is shown to this plight in conjunction with multinational profiteering publishing houses the more exploitative and ultimately callous it is). Further ambiguities are issues of temporariness in terms of change even at the level of the genetics of, say, grain the per se in terms of military and constabulary occupation of and policy about broader swathes of territory, and a 'vector overlay' in three-D without digitalisation through commercial-government-military satellite mapping. Terrain, terraforming, poem, casting poems in lines, in mnemonics. The sundial losing its shadow, its refuge, all day long.

We now have a literary as well as ontic endgame and mass extinction. Some people are gradually easing/merging this into/with a fantastical 'Doggerland'[23] fiction-desiring for a hunter-gatherer Euro purity of presence[24] that can remap according to earlier catastrophic climate-change events. They are vaguely seeking to normalise matters through archaeological retrieval of evidence of the continuance and persistence of humans – a new survivalism that is not denial but neither does it accept the personal need for dramatic change. Literature, especially fiction, occupies this position, as do *distracting* sciences of 'evidence' as justifications of our contemporary condition as intrinsic to the 'natural' arc of human 'development'. Pastoral, even in its negating and challenging-status-quo variations, can easily fall into the resist-but-ultimately-comply mode if awareness isn't omnipresent.

Pastoral has always been a vehicle par excellence for satirising social manners, class and wealth/leisure/comfort, but usually with affectionate bite (and that is arguably its failing), but Romanticism dragged it steadfastly into a 'high art' (for all its apparent openness to ordinariness and the idiomatic) of elegy, of lament for the loss not only of a 'Golden Age' but of the possibility of intactness. Consider Paul Alpers' claims, ventured in *What is Pastoral?*: 'The satiric potentialities of pastoral are commonplace – to the extent that in some accounts, satire is not simply an aspect or potential use of pastoral, but its main motive. And the extraordinary emphasis on the Golden Age in modern accounts of pastoral – far beyond what is justified by ancient or even Renaissance writers – is due to critics' accepting a structure of relationships which makes the elegy, in Schiller's sense, a definitive manifestation of

---

23   https://en.wikipedia.org/wiki/Doggerland.
24   For a deeply disturbing bonding of archaeology and oil exploration, and with special attention to be given to the word 'arguably' in relation to the incontestable science that fossil-fuel usage is causing an exponential increase in human-induced global warming, see this apologia: 'Professor Gaffney has mapped 43,000 square metres of seafloor terrain, using data supplied by oil and gas exploration companies. Today, fossil fuels have arguably played a big role in the current period of global warming, so there's an irony about these resources contributing to finding out more about the last great melt' (www.abc.net.au/news/science/2019-11-20/searching-for-doggerland-archaeology-palaeontology-scandinavia/11707174).

the impulse at the heart of this kind of poetry'.[25] Actually, Rosanna Warren[26] long claimed that pastoral included an awareness of rural problematics, which it does – but for me, never *enough*. I seek to lift pastoral 'beyond' satire and elegy into record-keeping and witness. The question becomes how we talk about that positioning, and how that becomes (necessary) heteroglossia with the poem. Which naturally charts a course that takes one back to forms of eclogue.

The writing of an against-pastoral is an issue of location. All locations of farming have been subscribed to nation-state and corporate power structures, so often by acts of dispossession. The pushing of land to produce more food for the necessity of 'feeding mouths' is one thing, but to ramp up to 'value-add', to profit to feed a small number of people's leisure and empowerment, is the corruption of locality and locale out of rapacity and greed. This exploitation of the body is the male field tripping, the geographising of the earth via a persistent and resilient patriarchy. In her essay 'Toward a Politics of Location', poet and radical feminist Adrienne Rich writes: 'Begin, though, not with a continent or a country or a house, but the geography closest in – the body. Here at least I know I exist, that living human individual whom the young Marx called "the first premise of all human history". But it was not as a Marxist that I turned to this place, back from philosophy and literature and science and theology in which I had looked for myself in vain. It was as a radical feminist'.[27] And in the eclogue, the unifying voice of the poet (traditionally serving the expectations of the privileged, not the 'workers') controls the singers/herders' voices *and* the voice of the song competition's 'judge'. The herders and the 'goddess' serve the poet's purpose of celebrating the privileged, who will inevitably seek to profit from the land of the pastoral. In reconfiguring pastoral, radical retakes of positioning of gender and identity in constructs of land *per* text are essential. This exists in the work of Canadian poet Lisa Robertson and American poet Juliana Spahr, and many others, but it also needs to happen at the level of how we all (as consumers of text) re-inscribe our presence of consuming locality and how we commune about it. Maybe the pastoral poem has validity in this.

There's a poem by Vénus Khoury-Ghata written out of experience of warzone Lebanon in which the pastoral implodes into a reformulation of gender and nurturing stereotypes in the face of catastrophe and survival – a de-pastoral of survival against brute reality in a conflict zone. In 'L'automne précéda l'été', she writes:

> L'automne précéda l'été d'un jour
> des jardiniers vigilants coupèrent plus tôt que prévu les cils humides de

---

25 Paul Alpers, *What is Pastoral?* (University of Chicago Press, 1996), pp. 30–31.
26 Kisella, *Spatial Relations*, Vol. 2 – Dialogue with Rosanna Warren.
27 Adrienne Rich, 'Notes Toward a Politics of Location', *Blood, Bread and Poetry: Selected Prose 1979–1985* (Virago Press, 1986), pp. 210–231.

la passiflore
et los horloges tricotèrent des nuits plus étroites[28]

How things keep on in such circumstances relies on resetting and persistence. Not the same, and adapting. But to forget how we got to crisis, and to not try to prevent the damage, is criminal. Pastoral has the ultimate responsibility because it has safe-distanced itself from the damage as much as it is ironised, lamented or celebrated. It should never be merely an entertainment. There is no dream of a pastoral, but the pastoral is infused with dreams of 'us' and 'them' – the readers and the actors we expect to do the doing.

It is hard to write while carrying out hard physical labour, but is it hard to think about writing sitting in an air-conditioned combine harvester with stereo, following the ley lines of a GPS around the paddock? The farmer-poet is the farmer who knows what's best for the land because they 'love the land', allegedly, even though it is stolen land (in Australia). Do we elide David Campbell's poems of rurality and Virgil's war-land-grant 'farming', do we take the pastoral lease out of the work of Judith Wright, or are these intrinsic to each other across the timing and spacing of global rural capital, for all their different 'takes' on it? Do we offset these imperialisms and (in Wright's case especially) anti-imperialisms with the active voice of singers of and on the land in an array of agriculture-nature elisions, wherein THE FARM does not represent THE FARM but acts of co-existence in which food is one part of growth and being? I think so, and I think so as pantheist and anarchist, as pacifist and vegan, as a believer in rights of self-determination, in the rebus being understood by the layperson and the dream being interactive but respectful. Maybe this is the spiritual-locality respect integral to international regionalism. To withdraw from Western pastoralism, see, for example the perspective of rural India,[29] and particularly the enactments of rural resistance to encroachment as exemplified in these words by Rajkishor Sunani, a Dalit poet, singer and activist from Karlagaon village, around 110 kilometers from the Vedanta alumina refinery in Kalahandi district: 'From my childhood, I have been a rebel. I protest against injustice', he says. 'I joined the movement [against bauxite mining in the Niyamgiri hills] in 2002–2003. I wrote songs to make people aware, and I travelled from village to village to spread the message of the movement'.[30] For me, peace and environmental activism and a justice of cultural and spiritual belief are the drivers of an activism of rectification.

But in the dream of farm as giving space, 'the farmer' requires the tools of a conventional poetics that elides and merges the 'rural' (colonial agriculturalism) with *Nature,* includes a dash and splash of self-deprecating humour (you know,

---

28 Vénus Khoury-Ghata, 'L'Automne précéda l'été', www.babelmatrix.org/works/fr/Khoury-Ghata,_V%C3%A9nus-1937/L%E2%80%99Automne_pr%C3%A9c%C3%A9da_l%E2%80%99%C3%A9t%C3%A9.
29 See https://ruralindiaonline.org/articles/the-singers-and-poets-of-rural-india.
30 https://ruralindiaonline.org/articles/the-mountain-forest-and-streams-are-our-gods.

as in how Australians like to 'take the piss', as the saying goes, through sometimes brutally satirical means … and out of themselves, too, as self-satirists … but not *really!*), and lots of national myth-making – adapted as science fact embedded in literary-popular canonicity from a montage poem such as Dorothea Mackellar's 'My Country', still wheeled out by right-wing media pundits denying climate change (and always misread and geographised as all-continent encompassing). As an aside, the paper referenced in a recent newspaper article entitled 'Climate Alarmists Are Brazen Opportunists Preying on Misery' cherry-picks history, has no understanding of frequency, change, effects of industrial revolution, and so on, and lays claims to the dead and their opinions/responses/feelings in a patriotic fervour of now-ism.[31] Pastoral needs to collapse in their hands when they try such tricks of the mob – the rural mob-ism of national militaristic agriculturalism; the nightmare of their pastoral dreaming![32] – desiring to keep Euro-farm traditions alive in colonised spaces and mechanise, chemicalise and genetically modify to increase production and profit. A false claim to community via common purpose and common need. Not the cooperative interactions and the mutual aid envisaged (and witnessed) by Peter Kropotkin but a retreat into a pastoral nostalgia of nature punishing but them not punishing nature: the landowners; pastoral equation – the state–private balance of capitalism and colonialism.[33]

31 Chris Kenny, 'Climate Alarmists Are Brazen Opportunists Preying on Misery', *The Australian*, 15 November 2019, www.theaustralian.com.au/inquirer/climate-alarmists-are-brazen-opportunists-preying-on-misery/news-story/00d6187186abc4b74e46f7d2b7903053.
32 While I was not thinking specifically of Bob Hodge's and Vijay Mishra's *Dark Side of the Dream* in writing this, I guess the spokes of the magic circle are all-reaching.
33 See, as a subtextual interest (though I am not validating all said in this piece by citing it): *Kropotkin, Self-valorization and the Crisis of Marxism* (https://la.utexas.edu/users/hcleaver/kropotkin.html). It carries this introductory note: 'This paper was written for and presented to the Conference on Pyotr Alexeevich Kropotkin organized by the Russian Academy of Science on the 150th anniversary of his birth. The conference was held in Moscow, St. Petersburg and Dimitrov on December 8–14, 1992. It was the first such conference to be held on Russian soil since the Revolution in 1917. Published in *Anarchist Studies*, edited by Thomas V. Cahill, Department of Politics, Lancaster University, Lancaster, United Kingdom, February 24, 1993'. The piece says:

> Where the economists (and later the sociologists of work) celebrated the efficacy and productivity of specialization in production, Kropotkin showed how that very productivity was based not on competition but on the interlinked efforts of only formally divided workers.
> When, for example, he turned his attention to the relationship between the urbanization of industry and the relative neglect of agricultural production, he did not merely attack the former and lament the later or evoke nostalgic pastoral images of the past. Instead, he sought out and explored situations where this ecologically and socially crippling specialization was already being overcome, as in the *culture maraichere* around Paris – where the wastes of the city were being reunited with the soil to the benefit of all. Such living examples, he argued, were manifestations of the counter-tendency of a cooperative interdependence and constituted at least one way forward in this domain.

Dreaming for me is fraught. I counted the number of times I used 'fraught' in a recently completed 'critical' book and it was frightening. What does the word denote and connote at once? Is it beyond rebus? In one super-vivid dream eclogue, I was trying to argue that it was more ethical to work at a wheat-receival point than to clear land on which these crops are sown. Why, asked my 'rival' singer? Because even within your own logic, productivity will increase by replanting trees, healing the land, cultivating less with higher yields in a healthier non-toxic environment. My rival laughed and sang me out of the picture. But I came back, and said the poem isn't part of it: land returned to those dispossessed, land-restoration, cleaner air and soil, a pullback of tech and property, and THE FARM will become us all as pure connotation – a rebus of a vast mixture of forest and plains, of mountains and rivers ... signing 'distance' – *far* – followed by the letter M, which is the valley I am living on the edge of. The rival in the dream eclogue correctly said to me: that's selfish and egotistical to use your geographical point of reference and interest as a universal signifier.

PART THREE

This section considers a number of poets' works and lives. From celebrations to obituaries, from investigations to elegies, the common theme is the tension (the condition of being 'fraught') between how a text is read and what the intent was behind its making, and also its publication. The key to reading the ambiguous relationship between belief (vegan anarchist pacifist) and reading a text justly and in its own terms is focalised, especially in the discussion of Alison Whittaker's *Blakwork*, in which a number of poems are set around an abattoir where family worked. I write of *Blakwork* that it is: 'this *decentring book of centres* ... this word of mouth book of occasional computer gambits ... of paddy melon paddocks (been writing a lot about those lately) ... of shredding the warped contrivances of racism ... of powerful blakwomen ... of growing up and observing the journey ... of family and belonging and country'. Much of this section is concerned with identity and belonging, and how such things are defined or refuse definition (depending who is doing the defining), as well as notions of community. The crisis of colonialism is said and unsaid in the crisis of textuality. Across these pieces I am ultimately arguing for respect for difference, for cultural diversity, for mutual co-existence, a primacy of Indigenous rights, and respect for the *paths* of knowledge. Poetry becomes an enactment of presence and its contradictions.

Celebrating Fay Zwicky

In her introduction to *Quarry: A Selection of Western Australian Poetry*,[1] Fay Zwicky begins, 'In selecting poems for this anthology, I have tried to present a range of attentive responses to living' (p. 1). This statement of intent might also work as an *ars poetica* for her own poetry and literary practice. Zwicky knew the complications of living entwined with the complexities of history and place, the injustices and the ill-distributed rewards of life. She was aware of her own failings, as much as she was aware of the failings of others. This twofold awareness was what made her such a remarkable poet – in her social dissections there is self-awareness; in her engagements with the traumas of history and 'the now', there's a sense of collective human responsibility.

Strongly conscious of *where* she was writing from – be it Perth, Western Australia or Florida, or cities of Indonesia – Zwicky was also wary of reducing place to a mere impression, to an easy descriptor. Place is made up of many co-ordinates that are constantly in flux, and even in her most satirical moments, she doesn't leave her pinpoint observations as the final word – the poem allows us to believe there are other ways of seeing. In the same opening paragraph of her introduction to *Quarry*, she writes: 'Seeking poems to bolster regional clichés did not play a part in my selection. The thematic range and very avoidance of stereotype (so often defined by and accepted from external and internal sources) will, I hope, allow readers freedom to discern for themselves what it is like to be human in a certain world' (p. 1). We have more of a possible *ars poetica* statement for Zwicky's own work here. The right to discern for ourselves – to be provided with knowledge but to use that knowledge in ways and contexts that we personally comprehend – and vitally, to ask, to consider 'what it is like to be human in a certain world'. To be human when so often humans are brutal to other humans; to be human when mere existence can be unforgiving and cruel (I hesitate to use the word 'fate'), but the key to this statement is in fact 'in a certain world'. For each of us, reader or writer, there are many worlds, though each of us has a 'certain world' in which we function – a sense of where we are and what is around us. We may doubt the veracity of existence, but we basically take our awareness of the world as reliable. Yet, of course, it is contestable by others and ourselves. In creating a poem, we create a certain world, and the humanity presented in it is contingent on that world. In a sense, all poems become processings, tools, and moments of survival. The poem doesn't just exist to entertain us, even inform us; it exists because without it a way of being human would not exist.

Zwicky was rigorous in her making of poems, and in part that was because there's a deep responsibility in creating these certain worlds where we might be human. An ethical and moral poet, she felt deeply that a poet must write with integrity or not write at all. This is evidenced in her own critical writing, her

---

1 Fay Zwicky, *Quarry: A Selection of Western Australian Poetry* (Fremantle Arts Centre Press, 1981).

social conversation that so many of us remember, but most vitally in the poems themselves, especially the poems of her first volume, *Isaac Babel's Fiddle*.[2] And shortly, I am going to consider the second poem from this collection, 'Survival Kit', in the context of managing to be human in *a world*.

It is worth recollecting that the subtitle of Zwicky's collection of essays, *The Lyre in the Pawnshop*[3] is 'Essays on Literature and Survival 1974–1984'. And it is worth considering her review in that book of *The Poems of Stanley Kunitz 1928–1978* entitled 'Awkward Survival', which she concludes as follows: 'For all the difficulties of having chosen "a damnable trade where winning is like losing", Kunitz is at his best in the survival stance, balancing between two worlds and refusing to fall: "The sands whispered, *Be separate.*/The stones taught me, *Be hard.*/I dance for the joy of surviving,/On the edge of the road."' (p. 225).

The quote from Kunitz is quite telling in considering Zwicky's *ars poetica*, of a contemplation of the liminal, but really, more a contemplation of hard and difficult edges and decisions we have to make for survival that are both rational and moral, an equation that troubles Zwicky's poems in so many ways. Rejecting sentimentality, while having a strong stance on the obligation of parent and teacher towards child and/or student, the issue is not one of hierarchy or authority but of trust and responsibility. And even more, it's an awareness that as parent or teacher one is likely learning more than one is teaching, and that these relationships, like that between creativity and rationality, might seem antithetical but need reconciling.

In her introduction to *The Lyre in the Pawnshop*, Zwicky writes: If it is true that creativity is the outcome of a struggle between spontaneity and form, then I want to look as possibilities of reconciling what are often assumed to be two antithetical forces' (p. 1). And in the next paragraph: 'For the teacher, the conflict lies between the subtle and insidious illusion of being able to reclaim the lost, and the simultaneous awareness that your students are often wiser, less lost than you are yourself' (p. 1).

What's being discussed here are issues of trust and perception. Trust in the sense of any relationship of responsibility that is mediated by a sharing; and perception in the sense of what experience and knowledge one takes to the process of teaching, of offering tools for survival. In a world capable of the Holocaust, Zwicky's poetry consistently repositions ways of perceiving history and responsibility to articulate its brutalities, its crimes. She constantly mediates her own position of authority to comment, while defining and questioning her own position in ancestral, familial and cultural ways.

---

2 Fay Zwicky, *Isaac Babel's Fiddle* (Maximus Books, 1976).
3 Fay Zwicky, *The Lyre in the Pawnshop* (University of Western Australia Publishing, 1986).

She also says in the introduction to *The Lyre in the Pawnshop*:

> My own origins, so thoroughly attenuated by generations of assimilation, give me no claim to sentimental atavism or self-repudiating utopianism. Yet Steiner's questions and Wesker's considerations ['writers of Jewish origins were asked to assess the role played by these respective cultures in their work' especially in the sense of the effect of Torah commentaries: the question of it being 'natural' to be 'writer' or 'scholar'] coincide with my own reservations connected with the mysterious act of writing. (p. 3)

And she qualifies this further: 'How does the poet reconcile the growth of his individuality with the demands of the society in which he lives?' (p. 3).

'Survival Kit' is a poem about a world of the poet's creation, but also a world into which she raises her children. That anxious dynamic of responsibility, teaching and being taught, imparting knowledge (often threatening and disturbing) and receiving awareness (often illuminating, redemptive), resolves into the form of the poem, into the rationality of line and metre, of shape on the page, and offers the mechanism for an expression of the contradictions of being human. For Zwicky, all poems, in a sense, are makers of contradiction, if not paradox (not the right word for her work – really, she *counterpoints* certainty and uncertainty, and the musical suggestion here seems apt), but there is unquestionable value in the mysterious act of writing, even if there are questions about the rights and worth of an individual doing the writing. It was never easy, never straightforward for Zwicky. Writing carried responsibility – in what is said, in how one listens.

Interestingly, when Bruce Bennett and Bill Grono anthologised this poem in *Wide Domain: Western Australian Themes & Images*,[4] they included it in the thematic section of 'Growing Up' (along with pieces such as 'School' by Peter Cowan, 'The Witnesses' by Dorothy Hewett, and 'First Love' by Kenneth Mackenzie). The poem begins:

> I have waited to be forty all my life (always a
> Sucker for precise reckoning), and
> Here is the year beckoning me
> To be where I always wanted, legitimately.

Poets have a thing about turning forty, as maybe we all do. Peter Porter wrote, 'On This Day I Complete My Fortieth Year'; John Tranter has played with turning forty. Irony is the only way one can deal with an artificial marker constructed more by social mores than any biological reality, and, of course, as literary trope. Zwicky does irony especially well. She manages that edginess between aloof poise and idiomatic sarcasm. A trigger word opens to a theme, an

---

4 Bruce Bennett and Bill Grono, *Wide Domain: Western Australian Themes & Images* (A & R, 1979).

idea that will be further critiques. From 'legitimately', we go to the next line's legal play, and the further play on the saying:

> *Dieu et mon droit*, a confirmation devoutly
> Wished for, a mark on the census that I am beginning
> Where I began, that nothing has been worth winning,
> That nothing has definitely been won,
> Or absolutely lost.

Dieu et mon droit is the motto of the British crown ('outside Scotland') – 'God and my right'. As a student of an Anglican Girls' School she operated under this directive. A confirmation that was contrary to her heritage and antecedents, but not to the desires of her mother's social desires in the Melbourne of Zwicky's childhood. And of course the play on Hamlet's great soliloquy in which consummation (death) is reckoned as the reconfirmation of baptism's promises. The equivocations of belonging and presence that mark the Australian colonial experience are ironised, but so is the world and language the poet is *able* to create, given the tools with which she's been raised. In there, approaching a sign of absolute social maturity, she is still searching and learning the human, appropriate (or not) responses to living. By the grace of whose God is society ruled? These are poor tools for survival, and likely complicate the presumed speaker's Jewish identity and heritage.

The second stanza of these four stanzas of uneven length confronts evasions of living, of life and its consequences – 'removing my glasses/At movies, chickening on violence even at one remove,' – avoiding, hiding behind the magnificence of music even when that music relates to the ultimate tragedy, the loss of children (by scarlet fever in terms of the poems on which Mahler based his piece) and the anxiety over the well-being of one's own children:

> Moping with Mahler, weak for my children, lead
> Bleater of *Kindertotenlieder*

This is harsh, tense, and even terrifying. A distance that Anne Sexton pretends in her own death-wish-fear poems is captured in Zwicky's poem in a strangely self-distancing and hardening way, which, nonetheless, emphasises the personal angst. In some ways, definitively *unconfessional* as a poet, Zwicky's issues and play with ironising her own deeply felt angst make her a poet of self-scrutiny, a poet who retreats into academic thought as a protection, but knowing it is a smokescreen to avoid the self-confrontations she wishes to expurgate in the public-private space of the poem. The poem is a space of a world, and the poet is a world, and that world or those worlds will end as they are written, as they are read, as they are forgotten. She writes: 'Bound to admit that I/Welcome the end of a world that I am' – note the 'a world', not 'the world'. The article is vital here. (As in Donne: *I am a little world made cunningly* … – 'Holy Sonnet V') And 'I am' is what I create, not what is. The persona also notes 'I rejoice/In the worm drinking dew, the lift as the leaf/Bursts its bud, gaiety in grief.'

The final stanza of this failing and yet necessary, clung-to, survival kit of teaching and learning (self, the reader, those who will listen), is a dynamic bursting of the bubble into a staged loss of control (irony always holds her hand). In the end, nature, the world outside 'a world' – those many other worlds that constitute our collective reality, and constitute existence, are going to remain indifferent to our fears, concerns, angsts, and our growing older. 'As flies to wanton boys are we to the Gods', and the eternal question relating even to the lesser or greater monarchs (and their mottoes): 'Did the/Nightingales carrying on in the woods of Mycenae/Give a damn for Agamemnon?'

And that's it – the poet standing alone, but with angst and concern for the world that are not hers. And of hers? Well, there are her fears and concerns and her aloneness. And learning to live with it, and those others.

Zwicky's poetry is recognised as one of the great accomplishments of Australian literature. She was also a remarkable teacher, and family stories will always centre on her having taught my mother, on me searching her out when I first arrived at the University of Western Australia from Geraldton and her saying 'Your Mum taught me about Wordsworth'. This brilliant teacher, who along with Dorothy Hewett and Veronica Brady, shaped my mother's perceptions of literature, and consequently my own, had that way of disarming largesse. A gentle irony, no doubt, but also an acknowledgement of the complexities and mysteries of both teaching and writing. Of learning to live, of articulating a world, of communicating with other worlds. As the poet, critic and editor of the great American poetry journal, *Poetry*, Don Share wrote recently in an interview with City Lights bookshop, 'Fay's Zwicky's *Collected Poems* – an utterly life-changing book!'

A dissenting imagination: disambiguations

Just a few days before she died, Fay Zwicky was given this magnificent volume of her *Collected Poems*,[5] her life's work in poetry, by one of its editors, and had the chance to hold in her hands the substance of her life's work in poetry.

Zwicky is one of four 'historically' significant Western Australian poets, along with Jack Davis, Dorothy Hewett and Randolph Stow. Born in Melbourne in 1933 and raised there, she arrived in Western Australia only in 1961 with her husband, biologist Karl Zwicky, having lived and worked for lengthy periods in the 1950s in Indonesia (she also lived for a time in Europe and spent further time in the United States).

Perceiving Western Australia as isolation, edge of continent, gazing into the flux of Indian and Southern Ocean eternity, Zwicky became an essential part of the city and its projection of voice into a broader Australia. As Lucy Dougan and Tim Dolin say in their introduction, 'Once in Perth, she made it her home. Her essay, "Neither Out Far Nor in Deep" explores the ways in which both

---

5 *The Collected Poems of Fay Zwicky*, edited and introduced by Lucy Dougan and Tim Dolin (University of Western Australia Publishing, 2017).

the Swan River, "that great consoling stretch of water," and the Indian Ocean "freed" her "to meditate": "My adopted parish handed me the very stuff of poetry ... A little rush of infinity that alters perspective however slightly and briefly permits a standing outside of oneself". It is certainly the case that Perth provided a place from which to write' (p. 5).

But there's nothing comfortable in this 'retreat' into the 'suburban', for Zwicky's Perth is also a place epitomising the distance and distancing she in some ways embraced regarding her own cultural heritages, and her own intellectual and cultural requirements. She came from what we call a musical family, was educated at Church of England girls' schools in Melbourne, and became more aware of her Jewish heritage as a consequence of the Second World War, which also took her father away from her, and her two sisters and mother, for six years. Dougan and Dolin have included a vital essay of Zwicky's, 'Border Crossings' (2000), in which she discusses her childhood and textual-musical influences, especially from the Anglican Prayer Book, and how she came to write her major work, arguably the major longer 'Australian' poem of the last century, 'Kaddish'.

Written in response to her father's death at sea (in 1967), Zwicky searched out language and languages for her 'Kaddish' – languages which needed to be drawn out of her heritage and identity, though they were not alien in the way that so much Australian indifference to her cultural values was. Not having any Hebrew, she entered the realm of speaking for the dead, maintaining a presence of memory.

It's not surprising, as she herself notes, that this liberation in entering the language and culturality she required for her lament came via American sources, especially Allen Ginsberg's poem for his mother Naomi, 'Kaddish'. But it was Zwicky's 'failure' to understand that the Kaddish was traditionally the domain of men that led her to dissent from tradition and make something radical, even rebellious – a trait of which she was sceptical and wary, but which she embodied in so many ways: 'the traditional order of priorities has always rankled with me and continues to do so' (p. 14). In poems such as the 'Indonesian poems' in *The Gatekeeper's Wife*, where Zwicky's first husband is remembered, love in memory is emphasised through loss – cultural referents are localised and grow in personal remembrance.

As time went on in Zwicky's writing life (which really gained momentum and traction when she settled in as a teacher at the University of Western Australia), she moved from a more formally and intellectually constrained diction in the poems that make up her first volume, *Isaac Babel's Fiddle*, to the looser American-influenced conversational line of the poems of later volumes such as *Ask Me*, *The Gatekeeper's Wife*, and her last, the masterful, which contains a number of her finest poems. It can be argued that in doing so she was actually becoming increasingly conscious of a mission to speak 'against our mutual obliteration'. As the formalities of the poems seem to become more relaxed, the intensity of their political and ethical gaze increases.

Ivor Indyk has appropriately located Zwicky's poetic purpose in the zone of the moral, and Zwicky is always a morally and ethically attuned poet, but she was constantly aware of avoiding didacticism and ideology, which she perceived as being the enemy of the imagination, and ultimately freedom itself.

I would agree that she avoided these traps all her working life, but I would also argue that her moral purpose was political, rebellious, and far noisier than her manners, her Anglican Church of England upper-middle class (Europeanised) cultural upbringing, might permit. Everywhere are the signs of a spirit in rebellion, but also a rebellion in language itself. I consider her one of the most intense and even angry voices speaking for the sanctity of the human spirit to have come out of Australia.

Other than a number of the late poems, such as 'Picnic' itself, in which the ease and strain of empathy work hand-in-hand, and 'Boat Song', the remarkable poem for refugees she published in the *West Australian* newspaper in 2014, it's easy to forget how 'topical' Zwicky could be regarding political events. 'Kaddish' is one such poem, though it's rarely if ever read that way. Neither are poems of voices such as 'Ark Voices', 'Mrs Noah Speaks', or 'The Potter' from the sequence 'The Terracotta Army at Xi'an'. 'The Potter' is surely Zwicky's sensibility again rebelling within the potter's male voice as contrary, as female-author provocateur, as voice of the creator against the tyranny of a deathly patronage.

In this sequence of voice poems, Zwicky's Euro-Australian inflections of ways of seeing, her Westernised modernity segue with tactile 'moments' and the archaeology of China's history, creating strange disambiguations reminiscent of Eliot. There's a political subtext of the self in these poems, but its subtextuality doesn't prevent the politics bursting out when confronted by horror, even if there's a struggle for the poet-observer's culpability in the failure to prevent horror – take 'Tiananmen Square June 4, 1989'.

It's through the imagination that the poet can quietly compel change. For one who wrestled with silence, as Zwicky did, we might consider that 'quiet' and 'silence' are different things, and the latter has a moral gravitas that 'quiet' seemingly doesn't, and yet it's in the quiet, the husky-voiced steadiness that the quavering, hesitant, and brooding anger resides, ready to burst out of its constraints. Rather than poem after poem, it's line by line that we discover this, lines that we can sense have been drafted and redrafted, left and revisited, maybe years after their inspiring events, like the 'Kaddish' that had to come, in time, in the way memory, knowledge, experience, and dealing with the quotidian allowed.

Here are a few such lines taken from early through to late poems about an array of 'subjects'. From 'Emily Dickinson Judges the Bread Division at the Amherst Cattle Show, 1858' – 'About my neck the acid victor's wreath'; from 'Talking Mermaid' – 'The waterfront is murmurous with attention', and 'Pure play is for the feudal few'; and in terms of the potency and failings of memory, and the politics of presence, from 'Losing Track', set in Jerusalem, the line tripping into the next with poise *and* anxiety, 'wondering how long can human memory stand/an absence trapped in strange geography.'

This last poem also finishes with what we might think of as a signature conjecture for Zwicky: 'You might say getting close to God without God.' This echoes Zwicky's notion of the quietly religious – to her core she wanted restraint to give liberty, the forms of Bach to liberate imagination, and even as her poetry 'freed up' in line and tonality across the decades, she still maintained the purpose of poetry, a purpose linked to form, restraint, care and craft, and manners. I can't emphasise this enough: though she skirted the bohemia of the arts, she remained ensconced in the security of Waratah Avenue in one of Perth's leafy suburbs. She ventured out, she encountered cultural difference, admired 'difference', but remained herself in her own journey towards enlightenment or, indeed, annihilation. This is the oscillating ambiguity of Zwicky not only in her work but in discussion around her work (and life). I don't see it as a duality between the ambiguous and unambiguous, but a mode of enacting a textual life in a distressed world. Not 'beyond ambiguity' as I understand it, but embracing the spectrum of ambiguity in the making of poems/music/text and interfacing this with day-to-day life.

There are poems of great sensitivity to alternative spiritualities and culture, such as the sequence of 'Indian' poems. 'The Temple, Somnapura', where an engagement with spirituality (something she imagined was required to be religious but was perhaps constantly unsure of in herself) is entered through dance and physical forms in non-intrusive, respectful ways – but always a scrutiny of the self, of the motives in writing even joyfully.

We also find in her poems a struggle to belong in her own culture – Zwicky's sense of herself as 'a dark-faced woman' ('Soup and Jelly'), conscious of her difference in the Anglo-Celtic regime in which she was raised. In some ways, she relished outsider status as a liberty in itself, a way of seeing in and out of national machines of control, but she also wanted to be part of community, and America seemed to offer that to her and her family.

But I am not as convinced of this as some, and I know America to be so polyvalent in terms of identity that what feels comfortable at one time can shift rapidly, and the joy is always restrained by the eschatology underpinning a democracy born out of slavery, civil war, and unfettered optimism in the capitalist enterprise. 'Four Poems from America' runs the full gamut of emotions of exposure and inclusion and still being outside.

Zwicky felt compelled to analyse the contradictory role of the poet in society. She was anti-oracular, but interested in the substance of the Pythic, of the myths of the oracle. Because Zwicky always utilised sculptural-musical qualities in her 'taut style', even when she is being chatty it is totally controlled prosodically – never excessive, and so formally balanced yet with life and zip in it, hard to achieve, especially when working with material from different cultural experiences, and certainly when dealing with vision, and public enunciation of private experience. Astonishingly, she always manages it without overextending or falling prey to what she found offensive: the self-serving pronouncement.

To find a way into any poet's work, repetitions of words and ideas are key. With Zwicky we find 'dead', 'dreams', 'spectre', 'pines', 'God' and so on, and an attendance to the distresses and affirmations around the presence and absence of children, the will of the adult and the will of the child, often seguing with issues of 'home and away', longing for return mediated by a desire to be away, literary referents, a polyphony of voices, and even when a personal arcana is deployed (she was cautious about obscure personal details), it always gives an impression that works in a 'universal' manner.

Her early poems especially were amalgamations of different discourses and impacted approaches to form – 'Totem and Taboo', with its totemics fusing with ambivalence, is a mini anti-epic, playing out Freudian neurosis, 'primitivism' and animism, 'fear and respect', and the convolution of original sin, phylogenetics and the fate of the father. Then a less 'impacted' approach comes into play with the later 'American poem'. 'A Tale of the Great Smokies' is like a novel, a fiction about receiving stories of that unstable sense of place which one desires in part – a kind of translationese of 'Americana' (to use Dougan and Dolin's term), in which dynamic equivalence allows emergence from speechlessness and private dialogues, Zwicky's extraction of one possible Odyssey in America. The shearing in this sequence acts as transference for a sexual tension narrative that manages not to be patronising because of its careful elevation into the mythic.

I use the word 'integrity' a lot when discussing Zwicky's work. And that is what can take us from an earlier poem such as 'Dogwood', in which natural beauty meets intellectual integrity that devastates the literary conceit, pathetic fallacy, to the sincerity of the 'hospice' and caring poems of *Ask Me*, where the irony is flattened to poignancy, which leaves the poet and reader looking askance in the face of loss, of conveying a situation simply by 'telling'. In 'Soup and Jelly' we get the full range of Zwicky's poetics of alienation and belonging, of outsider–insider confrontations – bigotry is experienced, and it is absorbed (though it is also present in the Fenian remark: to negate by othering in return). I find this one of the most moving poems I have read; here are two stanzas:

> 'Are you a foreigner?'
> 'Not exactly. Just a little sunburnt,'
> and I put the jelly down. I mustn't feel
> a thing: my smile has come unstuck.
> I place a paper napkin on his lap. He winces.
> 'You're a foreigner all right,' he says.
> 'OK,' I say. What's one displacement more or less,
> wishing I were a hearty flat-faced Fenian
> with a perm and nothing doing in the belfry.
> Someone like his mother. Or a wife who
> spared him the sorrow of himself.
>
> Now he grabs the spoon. 'I'll do it.'
> 'Right,' I say, 'You go ahead. Just ask me
> if you want some help.' The tone's not right.
> I watch the trembling progress of the spoon
> for what seems years, paralysed with pity
> for his pride.

Zwicky played the public against the private; she was the strong female voice at a time when poets in Australia were (honestly) divided as 'poets and women poets', sometimes as a positive affirmation, but mostly by bloke poets and critics as a hierarchy. Zwicky undid such false divisions in ongoing ways. What are certainties in a damaged world, a world in which she grew into the absolute confronting fact of the failure of humanity in the details and reality of the Holocaust? An altered world in which Euro-cultural normatives of memory themselves had been brutalised, fragmented, and even deleted, to be mediated through the distance (physical and conceptual) of an Australia in which vastness and the absurdity of the colonial intrusion made for displaced existentialism in the growing awareness of the girl born Julia Rosefield. And however distant a past is, and however close a present is, who one *is* is a complex array of past and present. As Zwicky writes in the early 'Summer Pogrom', 'Dead lie deep in me.'

God, which cannot be mentioned, occurs again and again across the *Collected Poems*. The relationship between God and humanity is strained, though the self, for all its failings, retains access in numerous ways to God, who remains tolerant, if disappointed. Zwicky's is a poetry of non-entitled ontology. In her final journal-published poem, gathered with other uncollected poems at the end of this volume, all chosen by Zwicky herself, we again encounter death, memory and God, a God puzzling in its absence and presence, its paradox of being in the individual life and collective lives of humanity.

Zwicky wrote many elegies across her life, elegies that express sincere and steady affection for those lost, that are also about the nature and complexities of friendship, and especially about how those left behind deal with loss, and how they maintain memories. Zwicky relied on there being other poets – though alone in her poetry in some ways, in others she was highly communal. Ironically, with great sincerity, in friendship and contestation, she addressed the dead and her friends and peers. 'In Memoriam, JB' ends with these lines, 'We only ever yield to love/when someone's dead or gone.' And this is a truth in Zwicky's textual life of moral integrity that struggled with the failings of the everyday, of her own obligations to her own conscience. But in its accuracy for her crisis of self is also a peace and resolution – we who loved her, even if she didn't love us, or some of us, continue to yield to her 'dissenting imagination', through which she was truly a rebel, even if she would have rejected the term.

Places we do or don't go to not only *in person*, but also *in writing*[6]

Let's begin at school in English class in the 'new buildings' around 1978, Geraldton High School, the new wing built to replace the asbestos demountable classrooms to the south of the old school main building. We are reading

---

6 'The inaugural Randolph Stow Address for 2019, *Writing the Place: The Process of Conjuring Landscape*. In conclusion to the address, Charmaine Papertalk-Green firmly anchored the interpretation of decolonising the landscape to the Yamaji perspective.' As noted by festival organisers in conjunction with John Kinsella in *Westerly*, 2019.

through Alexander Craig's anthology *Twelve Poets* – an in-class reading session to get familiar with some Australian poetry in a more concentrated way than the odd poem here and there in a general poetry anthology. I am lucky enough via my mum, an English teacher at the school, to already be up with a few Australian poets, especially Judith Wright, who is not actually one of the poets in the anthology, already established and well-known to school readers. These are newer poets, astonishingly eleven men and only one woman, but Gwen Harwood is no extra spoke on the wheel, she's pivotal. As Judith Wright looms so large in my imagination, I am shocked into a different way of perceiving 'landscape' via the poetry of a once-local Geraldton poet, Randolph Stow, whose poem 'Landscapes' echoes off the page:

> But the butcherbird draws all in; that voice is a builder
> of roofless cathedrals and claustrophobic forests
> – and one need not notice walls, so huge is the sky.

In the light of these lines, I actually start to ask myself what am I doing *here*, in this place, and do I belong? Here in Geraldton where we had recently moved, but more than that, here on this land, and further south where I was born, but where I am also culturally distant in so many ways. How do I connect with respect for this land I feel close to, and yet lack a way of understanding? I ponder 'roofless cathedrals', something I will ponder till the present day, especially when it's beneath the roofs of flooded gums, salmon gums and other ancient trees about to be bulldozed for 'developments'. But back then I am fifteen and unsure about *religion*, and especially about God, and I know I love the 'outdoors' and want to spend my time in the bush under the sky, yet I also want to book-learn and gain knowledge every way I can. Stow confuses and entices me to understand who I am, and what I might do where I am.

In this short poem by 'local' Randolph Stow, I realise knowledge comes in many ways, and I have to start to learn outside the usual routes. He is of a 'settler background', and yet there's something troubled and deeply unbelonging, something outside notions of 'heritage' and 'inheritance' in him. How can he write so intensely about 'here' and still not be 'settled' with 'here'? He both belongs and doesn't belong. I know that feeling, I tell myself! At fifteen I knew I was on Aboriginal land, and I asked and was told it was Yamaji land. I was told and listened intensely to stories of 'Champion Bay'.

Cathedrals are not necessarily as they *look* – the roof, the ceiling, in many ways, always aspirational, is also a block to truths and to insight into the spirit. Some insights might be mine to share; others won't be. And leaping 'ahead', but also of the same time, from Stow to the Cathedral-questioning and undoing poetry of Charmaine Papertalk-Green, in our collaboration on Monsignor Hawes, priest and architect, many decades later, I begin a journey that doesn't go from A to B and back again, à la Andy Warhol of New York, over whom I would obsess when in my twenties and thirties, but at angles and digressions I could never have imagined.

In writing place, I necessarily write about where I am, where I have been, and also where I am likely to go. This sounds obvious, but it's not, really. Because where I go has increasingly to do with issues of permission and intrusion and welcome. This can involve respecting traditional peoples' country, *their* land and culture, and whether or not they want me there, but it can also be an issue of encroaching against mining, pastoral or government exclusion and control as an act of protest in attempts to preserve native vegetation and wildlife. Sometimes the acts of visiting and trespassing and working out where one should or shouldn't go are not straightforward and require much conversation and interaction. This means there's nothing furtive or secret about it – quite the opposite, it's all publicly declared, though private conversations are kept just that.

Why is this relevant here? Well, I am talking about the places we do or don't go to not only *in person*, but also *in writing*. When writing the Geraldton area, which I still often do, I do so as one who has lived here during my teenage years and who has family in town, and visits maybe once a year or every couple of years, but also as one who is more often absent. I don't just get the right to speak of where I don't permanently live, though I feel I do get the right to comment on place-specific issues that affect the entire planet – the devastation of country, pollution, exploitation, and lack of respect. So, I need to find a way through in my writing that acknowledges my outside status with some inside knowledge.

Back to my teenage years. It's now late 1978, and I am fifteen, have been in Geraldton for close to a year – it's getting near Christmas holidays and I want to get out on pushbikes with my mate Peter and head to Drummond's Cove to camp on the beach, in the sandhills – a pivotal moment in my life that will *echo*, too, through my poetry and fiction. I don't think about anything outside the world being there for us to explore, use, learn from, intrude on, hide in. We head out on our bikes and take risks, perform that act of being teenagers working to reduce our constraints. But the Stow poem bothered me – it was called 'Landscapes', meaning there were more than one, or was it addressing all 'landscapes'? – and was it this one or others? – and something was missing, and I knew what it was, and didn't yet know how to put it. Ten years later, I wrote the first draft of a long poem about the nineteenth-century explorer George Grey and the fact that his intrusions were actually acts of *unexploring*, were acts of aggression and attack on Aboriginal peoples in the name of the Crown and progress, and had none of the vision and foreseeing his journals would later, in a variety of senses, congratulate himself on. That long anti-epic poem of mine would eventually, in a final draft, ironically be called 'The Benefaction'.

I'll give you a more recent example of my reprocessing teen years in Geraldton, and the issue of where my place might be in the imagining of the place – I am not denying the reality of presence, of the day-to-day, of living. I am talking about how we position ourselves in terms of rights and possession, the permissions we do or don't obtain, do or don't give ourselves to write ourselves into a place.

Sometime around 2014 when walking around the 'new' marina (new to me) at the bottom of Bailey Street, as I think of it in terms of my old school coordinates, a poem came to me, as it had to. I had been appalled when the old nurses' quarters opposite the old prison, which my family had lived in for a period in my teens, was knocked down to make way for a car park for the Coles shopping-centre precinct. Don't get me wrong, I am making no excuses for colonial buildings that represent the occupation of Yamaji land, but the building had stood a long time, been of use to people via the health aspect of things, and should not have been knocked down – it could have housed a number of homeless families, put heritage to pragmatic use. And that's the way I see any ill-gotten heritage – the markers of colonial occupation – in the rectifying use they can be put to. *Conserve* to make *use* of, I say. So, that house long gone, I walk down to where the railway workshops had been, down to the marina and the maritime museum area, and I see gains and losses. The coast remodelled and, along with public focuses, especially Aboriginal works in the museum which I take as positively affirming, and an attempt in the general curation to face the complexity of settlement, and the use of the sea, I am overwhelmed by the irony of messing with the sea – the marina was full of boats of those who were at least well-off, if not the wealthy.

My personal despair aside – and I appreciate many others may look onto such an enclave and not necessarily feel the way I do, and, further, the old seafront was stone-walled and full of railway intrusions when I was a kid, so it, too, back then, was intrusive – what redeemed 'place' for me was the sight and interaction with a sea lion. Its adjustment to the 'imagined' space was the roofless cathedral, or the de-roofing of the cathedral, that brought a greater spiritual truth to the place, to me, and possibly to itself, too.

This is the poem:

Sea Lion

Where I stood on the rocks in front of the train workshops
there's a marina and the growth urge of the Midwest middle class.
Large boats with sport-fishing ambitions sit in their pens – wine
and beer are quaffed amidships. Ladies with headphones and prams
jog along the boardwalk. Inside the maze of channels green water.

Where I stood on the rocks in front of the train workshops
huge chunks of inland stone ward off the Indian ocean. Builders
will tolerate no wrecks of pleasure craft within their remit.
But near the jetty not locked-off from non-subscribers
Tim spots a sea lion which bottles, dives, then emerges

alongside us – lolling, rolling, blowing stale air over green waters.
It dives under the jetty and we misjudge where it emerges
but it turns back and communes with us nonetheless.
I am guessing a sea lion would consider this 'relaxed', like us,
but maybe not because fish are on its agenda. But Tim is excited.

> So close! How the leisurists feel looking out from their cabins,
> or down from luxury flats overlooking their pride and joys,
> is another matter. What does it mean, this reclaiming of land,
> this enveloping of sea, the narrow opening to a shipwreck coast?
> Three and a half decades have passed. I feel no nostalgia, only grief.
>
> Where I stood on the rocks in front of the train workshops
> I fretted about the sheds and machinery behind me, the shored-
> up defences against rough seas, and opening to the right looking
> out to the islands, the crescent of beach where in the shallows
> I trod on a cobbler and knew blue murder was a toxin in the blood.
>
> Where I stood on the rocks in front of the train workshops
> I should have guessed what would come – the agonising expanse
> of God and science, the juxtaposition of machines and the sea, the inevitability
> of pushing out – nodules on the island continent, forces for and against
> isolation. We stayed as long as we could, watching the sea lion.

See, for me, Geraldton has never just been a take-it-easy, lots-of-sun, good holiday place; it was home, and still remains a distant home of the imagination (rightly or wrongly), with all the complexities of belonging that entails. I was both happy and unhappy in Geraldton. I worked in a lab, took mineral sand samples as ships were being loaded, and yet started to develop my strong anti-mining stance in life. I was young and full of contradictions. I don't look back with nostalgia, but I do look back with appreciation at the world-view I got from joining town with country, rural with sea. I was distressed by racism and violence and, as tracked in my 'white bloke' poems written in dialogue with Charmaine and Charmaine's poems of Yamaji life-experience, I was strongly affected by that violence, but I also learnt how to write poetry about such issues.

I have people I am still close to, and places within the area I feel increasingly close to. I always felt I shouldn't be at Ellendale Pool, which felt, if not off-limits to me, certainly sacred to others who were not me. I didn't understand why, and it's a place I feel both fascinated by, and deeply respectful of, to the point that I should leave. In some senses, I know it best through enforced absence. Now, this is not to impose on others; it's a feeling and it has been voiced in my poems and stories. But I still voice it. I think Stow, certainly looking back over his life, had similar misgivings and uncertainties, and he knew that place much better than me on a literal level.

Which takes me back to the idea of *heritage*, so vital to the region. Heritage is something both to embrace and to be wary of. Heritage can occlude the stories of country, and become just an ongoing way of denying the reality of colonialism. On the other hand, heritage can become a conversation too, about the intrusion and theft of country, and can lead to healing, to 'reconciliations' that are wanted by those dispossessed, not forced on them, and a way of showing the success and failures of justice regarding history.

Sadly, there are far more injustices in the heritage record than justices. So what do we do? We preserve as traces, as records of what was, so we can make what *is now* better. I am, for these reasons, haunted by the colonial buildings of Greenough Hamlet as much as I am by the few remaining wind-bent trees that make the postcards of the recent past, and the Instagram moments of the present day. They too easily become part of the status quo of sandplain that is only about farming, but should surely be about restoration of both Yamaji rights and also the country as it once was, and what it could have been and could still be under the guidance of elders who best know how to make land 'work' for people and for itself, for the other creatures that dwell on it.

Co-existence is what interests me in this: between the aspirations of people, and the aspirations of other life. Farming needs to co-exist with respect for country. And where farms meet the sea is a place of disturbance and questioning. I have connected with those farms, with the sea, and the disturbances of settlement and the guilt they bring. In my 1998 book *The Hunt*,[7] I open the poem 'A Tale from Sand-Plain Country' with these bothering lines (bothering to me, at least):

> Where the coast meets the sea
> Four hundred kilometres north
> Wheatfields go right up to the dunes
> Which shift with winds so strong
> They bend trees. Postcards are sold.
> Once the Devil played cards
> In a small stone pub
> And his opponents
> Noting his luck change
> As the stakes got high
> Checked to see if he'd been
> Marking cards under the table.

Rumours, stories, religion from far away brought in, in an attempt to overlay spirituality already there, but only stirring up the disturbance, the doubts, the wrongs. How does the language of recounting, whatever that language is, deal with this?

In the same locale, in those old Greenough Hamlet buildings, I find hope in the persistence of, say, swallows where few nesting places are left. The haunting and the nesting go hand-in-hand, maybe.

Swallows at Greenough Hamlet

> It's the tree-bending wind I grew through
> in my 'growth spurt' – when I went away

---

7 John Kinsella, *The Hunt* (Bloodaxe, 1998 and FACP, 1999).

for the Christmas break at sixteen and returned
to school at Candlemas, my birthday, at full height.

We walk through the hamlet, holding our hats,
stepping around the jail, which we won't visit.
The convent was a site of learning and no doubt pain –
it is cool and rudimentary and denies the wind access.

We go inside as blank as we can make ourselves.
and Tracy says it feels familiar, though she remarks
on the veils of the Presentation Sisters in a *fin de siècle*
photograph setting them apart – more like France

than Cork or Kerry. I don't feel a connection
until I walk into the room as chapel and see two
swallows fly from one high, round louvred window
to another, their shit over the floor, over the organ,

over the Bible open somewhere just past the middle.
I step back and let them settle in peace. Tim notices
a nest moulded into a high corner. The two birds
fly again then perch on the frame of a painting:

Tracy tells me it is probably Simeon holding
the baby Jesus – during Mary's presentation
at the temple. The swallows, still ruffled, touch
beaks and lift their forked tails to balance,

chattering intensely. Later, we read the building
is supposed to be 'haunted', but no static of expectation
interferes with our interaction, our brief cohabitation
with swallows who will fly fast every time

new visitors enter the building. Outside,
another pair of swallows follows us through shade
of a strong, bowed eucalypt, to pivot on wires
in driving wind, to call through the haze

where so many aspects of the four elements mix.
What was offered up in the temple was existence,
and no farmyard sacrifice, no holy acquiescence,
will occlude the glory of swallows making life.

What's interesting about going back again and again to a place one has lived in, but not actually 'moving back', is how over the years memories become more fragmented; so to compensate, you turn them into stories, to keep the threads going. In writing short fiction on Geraldton – and I have many stories set there, especially concerning the sea – I embellish or divert from an experience to make my story someone else's story, to increase the range of possibilities, maybe to tell myself more than I recall, or could have known. But in poetry, I try to join the fragments by returning and experiencing the here-and-now, and the poems build out of the past juxtaposing with the present; how I see things now merges with how I recall I saw things 'back then'.

Sometimes I see old schoolmates in the street and they don't recognise me, or maybe just pretend not to (fine!), and I try to think of how their perception of the place in which they've lived a large part of their lives has changed, and not changed. How many different stories are constantly at work in that place – counterpointing, augmenting, and probably frequently contradicting and at odds. When I started writing poems 'back' to Geraldton in the early-to-mid-1990s, I found I would write about school issues, about conflict I observed outside and inside myself, and especially about the beach.

My brother and I spent a lot of time skin-diving, and a lot of time on the sand. In Geraldton, I got a sense of 'under the water', and what I saw on my daily dives has informed the way I see the surface world now, especially as a most frequently 'inland' dweller. My brother, a shearer, but also a surfer who first stood on a board among the 'dumpers' at Back Beach before moving across to Neons, Explosives, Hell's Gates and other breaks as a thirteen-year-old, still lives between the world of coast and inland, both of them vitally part of his seeing the world. And it sticks with me, too. Here is a poem from a book I wrote with the writer Robert Drewe called *Sand*, because we dragged as much sand inside our house as there was outside, as we traipsed back and forth between beach and waves and reefs and home:

Geraldton 2 Coastal Prophecy

> The quality of sand ...
> Sunset Beach breaking at night,
> gulls arcing in the glow,
> the suffocating stench of weed
> heaped by storm,
> unravelled by those searching for worms ...
> the shape of kelp, of exotica: bull and antler,
> fan and sifters of currents,
> mainly ribbons like laminated book covers shredded
> endlessly, sand shoals thinning
> and the reef fish becoming scarcer:
> check out what a spear from a spear gun does to a snapper,
> ripping through and splaying its barbs, most often pulled back
> till the flesh rips out, and it swims at an angle away,
> a rock cod camouflage blown by a swirl of sand
> on a clear day less a dorsal fin, a tail,
> or the ray flat to the sand flapping airfoil
> and a movement not of the dry land, of the surface,

its barbs in the long cartilaginous extension
of its broad self, a shovel-nosed shark
suffering the same, and anemones sensing
and closing too soon as weighted by lead
and buoyant in the insulation of a wetsuit
you pass, all colours of the sea muted as things stir up
and a rainstorm of salt makes the shafts
of sunlight grey … rules of a savage storm,
lines of fast fish ripping along the shallows,
moving out deep, the flickering sea snake
walking water and engraving
with a diffuse and widening shadow,
the weed dumped again and again on the beach
sweating in the late afternoon, the breeze
coating all, with a layer of sand, a composting of the beach,
botany and biology merging, interphase;
crabs lift and launch at night also,
the sun's orange blast
having bored through the sand
by then, a glimmer dispersed by currents and tide;
morning: stiller almost cold, bit of a cray float
colour eaten off like a warning, bite mark of sea
and the ropes tangled and layered into the sand, cuttlefish
still flesh around their lipped anatomies, declarations
of aerofoil and escape, graphological
on the sea's diluted ink, shells where the sea
has been emptied and the conch is an analogue
from *Lord of the Flies*; recall as a school kid
sunning here, a friend of the family
visiting, crisping in her bikini: flew kites,
through sand, crashed into the low waves,
felt tired and hungry in that washed-out good way,
the ocean all out there and a place of retreat, staving off
the land's locks and weirs, eroding stone,
pools so deep they find no end to the water,
fields flowing down to edge water
and sand rolling in heaps,
shaped and reshaped and held down
by a scrub defying
rules of fertility,
the ocean breathing life into the green succulence,
the sun doing the rest.

This was written on a revisit to Geraldton in around 2006, staying in the Point Moore Caravan Park Chalets. Down on the beach from where the osprey craypot pole-sitting nest platform is now, down from the striped lighthouse, which was there when I was nineteen, where I had a picnic on the sand with a girl from high-school who was a poet (a year younger than me) … We'd talked about the sea and writing, believe it or not, and the fact that I had just moved to Perth to go to university – she stayed on in town. She was a poet and a fiction writer, and we both saw Geraldton as home, but also as somewhere you thought away from. To me, this is telling – when it is really your country, looking away can only take you deeper back into your home place, into your heritage, your real heritage, which is so much more than buildings, and when it is literally your country, into your ancestral and spiritual interconnectedness with place. As one without Aboriginal heritage, I didn't have this, and don't have it, and remember understanding this at eighteen.

But I wanted to write about this dislocation, and what I could reclaim, what I was allowed to reclaim, from my time living in Geraldton. And in some ways, what I felt I could talk about were the problems, the traumas, more than the many pleasures I had. A particularly traumatic poem that came out of my witnessing a terrible crime as a kid messing around on the Chapman River behind the old army training area, was about a sack of kittens thrown out of a car onto the sandy river bed. Something you never recover from. Rather than read that poem, written many years after I was there, and maybe a poem that had to be written 'away', I will read the first attempt I made to discuss it ... maybe written in the mid-1990s:

9. Chapman River, where ...

The off-colour of the water
in summer, the influx of the sea when the sandbar
broke through in winter. The sandstone cliffs
upstream where the river ate through history
and ignored settlement. Where human nature
was a sack of cats dumped down on the flats
below by persons unknown, driving a blue car
with covered number plates. Where an army reserve
backed onto the gorge, and you considered that
despite live ammunition nature had the best chance
behind the barbed-wire fences. Where bream grew smarter
along the lengths of a golf course, dragging red flesh
on endless runs, poisoning the unwitting with
their spikes. Where heat and water birds colluded
and something like myth made a ghost of itself
and got into your bones. When solitude
became reason enough for fear and the city
hundreds of miles South was always too close.

That was a first attempt to deal with the issue, but cushioned by other memories. For memories are cross-referenced with others, but the further we move away from them in time and place, what remains are often the most traumatic parts.

Water and land. Again, and again. Staying where we can look out onto the sea as if there are other places to go, but it's not what we want in Geraldton. I have learnt that, in my coming back, over and over: the need to let the sea be, not a place to cross, but an endlessness that converses with the immensity of land. I later wrote this in the place where we often stay, looking out at the sea and a lone pine tree being buffeted in the wind – a 'mast tree', like the Norfolk pines along Durlacher and Fitzgerald Streets … a ship mast but not an adjuster to bend to the breeze like the river red gums of Greenough (though they have little choice losing mutual support in such vegetation-cleared spaces!).

The Sway of a Coastal Pine Tree

A lipidic white-capped sea, low
coastal heath, tether tableaux
to breeze bending the old pine
towards them, its sway on rebound
bringing it back to lash sunset.

Bright dark matter mixed
to force back to where the breeze
has blown, to fill compulsive
need, sweep to vacate and occupy –
lean to resist, impelled.

Pine is ritual, drawn back
to depths where appearances
are made and blessed, mast-like,
bent against a tidal surge,
branches radiant with drowning.

Confess, to balance or divine
a flow, draw needles against compasses,
steer towards an anchorage,
high up in the rigging, less rigid,
    breeze-dried waves,

  arrangements of vastness.

Whose rituals are they, these non-native, introduced pines? They belong, as they've been planted and nurtured, and are identified in the centre of town as heritage, living heritage, and yet they're not. And this is the crisis of presence, of settlement. How do we talk about it? Well, literature is one means, and over the decades I have realised that literature is not about the self, but about ongoing conversations with others. How do we change the architecture of what we know as dwelling to become roofless cathedrals that respect not only all forms of worship, but the fact that buildings of worship are built on other places of worship, and that the stone and wood of these buildings is the stone and wood of a much longer-lasting permanent presence? It's not irony to say that the stone cathedrals are the temporary structures, and the places of Yamaji worship are the persistent and permanent ones, no matter how hard the ongoing colonial survey had tried to erase them.

Working with Charmaine Papertalk-Green on our book of poems, *False Claims of Colonial Thieves*, has been for me a personal addressing of what, essentially, is not mine to address, outside the fact that I have few rights of comment, even if I am an avid observer. But through her generosity as a Yamaji woman and poet, I have been able to talk over these 'issues' in poetry, and what we have done is there for people to read and talk about themselves. I'd like to finish with two poems, one of mine read by me, and one of Charmaine's read by her.[8] It seems appropriate to return to Ellendale Pool, where Stow is referenced on a sign, and over which he may or may not have felt comfortable. Randolph 'Mick' Stow and Charmaine Papertalk-Green are both great poets of this region, but Charmaine is a poet of this country.

Peacocking at Ellendale Pool

Speaking a truth doesn't disabuse
as the martins and swallows fly in & out

of the cliffs, and the *pool that is bottomless*
reaches beyond all prospects of drought,

and the kestrel positions itself for the edges
of chaos, and campers wade into amoebic

meningitis – *into the cells* – on a thirty-eight
degree day. Randolph Stow is celebrated

on a sign in the eye of the land, and we are informed
that he wrote *A Haunted Land* and *desire*

troubled this enclave, eye of the fillet,
its bloodied history. And then he was gone,

ensconced in Suffolk, away from his troubled
identity, or the lapses in identity that left

him stranded. And among those *revenant*
thick white river redgums (felled so readily), caravans

& willie wagtails, and a long-nosed dragon
in a swamp she-oak flashing point to point,

---

8 It is essential to understand that Charmaine Papertalk-Green read her poem 'Creation Markings – Ellendale Pool' to the audience in the Geraldton Town Library, when the first version of this paper was delivered. She read the poem on her people's land, her community's country, in her space for speaking.

and the public gorging itself on the scene,
that interlude in a thermonuclear world,

pastoral country up to its edges, and another sign
speaking of the 'Indigenous connection' – thriller

subtext, crime drama, blockbuster and award winner,
as if it's a connection 'we' *might* take under advice!

This land that never stopped being Aboriginal land,
and *it* allows us to walk its erosions without being

plunged to the bottom of the bottomless pit.
Such decorations of the literary! Such gifts of *English*!

Charmaine Papertalk-Green reads her poem 'Creation Markings – Ellendale Pool' to the audience in the Geraldton Town Library. This is her land, her community's country, her space for speaking and final words and all presences and futures and pasts.

'Precise poems' are more ambiguous than we might think: on Judith Wright's *Collected Poems*[9]

I wish to celebrate this new edition of Judith Wright's *Collected Poems*. It is a book that should be kept permanently in print for so many reasons. If Wright's superb selected, *A Human Pattern*, is a distillation of her work, it is not the sole repository and dwelling-space of her greatest poetry. Many of the poems left out of that collection warrant this appellation as well.

Further, Wright (1915–2000) herself half-lamented the loss of context that comes with the passing of time, the 'forgetting' of reasons, the pressures and necessities that underpin the writing of a poem; and what better way to regain some of that context than by the conversation, the mutual reinforcing that comes with publishing a *Collected Poems*. Those earlier poems, Wright distanced herself from, because of a growing awareness and absolute commitment to fairness and justice, to a treaty with Indigenous Australia, for acknowledgement and restitution in terms of cultural richness, diversity and presence, land rights and compensation for what has been stolen. Poems that in 'their time'

---

9   This chapter, which acts as a Foreword to the Fourth Estate 2016 edition of *Judith Wright: Collected Poems 1942–1985* has an unusual textual history. Originally written as a much shorter version to introduce *A Human Pattern: Selected Poems* (of Judith Wright) published in the UK by Carcanet in 2009 (and collected in Vol. 1 of my *Spatial Relations*), I was asked to expand it (to almost twice the length) by HarperCollins Publishing for their new 2016 Australian reissue of the 1994 collected. So here it is, complete, in its zone among my other related and interactive commentaries. As noted, none of my texts lives in isolation.

might have been considered socially aware and 'fair' by her predominantly white English-speaking audience, yet that she came to doubt because of those very reasons.

But Wright was also the ultimate poet who understood that a poem is a guide to the imagination and, as she indicates, a guide to understanding herself. This collected, to which she added her own typically concise and illuminating preface, is a map of the self as well as for viewing, critiquing and experiencing Australia, and by extension the 'wider world' all peoples occupy.

This collected is a document of mapping of place, language, cultures and the self. Remarkable love poems, poems of intense intimacy, engage in dialogue with poems of great social and ecological concern. As the work of an environmentalist, Wright's poems were advocates for the natural world while always being poems of inner human landscapes as well. They are about observation, history, loss, obligation, beauty, and the self-empowerment and collective empowerment of all living things. From her generations of colonial heritage, she managed to look at herself and where she came from, and reconfigure it into another way of belonging, another way of conversing with an ancient country and its Indigenous people.

Poets and critics often ask themselves and each other who the audience for poetry is. What is its demographic? Inevitably, different 'kinds' of poetry are apportioned and even relegated to different audiences. This is patently ridiculous, because poetry is available to all of us whenever we can access it. What might not speak to us can do so if we listen with different ears. What Wright notes as 'context' (or a lack of it) is what readers might search for in understanding a poem, but it's also what they bring to the poem. And this, I expect, also delighted Wright. She was never closed to different approaches to the 'meaning' of her poems.

I celebrate this volume because its audience is humanity, and if we travel with it we will grow as it grows, and as the reachings-out to the land and its peoples are made, we might reach with them. The crisis of belonging and presence is at the core of the Australian 'identity' – that mysterious shared something that goes outside nationalism, that connects migrant peoples from all over the world to the conflicted penal-colonial shifting sands of state, and the aggressive occupation of Indigenous land, the theft of country itself.

Australia is many people and many peoples placing great pressure on vulnerable ecologies, and often promoting 'progress' as opposed to 'conservation'. Across the time of colonisation (it's ongoing), there have been many versions of Australia, and the 'setting' and particularity of these many spaces are caught by Wright in local detail that branches into a consultation with wider myths of 'Australia'. In the fascinating poem, 'Country Town', (not included in *A Human Pattern*), part of the collection *The Moving Image*,[10] which appeared just after the Second World War, we read:

---

10 Judith Wright, *The Moving Image* (Meanjin Press, 1946).

> This is the landscape that the towns creep over;
> a landscape safe with bitumen and banks.
> The hostile hills are netted in with fences
> and the roads lead to houses and the pictures.
> Thunderbolt was killed by Constable Walker
> long ago; the bones are buried, the story printed.

The matter-of-fact tone, the reportage-like statement, the 'signing-off', are an early example of Wright's compassion and irony working hand in hand. This was her genius – the ability to combine tones with equal conviction and passion. This is about the authorities' desire to control *the land*, the 'wilderness', even the 'waste'; to throw the catchment of the *cordon sanitaire* as wide as possible and bring all rebellions, people and peoples, all nature under its supervision.

In her remarkable collection of non-fiction, *Born of the Conquerors: Selected Essays*,[11] in which she is a vital participant 'in attempting at last to do something to redress old wrongs' (p. xi), Wright investigates the issue of so-called 'wilderness' and 'waste':

> Our own dreams have shrunk to more realistic proportions, and our politicians now merely want to sell as much iron, coal and uranium as possible from the still untamed north and west of the continent, regardless of the wastelands which will follow. The concept behind this ambition is of course still the same – the Wilderness must be turned to account even if in the process it becomes an even more unproductive Waste – and the psychology behind it is I think also the same: a continuing and deeply instinctive fear and dislike of the unknown, of country of which man is not in control and which pays no tribute to this economy and his technological powers.
>
> The old recoil from the Wilderness still exists even when unoccupied forest country has been stripped of its dangers. The last of the Aborigines, of the bushrangers, and even of almost all the cattle-duffers have now been cleared from the bush, and the cities are becoming so intolerable that city-dwellers at least are in search of relief from them in natural surroundings as different as possible from the crowded smog-ridden streets. The value of wilderness for its intrinsic beauty and its quality of solitude is now in much more demand than before. But private interests of grazing, mining and other considerations, reinforced by the judgements of English visitors to whom Australian landscape seems as unattractive as it did to Barron Field, emphasise the old fears: wilderness is seen as the breeding-ground of innumerable predatory dingoes and grass-eating marsupials ready to descend on the human settlements, a source of bushfires, and a potential danger to bewildered bushwalkers. All these perils are deeply implanted in the European psychology, and we have to take them into account if we are to understand what the concept of Wilderness means. It is Outcast Country, such as Cain and Ishmael were banished to, and it is Danger Country in which unknown and mysterious and therefore hostile things survive. Worse, it is Waste – unproductive land which contributes nothing to the national or the private income. (p. 23, 'Wilderness, Waste and History')

---

11 Judith Wright, *Born of the Conquerors: Selected Essays* (Aboriginal Studies Press, 1991).

In talking of 'landscape' in 'Country Town', Wright seems to subtext a land previously 'scaped' (in various ways) by Aboriginal people, and re-scaped by colonialism. There's an irony in her use of the word 'landscaped' as there is in her use of the word 'wilderness', a term widely considered problematic, but which Wright appears to employ with full consciousness of Indigenous presence. And there's also the haunting of exile – 'looked like another country and wrenched the heart' – the re-scaping of land to recreate the image and pragmatics of (a European) 'home': loss on so many levels.

'Country Town' already asks the questions Wright would investigate further and further and with much self-scrutiny. She never excluded herself from complicity and responsibility in the wrongs she observed and traced in her poetry and prose. The poem begins with a fusion of lament, regret and something close to exasperation:

> This is no longer the landscape that they knew,
> the sad green enemy country of their exile,
> those branded men whose songs were of rebellion.

It is a land that refuses them, and yet offers sanctuary from unjust punishments and abuse, from the brutality of the Crown. This is a paradox from which Wright's concern grew, transformed and became so complex and multilayered, while retaining clarity of vision, the desire for justice. These men long for the loved ones of Ireland and Britain, console themselves with rum, and try to understand country. In some ways, they belong more in their exile than the colonisers who wish to consume and change and control. But Wright is also subtle, and is of the colonisers herself, if in many ways outside their towns. We read:

> And yet in the night of the sleeping town, the voices:
> This is not ours, not ours the flowering tree.
> What is it we have lost and left behind?

In this, Wright captures the sense of internal exile many colonisers felt, caught between the desire or need to 'leave' their home countries, and the longing for home. But there's also the sense that the signs of the land are readable by others and not themselves. It is an 'early' poem that tracks the ravaging of land, exploitation of people, loss and desire, a haunting that can only increase.

We also read in *Born of the Conquerors* this summation of how Wright's awareness of the presence, dispossession and absence of Aboriginal people in places she knew moved to a more active understanding of the crimes committed, and a need for restitution by 'white' Australia to Aboriginal people. And by extension, we might consider why we move from suggestion and intimation of wrongs done to Aboriginal people as they are 'part' of country in Wright's earlier poems, to a more overt consideration of independence, liberty, agency, Aboriginal law and custom, culture and country in her poetry (see the poem

'Two Dreamtimes' and 'to where I stand with all my fathers/their guilt and righteousness'), essays and other writings:

> My father once told me, looking out from the escarpment of the tableland across the gulfs which are now part of the New England National Park, of the driving of an Aboriginal group suspected of killing cattle, over the cliff opposite. That story lodged itself in my mind [...] A bora ring and sacred way survived not far from my grandmother's home, and the paddock was named the Bora Paddock – I wrote 'Bora Ring', about that. I am told the ring area has now been ploughed; and a very old carved tree near the woolshed on Wallamumbi where I was brought up has disappeared too. They were some of the last signs of occupation stretching many thousands of years into the past, but they were not thought worth preserving.
>
> I spent a couple of years at Sydney University in the then new anthropology course. But for anthropologists, it seemed to me, Aborigines seemed little more than objects of study. For many years, historians appeared to regard them as either invisible, or mere obstructions or occasional assistants in the exploration of the continent. Those attitudes have died hard.
>
> It was not until I was in my forties that I was able to meet Kath Walker, as she then was, and to get educated in the realities of Aboriginal life. (p. xi)

One of the delights of having here the full range of poems is to rediscover those that brought wonder and epiphanies when first encountered. I remember reading 'Flying-Fox on Barbed Wire' from *The Two Fires* (1955)[12] when I was a teenager in the 1970s, and remaking the poem in my head with a local bat the victim rather than a flying fox which, since I was in Geraldton on the mid-west coast, was unknown to me outside books. What caught my attention, and really became a key to understanding not only Wright's poetry, but a lot of other poetry, were the seeming contradictions. The celebration and fear, the damnation and liberation, the anthropomorphising mixed with respect and distance: familiarity and alienation. How could such contradictory factors work in a poem and make absolute 'sense'? It all added up to more than the sum of its parts. I could feel and hear and see the wounded creature. I could sense its resistance. I understood the hand of human interference and also responsibility: it was human-made barbed wire that caused the hurt and a human hand that freed the creature.

> Little nightmare flying-fox
> trapped on the cruel barbs of day
> has no weapon but a wing
> and a tiny scream.

The creature is night in day. Pinned as in a museum display, but alive:

> but stabbed with a pin its velvet hand
> and hung it in a hostile land.

---

12 Judith Wright, *The Two Fires* (Angus & Robertson, 1955).

Here is the violence of colonial intrusion: the barbed fencing of space, the realigning of lines of movement and communication of the flying fox, the victimisation of the creature. It is made hostile in its own world. The persona/e releases the victim: preventative measure against its 'needle bite' is not defence against a weapon; it's a fact of being. The flying fox is not attacking; it has been passively attacked by the wire. It will return to its night, the humans to the brutality of their day. It is worth noting that Wright only creates her sensuous images for a purpose: they are never gratuitous, never images for images' sake. Hers is an art with purpose and conviction.

Another delight of having the *Collected Poems* is that we can see the gathering of Wright's birds again. Originally published in volume form by A&R in 1962, they were later republished in the National Library's 2003 illustrated edition of Judith Wright's *Bird* poems with an introduction by Wright's daughter, Meredith McKinney, who notes that many of these poems were written for her as a child, but also for 'maturer ears than mine'. She writes:

> 'Whatever the bird is, is perfect in the bird', says Judith Wright in her poem 'Birds'. The poems of this present volume not only offer intimate portraits of many of the birds that were dear to her, but each poem in its varied way reaches to touch each varied bird's 'perfection'. They are the poet's way of becoming one with the creatures she loved. (p. 2)

And this holds not only for the wonderful bird poems, but for all Wright's nature poetry: hers was an environmentalism formed from both intellectual and emotional empathy. McKinney adds:

> The poems originally collected in *Birds* were written during the 1950s, the first decade of Judith's time of living and writing surrounded by the lush rainforest world of Tamborine Mountain in south-east Queensland, and most come directly out of that world and time. This was the happiest decade of her life, when she at last felt she had truly come into her own as poet, lover and mother, and the abundance of Tamborine's natural world and its birds spoke back to her of her own sense of abundance and delight.

It seems appropriate, given Wright's daughter's proximity to these poems both physically and spiritually, to quote from 'Eggs and Nestlings' with its sense of Blakean contraries, a Hardyesque understanding and empathy with the non-human, and John Clare-like innocence of observation (that in both Wright's and Clare's case was far from 'innocent', but always capable of wonder). The child sees 'three pale and powdered' eggs in a nest, and is later called by her mother to see the broken shells and the nestlings. Wright is a master of 'closure' that also offers metaphysical questioning: nothing is polite or comfortable in a Wright poem, no matter how well packaged in its 'verse form' and control of language it seems. The poem concludes:

> Those yellow gapes, those starveling cries,
> how they disquieted my eyes! –

> the shapeless furies come to be
> from shape's most pure serenity.

Furies and serenity. And we have an echo of Blake's 'eternity' in there as well. Disorder and order are shaped from the same materials. For such a committed activist, Wright's poetry of activism is rarely didactic. She sees, reads, listens, experiences, processes, offers. We tell ourselves. We converse with the poems.

With her concerns for the biosphere, Wright also developed a potent irony that could be disdainful while retaining a 'light' touch. Of Canberra and its political machinations, she wryly notes:

> Considered as an ecosystem
> Canberra is impossible.
> No balance between input and output;
> a monoculture community
> whose energy goes entirely into organisation.

Or the pastiche of the serious that is deadly serious in its underlying accusatory irony, in its lament for the future we blithely allow ourselves to (un)make:

> Ladies and gentlemen, we have returned
> from our foray into the future.

Hers is a wide arc of experience and poetic focus. And it stretches across the world: Hawaii, New Zealand, the myths of Ancient Greece ... Close observation of the 'termite queen' brings classical and psychological allusion, the epic and the minutiae of life, analogies of human struggle and animal selves; the case-moth up-close and the platypus is nearby. What's exciting are the many modes of address, the way the voice moves from poem to poem: speaking to a friend, speaking with an ironic grandeur, speaking carefully and compassionately, the poet standing outside her own experience and analysing it, declarative and almost conspiratorial (see what I see, if you look closely), the 'you' who is close and the you who is distant, the informative 'I', the chatty 'I', the lonely 'I', the loving 'I' and 'we'; address to the subject of the poem, listening to the subject, apostrophe, statement and question, rhetoric and lyric.

***

All human life works out of patterns, makes patterns, and leaves its mark, its imprint, to some degree or other. Judith Wright wondered at and investigated the complexity of design with a secular vision but a spiritual intensity. More than five decades of writing and thinking led her to feel that though all people had patterns in common, not all people considered or used these patterns (consciously or unconsciously) in just ways. The poem is a pattern, the land is a pattern, 'flora' and 'fauna' are patterns, society and communal groups are patterns. We are monadic and dyadic at once. And choices are made. The poem is a pattern and an exercise in free will. But when the distance between how we live in an environment and how we respect that environment grows too great, those patterns are disrupted, and become self-defeating and damaging to the networks of patterns that co-exist to make the world that is.

Though her poetry and worldview were so centred not only in Australian landscapes, flora and fauna, but in the idea of Australia with its mass of contradictions, affirmations and negations, Judith Wright was truly a world poet. From her pastoral origins on the family station in the New England tablelands, through to days near coast and rainforest in Queensland, and finally her much-loved inland acreage in the bush outside Canberra (at Braidwood, New South Wales), Wright looked inwards into Australia, and in doing so made the local poetically universal. Her dedication to place, and as her life went on, increasingly to environmental concerns and Indigenous rights, was part of a life-dialogue with her origins and their implications in her writing.

One cannot separate Wright's poetry from a political agenda, even in her earliest poetry which is less compensatory, less prone to self-critical considerations of her world as made by her family, and families like hers; of the destructive effect of 'pioneering' on the peoples whose land was stolen, and of the damage done to the ecology of those places.

But Wright is a poet in whom all aspects of the human condition are present in even the most scathing analysis of human greed and foibles. A poet of apparent formal conservatism in equal strength to her political radicalism, Wright needs to be formally re-read if one is fully to understand how much she was actually pushing the limits of formal diction and prosody in order to say what she felt needed to be said. It is true that later in her life she expressed doubt about innovative poetics, but this probably came out of a sense of exclusion, and maybe, too, of being misread in her dynamism.

Wright was an innovator in the way she wrote about flora and fauna. Though she separates human and animal causality, her poems so often consider not only the rights of animals themselves, but even the complexities of writing animals within the constraints of the poem itself. Here, she often uses form in a self-ironising way, subjecting the persona to the agency of the animal being discussed. In 'Platypus' (an animal exploited in life and in literature for being considered physically bizarre), the poem sets the animal against the persona's childhood memories of its rippling brilliance, and a history of consumption, environmental degradation and pollution, to arrive at the following:

> But at this late midnight
> suddenly my mind
> runs clear and you rise through.
> I sit and write
> a poem for your sake
> that follows a word –
> platypus, paradox –
> like the ripples of your wake.

Wright was a school standard for decades; it was through my mother, who taught Wright in her English classes, that I came across her poetry in my early childhood. One of the earliest poems I wrote was a less than successful imitation of 'The Old Prison'. I mention this because so many Australian poets of my generation cut their teeth on such poems. First, because they were what was taught, but second, and most importantly, because they combined formal attributes that one had to learn even if one wanted to overturn formal conventions; and third, because they seemed to speak for at least part of the experience of being a child in the Australian school environment. For those of us with rural connections, possibly even more so. Here are the last two stanzas of 'The Old Prison':

> Who built and laboured here?
> The wind and the sea say
> – Their cold nest is broken
> and they are blown away.
>
> They did not breed nor love.
> Each in his cell alone
> cried as the wind now cries
> through this flute of stone.

This presents a particularly relevant sense of the isolation and torment of convict prisoners (who likely made their own jails), and also of the imprisoning nature of 'pioneering': the sparseness and abandonment to the elements of markers of colonialism (and penal servitude) as an implied juxtaposition to the omnipresent markers of 'civilisation' in the places or country/countries of the prisoners' origins or heritage. A seemingly simple painting of abandonment becomes resonant with political implication. This poem appeared in Wright's second book, *From Woman to Man*. If we leap ahead, thirty years later we find this stanza in the poem 'For a Pastoral Family', in section 2, 'To My Generation':

> If now there are landslides, if our field of reference
> is much eroded, our hands show little blood.
> We enter a plea: Not Guilty.
> For the good of the Old Country
> the land was taken; the Empire had loyal service.
> Would any convict us?
> Our plea has been endorsed by every appropriate jury.

There are some vital and subtle shifts between the voices in these two poems, while essentially they remain the same. Wright is often considered to have become more radical as time went on, but I'd argue the signs were clearly there from the beginning. Both these poems deal with the effect of time and (false) justice. Both are about erosion and loss because of damaged presences in the first place. Both are about 'nature' taking back in the face of an Ozymandias-like effort to dominate and control. But much more than that, both deny that 'nature' is reason enough to ignore the implications of wrong-doing. In 'The Old Prison' we get no sense of the prisoners' wrong, only the bleakness of the jail being there: it has become in its failure (as it always would fail) an embodiment of loss and futility, it is of the bones of the land. In the more direct criticism of the 'To My Generation' piece, there is an accusation of injustice in justice itself, that the law that imposed on the land in colonising was an anathema to that land, and ultimately 'its people'.

Comparisons like this between different points in Wright's writing life generate much understanding of her greater vision. Take the very early 'Bora Ring' from her first book *The Moving Image* (1946), then 'At Cooloolah' from her third book, *The Two Fires* (1955), and finally 'Two Dreamtimes' from the much later *Alive* (1972).[13] All three poems are concerned with the relationship between Indigenous cultures/country and colonial Australia (in its various manifestations). 'Bora Ring' might be said to take a more patronising look at the 'issue', in the sense that absence is noted and responsibility (for the damage done to a brother person) focussed through a Biblical lens:

> The hunter is gone: the spear
> is splintered underground; the painted bodies
> a dream the world breathed sleeping and forgot.
> The nomad feet are still.
>
> Only the rider's heart
> halts at a sightless shadow, an unsaid word
> that fastens in the blood the ancient curse,
> the fear as old as Cain.

At first glance this seems a typical colonial guilt poem: the colonial rider/inheritor feels discomfort because of a violation of the basic Judaeo-Christian principle of justice and loyalty to a brother. Out of this, we might surmise noble sentiments within a noble-savage construct. In this context, the use of the figurative to equate Indigenous spiritual presence with the literary (derived from the Biblical) ghost is further evidence of appropriation ... another classic example of poetic sentiment separating from implications in the real world. But there is more to this than we might think. One must remember that this is a projection through the eyes and collective inherited sensibilities of the rider. It's his way of *understanding* in an inchoate way – the poet translates his disturbance and sense of guilt into the discourse he comes out of. There is, in the least, an acknowledgement of broader cultural culpability for wrong done here. Again, an issue of justice.

'At Cooloolah' is one of Wright's masterpieces. It taps into the 'issues' of 'Bora Ring' but goes much further in its metatexts and broader implications. In

---

13 Judith Wright, *Alive* (Angus & Robertson, 1972).

the following two magnificent stanzas, the idea of conquest and occupation is overturned without any sense of a romantic resonance to appease guilt:

> but I'm a stranger, come of a conquering people.
> I cannot share his calm, who watch his lake,
> being unloved by all my eyes delight in,
> and made uneasy, for an old murder's sake.
>
> Those dark-skinned people who once named Cooloolah
> knew that no land is lost or won by wars,
> for earth is spirit: the invader's feet will tangle
> in nets there and his blood be thinned by fears.

From a contemporary viewpoint, there is a more recognisably 'post-colonial' deconstruction of the positions of the coloniser and colonised here. There is a sense that colonisation has failed at anything more than murder, that the invaders will always be the real losers. Extending this, we might see that no hybridity is possible in the face of such crimes, and in the face of such spiritual and cultural strength existing in direct conjunction with, and coming out of, a land that the invaders can only abuse and misunderstand. What makes this a technically as well as politically radical poem is that the image-making, so characteristically rich (Wright is one of the great image-makers in Australian literature), is beholden to the implications of the message – what is being said struggles against the physical confines of stanza and line, and the very ability to express and discuss the horrific implications of the invaders' actions. The calm of the stanza pattern is belied by the trauma of what's being said. It is characteristic of Wright to undo and ironise form through strong political purpose.

'Two Dreamtimes' is dedicated to 'Kath Walker, now Oodgeroo Noonuccal', Indigenous poet and activist, and Judith Wright's close friend. It is significant to note that Walker changed her name as an act of resistance and reclamation at the time of the (very white) Bicentennial Celebrations of the First Fleet's arrival in Australia in 1788 (and thus the title was emended to note this name change for the *Selected Poems* originally published in 1990). This poem is fraught with contradictions in Wright's effort to find kinship, and break out of the binary she herself cites, of the conqueror and persecuted. Common ground is found in gender. Wright spent her entire life writing poems of empathy and insight into what it means physically and ontologically to be a woman in a patriarchal world, but even more, writing poems as an affirmation of human complexity, agency and identity. Wright projects her own sense of anger and humiliation at where she comes from, indeed who she is, into her effort to find spiritual connection with Oodgeroo, her 'shadow-sister'. One feels the necessity of the poem is on her side, and there's a tacit acknowledgement of Oodgeroo's likely graciousness in accepting such an address. The tension in the poem manifests in the apportioning and accepting of blame on the poet's part – no longer the distance of voice in the previous two poems I have mentioned in this context, but the poet herself:

> Over the rum your voice sang
> the tales of an old people,
> their dreaming buried, the place forgotten ...
> We too have lost our dreaming.
>
> We the robbers, robbed in turn,
> selling this land on hire-purchase;
> what's stolen once is stolen again
> even before we know it.
>
> If we are sisters, it's in this –
> our grief for a lost country,
> the place we dreamed in long ago,
> poisoned now and crumbling.

Wright claims a kinship to the land, and a loss. One confronts degrees of belonging – childhood spent in a particular place, older pioneer family – in the face of tens of thousands of years of family presence. This is not benign, there is a passionate urge to be part of the land because it is deeply felt, and though there is necessary contrition (justice again), hopes of redemption and ultimate connection come through friendship with an Indigenous Australian. The parrying and dialogics of the poem show an awareness of this irresolvable irony – it is the same faced by the rider in 'Bora Ring', just a more direct way of trying to overcome the guilt. One might consider this a form of appropriation, but in the context of Wright's activism for land rights and Indigenous rights in general, we are forced to reassess. Poetry is based in the act of comparison: of creating allusions whose sources the poet knows, having seen something outside the readily described but wanting to allow another to enter into it. Creating the pictures in our heads that, in the end, don't need the words. This is what Wright is doing. It's a life's writing process. It's a technical, philosophical and political agenda.

If Judith Wright has a greatest poem, it might very well be 'Naked Girl and Mirror'. A girl conversing with herself as woman in a mirror (or the true self conversing with the socially constructed self, ruled by vanity and expectation, entrapment and disappointment). Reflection becomes illumination and obscurity. Its longer lines, its address to the self – the internal 'other' – its dialogue between soul and body resolved as a soul-body conjoining that remains as a secret self throughout life, that a partner can never know – the inner girl that the grown woman might forget but who defines her deepest freedoms and identity – the poem is unmatched, to my mind, with any other with its subject matter I have read. The self-accusation, the call for agency that won't come in the living world, and the tension of self-address, often using a staccato line with multiple caesuras in conjunction with distended iambs, are disturbing. The poem's power rests in the addressing voice's denial that the grown woman can ever know her real inner self, when they are in essence one and the same. The forces and conventions of a society in which women are forced to role-play from birth to death, but especially from puberty on, don't overcome the soul even if they constrict the body. The poem is self-accusatory and self-liberating, a poem of compliance and resistance. In the end, not even male (we assume) lovers can get ownership of the inner self which the woman is taught to deny even to herself, but which is so desirable to the controlling lover:

> Yet I pity your eyes in the mirror, misted with tears;
> I lean to your kiss. I must serve you; I will obey.
> Some day we may love. I miss your going, some day,
> though I shall always resent your dumb and fruitful years.
> Your lovers shall learn better, and bitterly too,
> if their arrogance dares to think I am part of you.

Irony and empathy work together. Wright always wrote out of self-knowledge.

The list of Wright's influential poems is long. And when I say influential, I mean to the extent that generations of Australian schoolchildren knew them if not by heart then something close to it. Wright's work was used for teaching readings of Australian landscape (within the European way of seeing) and as affirmations of pastorality. This she later rejected, though her selection in *A Human Pattern* contains two of the poems she viewed as most problematically affirming in this context, 'Bullocky' and 'South of My Days'(probably the two best-known Australian poems outside the work of Banjo Paterson). Her poetry was used to introduce social issues (see 'Metho Drinker' ... one of my classes spent an entire lesson discussing the obvious meaning, but one difficult for schoolchildren, of 'His white and burning girl, his woman of fire,/creeps to his heart and sets a candle there' – the sexual, even romantic, substitution of alcohol in a perverse and horrific irony eluding us until prompted). It was used for discussions of Indigenous rights, and environmental issues. Wright was identified as definitively Australian, and was sold to us with a nationalistic affirmation she would have found disturbing but maybe also pleasing at the same time. There is that parochialism in her work, but it's not an uncommon attribute in poets of world standing. Other nations affirm their own through affirmations made by others of their own.

Spanning a large part of Wright's working life was her relationship with the philosopher Jack McKinney (who died in 1966; though he and Wright married in 1962, they spent many years living as a couple prior to that). McKinney had played an intensely intellectual role in feeding her poetry. Wright suffered deafness and eventually impaired vision toward the end of a vital and busy life. That busy life also included her helping to found the Wildlife Preservation Society of Queensland, raising a daughter, advocating for many other poets, fighting for Indigenous rights (including helping Nugget Coombs found the Aboriginal Treaty Committee in 1979), and standing up to governments in Australia over numerous social and environmental issues. I wrote to her a couple of times near the end of her life, and received back one fax in large letters and a card. They were the two most important short communiqués of my life even though they were negative replies to my requests for poems – she pointed out that she didn't write poetry anymore. She had said what she had to say, though she never stopped fighting for just causes. I am an anti-nationalist, but she would have understood that, as her version of nationalism was about country and the local, not about power and might. In her last book of poetry, *Phantom Dwelling*, she wrote these lines ('Brevity'):

> Rhyme, my old cymbal,
> I don't clash you as often,
> or trust your old promises
> of music and unison.
>
> I used to love Keats, Blake.
> Now I try haiku
> for its honed brevities,
> its inclusive silences.

Is there a new poetics in this? Her last book contains long-lined poems as well, but maybe reconciles the above declaration with her older prosody in the wonderful 'The Shadow of Fire: Ghazals' which, loosely using the internal structures of the ghazal, brings the 'shorter' and 'longer' together, and frees this strictest of forms from rhyme and repetition, reforging it in a landscape of her mind, stretching over her life. In these poems the personal address to the world around Wright reaches as apogee – a Sufi-like affirmation of all existence grounded in her familiar sense of the real, her down-to-earth practicality. The land is no game, but poets do play games. And whatever one's views or aspirations, we are neither all one thing nor all another. With the power to write of 'issues' as she did, it is easy to forget that Wright was a great poet of love and affirmation, and a great celebrator of beauty, especially in nature. Often this is anchored in the brutal irony of the abuse of nature (see the powerful 'Extinct Birds') or with foreboding and warning, but in the end it was an expression of the sublime. *A Human Pattern* finishes with these lines from the ghazal 'Patterns'; patterns were something that fascinated Wright and her philosopher husband – they had majesty but were never without social implications. Her poetry thrived on what seems, often, paradox:

> That prayer to Agni, fire-god, cannot be prayed.
> We are all of us born of fire, possessed by darkness.

Wright is an elemental poet. So much fire, water, earth and air is in her work. And of course that necessary fifth element, quintessence. The senses, birds and animals, women and children, and landscapes, all inhabit her work. She is often called a poet of nature, but I think she is far more a poet of human contact with the land in which humans and nature are differentiated. This is not to say they aren't part of the whole, but rather that poetry is an exploration of the distance humans create between themselves and nature. Between ideas of 'Eden', and the world they 'scape'. In the end, Wright was entirely sceptical of the Western aesthetic triumphing over the land, or even representing it, and I have often wondered if this was the real reason for her poetic silence late in life.

So, I celebrate this collected. Judith Wright was one of the greatest of twentieth-century poets, whose work is timeless. Her precise poems are more ambiguous than we might think, and this is their brilliant deception. Her influences were many, and ranged over many cultures. She learnt from Oodgeroo, she learnt from Urdu, Persian and Japanese poets, she learnt from Christopher Brennan and the colonial poets. She was never closed. Her work grew and continues to grow. For some of us, it is the reason to read and write poetry. And for generations of Australian poets she was a reader, editor, critic, friend and colleague who helped keep the conversation going and becoming more generous, open and committed. Unambiguous positionality, with a respect for the generative potential of polysemous figurative ambiguities of allusion and even elusiveness.

On Georgina Arnott's *The Unknown Judith Wright*[14]

In a book of many questions and not a few premises, maybe the core approach of *The Unknown Judith Wright* can be summed up in Georgina Arnott's statement: 'What is surprising is the extent to which Judith's life narrative has remained un-contextualised, perhaps even unchallenged, by literary critics, cultural historians and biographers with recourse to ancillary material' (p. 183). Arnott is accurate in this, and looks to rectify a small part of the 'omissions' by considering, in particular, Judith Wright's apparent unwillingness – even as she moved towards disavowing aspects of her colonial inheritance – to see the complicity of her Wyndham ancestors, especially George, in the systematic *brutality* of dispossession of Aboriginal peoples.

As we journey from the imperial project of Wright's ancestors, especially George Wyndham, and the legacy and cost of the squattocracy in terms of invasion of Aboriginal lands, to the 'recovery' of anonymous poems in Sydney University journals and their part in a possible pre-history for a number of Wright's prominent early *avowed* poems, one gets the feeling there are two books, at least, happening here.

Wright's university years come under scrutiny as a formative period of her social, ethical and writerly development, in a way not done before. Did Wright's studies in philosophy, history (which she failed), English and anthropology affect her development as writer and activist more than she would have had us think? What of charismatic lecturers? Her social circles? Her accommodation in the city? Arnott shows the effect of these is at least likely. But what results is an argument equivocating around what Wright later in life doesn't remember or couldn't confirm (say, in her historical research). Now, residues and traces are left by all experiences, and this argument is fair enough, but it's

---

14 Georgina Arnott, *The Unknown Judith Wright* (University of Western Australia Publishing, 2016).

a wilful argument. Unsurprisingly, Wright at university is both self-liberating and self-constraining, and there are also external family forces at work.

Yet Arnott's project is a worthy one. It is appropriate for her to seek to expose the lacunae and misprisions in Wright's own representation of her past to suit her later beliefs. To those of us who, like Arnott, grew up with Wright's poems, and have thought about these poems in the context of her life and her other non-poetry writings, it actually comes as no surprise that Wright sidestepped harsh realities (though she also confronted plenty of them) in telling her family history, in different ways at different times.

There are few, if any, colonial progenitors who cannot be held accountable for dispossession, and whether they arrived on 'settled' or 'unsettled' land, they enacted an ongoing denial of presence and agency, and inevitably physical harm (directly or indirectly) on first peoples. Arnott notes, 'Researching Judith's family history, I gradually developed the view that the Wyndhams directly dispossessed Aboriginal people, rather than only occupying and cultivating areas already "settled", as Judith suggested.'

Arnott is stating what needs to be stated, noting of George's legacy that 'Judith interpreted it in the best possible light.' What bothers me is the tendency towards rhetorical double-play in Arnott's argument. Obviously, Wright's was an ongoing process of examination and coming to grips, attempting (at least) to stick with the evidence she had, while trying to cling to some hope of good faith in what is, as implicated by Arnott and known by all those with indigenous heritage (and others), a tale of horror.

Occasionally, we get the sense Arnott is forcing the mid-1930s' Wright to fit our contemporary understanding of things: 'She became the quintessential Modern Woman ... She was neither sweet, nor innocent.' In attempting to match the construct of the Modern Woman and a 'transgressive sexuality', which ultimately remains guesswork, Arnott creates a somewhat overdetermined demi-portrait of a direction-changer in the pastoral inheritance, who, as she got older, would become genuinely radical in a way her privileged upbringing does *and* doesn't prepare us for. Sensuality and desire are evident in Wright's work from the earliest, but we don't need evidence, surely, for its validity and presence?

Strangely, Judith Wright seems absent from this 'biographical story' of her first twenty-one years, which often seems more like an unprocessed PhD thesis than an organic writing of part of a life – Wright is often a cipher for an argument. Maybe this is because it is environment – 'nature' – that seems so secondary in this analysis. It never can be in considering Wright.

Ironically, in part, this might be because Arnott is a competent but not intensely astute reader of poems. Sometimes Arnott misses the polysemous nature of poetry writing. The poem is not a document, but a living entity, which critiques the conditions of its own production.

The last chapter of the book makes valid arguments for Wright's authorship of anonymous poems in university publications. As Arnott suggests, *if* these poems *weren't* written by Wright, we do need to at least ask about their influence on Wright's acknowledged verse.

But, again, Arnott's readings of these poems are conventional – some dynamic correlations are missing, but maybe this is in keeping for a book that opens doors to further investigation, to a *certain* amount of reconsideration of Judith Wright as poet, activist and even historian.

On Alison Whittaker's poetry collection *Blakwork*: a letter to an editor[15]

I think *BlakWork* an extremely powerful book and a major work of poetry. Though I am an animal rights vegan of thirty plus years, I believe in everyone's right to make their own choices and relate to their own heritages and traditions as they will. I think her abattoir pieces are intensely powerful and obviously disturbing in a variety of necessary ways, but also disturbing to me in ways others might not find disturbing. With poetry, this is as it should be – and this is a book of confrontations with an ongoing colonialism that often doesn't recognise its own cultural impositions (because it's a colonial act to think that they are not cultural impositions).

Whittaker confronts the expectations and manners of 'polite society' (I come from impolite society), but I am also caught between two positions regarding the meat industry – I understand and respect the arguments of family, connections re what has been stolen ('hunter gatherer'), and the bigotries that circulate around this theft, as well as the human underpinnings of a reality, but I am also contradicting myself if I support an attack on those who protest the meat industry (including myself). It is possible to support both positions in the context, and within their contexts. Unless we consider positionality and culturality in such discussions, we end up with no justice in any form. The texts created by the poet offer many points of entry and exit, and allow me to be who I am and respect the author and the culturality of the book. To me, as reader and activist, this is essential. I learn how to better act by enacting a process of reading and understanding. The paradox becomes generative – I can move beyond my own ambiguities in how I am able and how I choose to relate to the text, to its knowledges.

This is a book of great humanity and empathy for those whose voices have been suppressed or manipulated by dominating mainstream cultural discourse. I admire that Alison Whittaker's intense and focussed style lets so many *other* voices speak as well – even shout out … sometimes whisper.

It's an innovative poetry, but not just for the sake of being 'innovative. Maybe it's because the speaking-through can only be done by pushing the conventions of English (language) to the limit, of breaking it up into something more flexible and dynamic rather than reconstituting into a more 'universal' vehicle for expressing truths – that is, working with language that can take the stress of what it has been part of (un)making – marginalisation, dispossession, indifference, brutality, exploitation.

---

15   This is an expanded text of an earlier letter to the publisher-editor of this brilliant book, *Blakwork* (Magabala Books, 2018) – some of what I said became a comment on the back of the book.

But Alison Whittaker is no 'wilting violet', no way! – this is strength and confrontation and undoing of all polite colonial conventions that have been used to mask the ongoing horror. Alison Whittaker's poetry is a living tool, an older precolonial tool with contemporary immediacy. And *this* is one of the reasons I'd personally challenge the meat industry – aside from what I see as mistreatment of animals and an exploitation – it's also part of the colonial over-riding of tradition and an ongoing exploitation. Alison Whittaker is fully aware of these issues, and makes her narrative/s aware and expansive in their social and personal understanding as she makes her points about family, the legacies of colonialism, survival, strength and pride, and I guess that's how I can read and accept what she writes – she knows *what* she writes. She and I would agree on many things across the picket lines at the abattoir, as I am trying to stop the killing and she is challenging who and what I am, my knowledge and my motives. I've been around a long time and I think that I am consistent in my beliefs and their application, as she is with hers, so I am sure we could find mutual respect. This is why such a book of poetry is so important – it creates a nodal point in the nexus of conversation. 'I' learn from it, and grow towards different forms of activism and respect.

The technical versatility of this book – and again, a versatility not because of *style*, but out of *necessity* – is fabulous. The prose poems, the fragment poems, the song poems, the wordplay poems ('Trope' is brilliant ... and disturbing), the poems undoing and remaking the coloniser's language, the history-story corrective poems, the powerful legal unpicking poems ... are really tuned into the overall speaking of the book, its blak affirmation, its resiliance as narrative and protest as affirmation and corrective – its necessity.

I don't think there's been any effective decolonising in Australia, not really, but this book provides a powerful tool to help us all on our way. There's a cosmology in this book, and it translates into parallels that *can* maybe co-exist. It also tests notions of the colloquial, idiomatic language, and the fact that what is said is in how it is said – social history is the speech we hear, speak, pass on. Further, I think Whittaker's added a completely via a new range of ironies to poetry! In America there was a movement of disruptive poetry and poetics in the 1970s–1990s called l=a=n=g=u=a=g=e poetry – it messed with syntax and 'meaning' to challenge convention and conservative America ... I think she has made a new (re)LANGUAGE poetry that does something similar, but very very different as well. Alison Whittaker will ultimately always keep one foot (at least!) firmly outside the 'academy', as will her poetry. It's the most *disruptive* and necessary poetry I've read since first reading (and hearing) Lionel Fogarty's work.

Even if I wear the bloody clothes of colonial legacy I want to keep scrubbing at the stains of who I am as long as possible, even if they are impossible to get out!

So, for this *decentering book of centres*, for this word-of-mouth book of occasional computer gambits, for this book of paddy melon paddocks (been writing a lot about those lately), for this book of shredding the warped contrivances of racism, for this book of powerful blakwomen, for this book of growing up and observing the journey, for this book of family and belonging and country, for this book of connection and refusal, for this book of intellectual brilliance, I say, Yes!

Non-ambiguous: dispossession and culpability – on Ambelin Kwaymullina's *Living on Stolen Land*

Living on Stolen Land[16] is a statement of resistance and healing and pathways to repair and justice, come out of the collective genius of Aboriginal knowledge as committedly and concisely expressed by gifted thinker-storyteller and justice-seeker, Ambelin Kwaymullina.

Settler-colonial society might equate this document with a manifesto, but it's much more than a manifesto can ever be – it is a statement on behalf of Aboriginal peoples about what is shared in the experience and consequence of dispossession, about suffering the ongoing pain of settler-colonialism, explaining how non-linear time and holistic knowledges extend beyond the quantifiable, into a way of being that is immense, sensitive to all shifts and connections surrounding the land, the community, and the individual.

It's about listening to thousands of years of knowledge, and learning reciprocity; how to hear and to respect silences, too. As we encounter the overt evidence of structural, explicit and unconscious bias, settler-colonials are offered a way through to understanding better how they can rectify the ongoing, persistent and toxic injustice.

This is a call for 'partnerships on pathways/to all knowledges' and respectful relationships between Aboriginal peoples and settler-colonials, and how they might best be achieved.

Kwaymullina's work tells the truths of dispossession, theft of knowledge and land and the people themselves, and also shows the strength and resilience of Aboriginal people and their cultures in seen and unseen ways of resisting this assault.

This is a work of voice that is both statement and poetry, creating its own way of expression because it needs to. It escapes the settler-colonial categories in the same way a hill has its stories its people understand and listen to. It is outside the settler-colonial narrative, and offers a shared Indigenous story possessed by the many Indigenous thinkers who are part of communities of voice of resistance.

Although I really have no right to make a subjective comment, as I live on stolen land and am incapable of finding my way through to the justice I know I must help be made, nonetheless I believe this to be one of the most important statements on restoration to the dispossessed, on how all of us might go about the essential processes of decolonisation with sensitivity and awareness, that has ever been articulated.

16 Ambelin Kwaymullina, *Living on Stolen Land* (Magabala Books, 2020).

There are probably many words spoken in community along these lines, and others written in different ways, but in this way, in this form, Ambelin Kwaymullina has done a service to us all, and I am grateful – I hope without any expectation of gain from it other than how better to respect, partner, listen and interact with all indigenous people and their communities. It is beautiful and compelling writing – a guide that offers clear paths, gives answers, tells truths so readily suppressed by the self-interests of settler-colonialism.

On Glen Phillips's *Collected Poems 1968–2018: In the Hollow of the Land*[17]

Glen Phillips has been a poet all his life and, at the time of writing, is in his early eighties. I celebrate his life's achievement as a poet. This collected poems in two volumes represents about a quarter of his poetic output, but it is a good, strong and fair representation of his practice, concerns, interests and purpose.

For a poet whose range in both form and geographies is expansive, it is the act of making the poem that unifies his oeuvre. Phillips is fascinated with the workings of language, as his work in Italian and Mandarin pinyin attest. The poem itself is a containment of expanses, a focussing down of the infinity of life into distilled moments, into observations and experiences contextualised within a longevity of presentation. Above all else, Phillips is conscious of what making a poem means, and the responsibility of being a poet, a singer.

His early childhood was spent around Southern Cross in the Western Australian wheatbelt. But it is important to consider Southern Cross's mining underpinnings as well, because growth and extraction are both parts of the 'settler'/colonial environment of presence that is remembered in so many of these poems. Phillips's father was a school teacher; his maternal grandfather had a farm near Yenyenning. His recollections and poetic settings for his memories are imbued with those connections as well as his own world's very specific stretched horizons. One of the main issues any poet negotiates is how their childhood experiences set or offset their adult ones. Phillips left the wheatbelt at a relatively young age, but has since spent his life reconnecting with it, travelling through it, conversing with what is, and isn't. His work has always had a consciousness of the land being stolen from Aboriginal peoples, but as his decades of writing 'home' have gone on, there's been an increase in his awareness and expression of what this means in terms of his own growing up, his own presence.

The compilings of memories have become more imbued with what they really meant beyond the understanding of a child of the white wheatbelt (as a construct of agricultural devastation), and also what was actually going on at the time. Phillips's memories are both celebratory and questioning, and in building a document of presence, he is also building a document on intrusion. There's

---

17 Glen Phillips, *Collected Poems 1968–2018: In the Hollow of the Land* (Boffins Books, 2019).

a remarkable poem in Volume 1 entitled 'Foot Printing', that works with the issues of knowledge and distance, of innocence and reality, of a boy wanting to quiz a Noongar woman on bush lore while the fact of her working for the white townsfolk offsets this:

> I followed her then to the clothesline,
> propped with a forked stick, bush cut,
> which her wild-bearded walkabout man
> had sold us for a shilling months before,
> and saw her footmarks in the yard's red dirt.
>
> Bursting with questions about snakes,
> birds, lizards, wild honey, yams and bardies;
> or hunting habits of dingoes, specially
> where young kids were concerned,
> I carefully tried my own feet in her prints.

This is devastating in so many ways. The child's feet cannot tread in those footprints, and yet his 'innocence', his particular way of seeing, is re-envisioned by the older man trying to make sense of his own presence and its consequences.

This celebratory unease has grown in Phillips's later work. But his earlier work is more exuberant in its engagement with place – landscape and how we commune with it are his driving force. The exuberance extends to how one encounters 'new' places and creates context for them through juxtaposing with places one has experienced. His China poems, extending back to the mid-1980s, do precisely this. They try to understand, above all to respect, and to self-situate in order to understand and respect. Access points into different cultures are often literary or artistic, and very often historic. Memorial museums, the grim reality of suffering people have endured and how they publicly discuss it, gradually harden the exuberance into broader critiques of the human condition, and the self. So, we get the strong imagistic sense of nature as experienced by the self, so characteristic of classical Chinese poetry, but that personal awareness and stillness are juxtaposed with the rapid and complex flow of the modern, the harshness of history. It is truly worth considering his poems that compare Shanghai across its period of extremely rapid change from the 1980s onwards. They are observation and comment poems on one hand, yet also entwined with personal interactions, with life's experiences elsewhere.

Phillips takes this dynamic to Italian landscapes and cultural experiences in intense ways. His familiarity with the Italian language, his writing poetry in Italian, his wife having Italian heritage, all fuse his poetry to the poetry of his 'other home'. Interestingly, as Phillips's Welsh mining grandfather informs the texts of now with his presence, stories told of the early twentieth-century entrapment below ground of an Italian miner, and his rescue by a diver brought in by train from Perth, subtextually interweave the poet's and the subject's heritage, landscapes of origin, landscapes of familiarity, making for a matrix for understanding not only belonging, but also alienation and loss. How do we talk about these slippages? Phillips offers some suggestions, and it takes moving from the wheatbelt to Tuscany or Palermo, to Shanghai or Mongolia, to get a sense of how. And this is where the collected poems' structure serves the reader so well – the poems of different landscapes and even languages and different points in time are interwoven so they create a dialogue across time and space. This is an essential critical and political choice of presentation and questioning of what a single poetic voice actually is and can be.

There are so many entry points across this collected that it's worth citing a few. One of the dominant modes of address – and so many of these poems address 'us', or a loved one, or a friend, or a place, or a point in time, or an 'issue', or a wrong – is the love poem. We could say that love is his greatest concern – outside 'landscape' as thing in itself, but also as visual representation, for as the drawings that appear throughout the work suggest, Phillips is the most visual of poets. Yet interestingly, love and landscape are so entwined that it would be painful to separate them. As he celebrates the details of flora, or of, say, the moon over the salt lakes, or the light of salmon gums, he celebrates them in the context of human experience. Humans are always close, even in isolation. The absence of the human often bespeaks wrongs and trauma, though he is also deeply capable of celebrating 'nature' in its own terms. His 'Birthday' love poems jump around in time and place, and are a distinct narrative thread through the work, so often fusing emotion with place – many places. We might also identify how a past makes a future, bringing us to ask, say, how the violence of white kids in wheatbelt towns is entangled with violence towards the land. But it's in the places of damage, such as the gravel pits, that discoveries of self are made as well. There is almost a tension between what some might term 'nostalgia' and others might term 'documentation'. We could suggest that it's a case of the consequences of nostalgia, and in this Phillips makes a unique contribution to creative settings of memory.

The key to all this is to understand that when Phillips fuses Chinese traditional knowledge, say, with seeing the town of Southern Cross, he does so not as appropriation but as celebratory fusion in the hope of increasing his own seeing. It must be remembered, for example, and as he states to a Chinese visitor, that the goldfields were the home to many Chinese people as well, and there is a dialogue there if we listen, and the poem is a space in which neglected, suppressed, disrupted or disrespected dialogues might occur on different diegetic levels – and this makes it no less complex or fraught. This is something I know Phillips is highly conscious of. Can this be done without imposition? – ultimately, probably not entirely, and the ambiguous registers of poetry seem to 'offer' a lot of leeway, but in the end it's a personal act of negotiating how we do and don't speak about different cultures, no matter how strongly we might feel we overlap with them. The history of Anglo-Celtic Australia is constantly being challenged. I reiterate, these 'usages' of cultures outside his originating culture always happen in dialogue with people whose cultures are being conversed with. It's essential to know of Phillips's deep friendship and sharing with others outside his own direct heritage. Again, the celebration that means we have creativity and a valuing of 'landscape', rather than destruction.

I should add that Glen Phillips and I spent much time travelling through the wheatbelt (including staying overnight in the Southern Cross Hotel – an epicentre of memory and response!) and talking over things: the minutiae of flora and fauna, the impact of farming, but especially the grim reality of ongoing colonisation. Without speaking for anyone else, I will say there's an attempted (for that's all it can be) act of restitution in all this, which extends out to the wider world and a desire to celebrate humanity and its right to intactness, to appreciate the world around it without destructive forces hindering or removing this right. It is also the key to celebration in his work. I have met few others who so value and respect the act of writing poetry, and the existence of poetry itself.

A poet's personal appreciation of Les Murray (in memoriam, April, 2019)

It's not a simple portrait when painted from this angle: a complex person, a brilliant poet (genius user of language), with some terrible politics. But it's still a deeply admiring one – admiring Les Murray's land-language poetry-making, his melding of observation and how it might be resolved in meaning. Though the poet's world was rural, it looked out to the world at large, a broader world he was always conscious of but was never going to bend to. The world could come to Bunyah, New South Wales, as he went out and read his poems to an international audience.

A traveller who could bring the 'ultrasound' of a bat into a room, he could show empathy for autism and different ways of perceiving the world with such linguistic intensity, such backgrounding of reading and seguing the 'ordinary' with 'high culture', that an audience could be wandering alongside him around his chosen locales. Les Murray had a way of drawing you with him, of making a poem count as a personal address, and an exchange in the paddock. Sometimes, it was that literal and that abstract at once. Like many others, I could identify with his 'sprawl' and with his 'dream of wearing shorts forever'.

Les and I stood on 'opposite sides' of the political fence, but usually got on pretty well when we met in person. I arranged his reading at Kenyon College, USA, to a packed auditorium, and on that visit he formed a friendship with a colleague, a connection on levels my interaction with him could never reach. But then again, when he was visiting Western Australia, as he did many times over the decades (driving across on at least one occasion), he even came out to my uncle and aunt's farm, Wheatlands, outside the town of York, and was serenaded by my aunt's Sweet Adelines group.

He loved it, and they loved him. Copies of his book were in many farmhouses – and that's really it. Les spoke to people on the land. He and I had a little distancing over my blaming of salinity on rapacious farming practices, as he took the 'battler'-farmer side of things, but salt is a reality of agricultural

Australia and it is more than a metaphor for colonisation. We also had a healthy disagreement over his brilliant poem 'The Grassfire Stanzas', in which he writes, 'August, and black centres expand on the afternoon paddock,/Dilating on a match in widening margins' and I argued that you could say that he was unconsciously commenting on white colonialism's spread over Aboriginal lands and black cultures. I had applied the theory of Vijay Mishra and Bob Hodge to his work and he disagreed. He was speaking for the people who were farming the land.

But he wasn't 'just' doing that, this self-styled bard of the people; he was working through the inflections of culture that inform any language, and in this case a language that had pressured and sometimes erased the languages of the people whose country it had been and still is. It has long been debated whether his astonishing 'Buladelah Holiday Song Cycle' is an example of appropriation, fusing the song of people whose culture has tens of thousands of years interacting with and on country, with the Euro-colonisation in a positive conjoining way.

What I will say, regardless of what Les said to anyone else, is that in conversation with me, I saw that he fiercely considered Aboriginal culture as something to respect and learn from. However he is viewed in these debates, in my experience of him, underlying it all was a wish to be respectful, to go beyond the genius of his own language-making of land into a language-making out of land that was beyond all colonial poetries or post-colonial poetries.

Les Murray had one of the most fervent and avid intellects I have encountered. When he came to Cambridge to read, he engaged everyone he could in contesting conversations about epistemology and learning, and what power gathered around elit(ist) access to knowledge. Though a university man himself, he was additionally a fierce autodidact, whose facility for 'foreign languages' informed the etymological plays and departures of his poetry. Les told me he didn't trust the avant-garde poets of anywhere or any time, but strangely, he shared more in common with many experimentalists of poetry than with the more conservative traditionalist poets who lionise him.

Les liked the fact that, of the few books I managed to hold on to when I reached rock bottom in my personal life in the early 1990s, one was J. H. Prynne's poems, the other was Les's selected poems, *The Vernacular Republic*. The generative nature of language in preserving rights and preventing, say, the rural being overrun by city decisions, or of a sovereignty of rights outside the power elites imposing their own versions of culture, caught my attention. And then we'd disagree. And then, occasionally, swap a letter.

I sent him a postcard from Ireland in December 2018 to congratulate him on turning 80 – I am not sure if it found him. Les, I respect your confidence in the glory of God and an afterlife, and I am sure your poems will continue to carry many of us in many different unforeseeable ways. And you know what Les, you were bullied as a kid and you knew what it was like and didn't like it – when that sense of things shines through all your learning and language artisanship, it's like nothing else. Thanks, mate.

On Les Murray's 'The Broad Bean Sermon'

> like edible meanings, each sealed around with a string
> and affixed to its moment, an unceasing colloquial assembly

This poem doesn't pontificate, it observes and relishes, unwinds its length in three-line stanzas, as compact but also driven, each to his own, as humans. Celebrating abundance and difference, the lines of growing beans are order and disorder. Murray manages to present the most specific descriptions of an almost personalised bean-pod, while working in the human world of need: for spiritual and physical health. The bean is the conceit; the act of picking is the focus – gathering what has been planted. You'll miss some the first picking, but go back again and again and they'll yield. This poem's overwhelming optimism is not only in its literal fruiting, but in the bounty available to all people. But these bean plants, 'a slack church parade/without belief' are, in their kinking and leaning, all of us in our mortality, too – none of us perfect. The 'edible', vital as it is, in the end is a word, part of language – affixed to its own moment, as is the bean-pod on the bean plant, and in its moment of harvest. The language tree is the bean plant; it is each of us together, separate, going through the cycle of growth and death. In this poem the plant serves a human purpose, but it's ultimately an affirmation of existence. That gathering and slackening and gathering-again rhythm shares a special familiarity, a nod and a wink, with the reader.

IM Bruce Dawe, 2020

The poet Bruce Dawe, who wrote his first poems in his teens under a pseudonym, died on 1 April 2020 at age 90 as one of Australia's best-known poets, respected by a wide and diverse audience. This diversity would have mattered to him. His work was widely honoured in his lifetime.

From a working-class background with broken schooling in Melbourne, then later ongoing commitment to part-time education, through to receiving a PhD, he eventually became a teacher and academic in Queensland. Dawe's earlier work-experience (his many jobs included being a postman, working in a battery factory, and serving for a long period with the RAAF) provided the 'lived life' feel of social familiarity in his poems.

Born in Fitzroy, growing up in Victoria and spending time working in Sydney, Dawe eventually taught in various institutions in Queensland. Apart from writing many books of poetry, he also edited a poetry anthology, *Dimensions*, published fiction, and collated *Speaking in Parables* (drawing on Christian, Jewish, Buddhist, Islamic and Hindu writings). Though he was a social commentator on the secular, his religious sensibility often underlay his moral positioning toward the material and secular. When I interviewed Dawe in 1998, he said, 'what we do is to deify the secular in one form or another, isn't it?' That statement, also a question, shows something of his poetic practice, too.

For decades, when you went into a second-hand bookshop in Australia, even if there was no poetry section, you'd find at least one book of poetry, and that book would be Bruce Dawe's *Sometimes Gladness*. It wasn't simply about a discarded book looking for a new owner, but the inevitable circulation of a school standard across the country. Innumerable copies of the many (updated) editions of this timeless classic were in high-school kids' bags, lockers, bookcases, desks and maybe scattered on their floors after a heavy study session.

At school in the mid-to-late 1970s, I too studied Dawe's poetry, and as I look through my bookshelves now I find three copies once owned by an in-law, by my mother, and by a stranger whose school form number is written after their name – on top of whiteout, because underneath you can make out another name and another form number. New editions with new poems came along, but at the book's heart was a remarkable body of socially aware, socially critical and socially investigative poetry that had coalesced by the mid-1970s.

Here was a poet who spoke with 'the voice of the people' (or 'a people'), who knew all the tones of irony and satire from the world he'd grown up in, lived in, and the world he saw beyond Australia's borders. He translated the satirical ways of other literature into Australian contexts. I use the word 'border' because Dawe's 2016 collection, *Border Security*,[18] shows his ability to empathise with human vulnerability when faced with officialdom, with the trappings of power (what we do or don't take through customs, and how such barriers work on our conscience). What are the real and imagined barriers between people?

Always behind Dawe's seemingly playful banter with us, his readers and public, is his commitment to sympathy and connection with the less empowered, the disenfranchised, downtrodden, neglected and exploited. He differentiates between the human foibles shown and exercised by power, and those of people who have little or no power. Dawe wrote against tyranny, brutality and totalitarianism. He wrestled, sometimes subliminally, with issues of masculinity.

Yet it was also in his 'topical' teachability that sometimes school kids missed out on Dawe's lyrically tender side – where irony, pathos and excoriating acerbity are put on hold to show the gravity of personal loss, of the essence of living shared by all.

I will never forget a school lesson in which we studied 'A Public Hangman Tells His Love', a 1967 poem about the Ronald Ryan hanging in Melbourne, that works like a disturbed love letter or a paradoxical letter of estranging yet familial tenderness between executioner and victim. It shows not only the brutal wrong of state execution, but the way in which we can be affected by tone and expectation with seemingly 'ordinary' language-use. That poem, written about what became Australia's last 'legal execution', begins:

---

18 Bruce Dawe, *Border Security* (University of Western Australia Publishing, 2016).

Beyond ambiguity

> Dear one, forgive my appearing before you like this,
> in a two-piece track-suit, welder's goggles
> and a green cloth cap, like some gross bee – this is the State's idea …

And this epistle, almost apostrophe – is signed off:

> Be assured, you will sink into the generous pool of public feeling
> as gently as a leaf … Accept your role. Feel chosen.
> You are this evening's headline. Come, my love.

What Dawe achieves here is horrifying and deft at once – implicating not only the state, but all who acquiesce in this kind of treatment of another living being; always speaking about power, but examining the often compromised nature of the generic 'public'. He appeals to our consciences by revealing our ways of dissembling.

At the end of that lesson, I was browsing his other poems to hand, and came across the remarkable 1964 lyric, 'Elegy for Drowned Children', where Dawe's rhetorical, conversational questioning mode becomes public and private in its implications at once:

> What does he do with them all, the old king:
> Having such a shining haul of boys in his sure net,
> How does he keep them happy, lead them to forget
> The world above, the aching air, birds, spring?

I understand why I was taught 'A Public Hangman' because of its 'topicality' and moral gravitas and necessity, and yet I wondered how closely connected the two poems were: both concerned with disempowerment and all its complexities. Both seemed to come from the same psychological place.

And Dawe, though such a 'readable' poet, a poet who speaks with people as if they will get him if they want to, also deals behind the screen of the page, with the personal behind the political.

Whether writing against the intractability and consequences of war in a quiet, understated but overwhelming way, getting at the root of the problem, or laughing with us about sports obsessions (Australian Rules Footy!) and group behaviours, he was always with us, and remains with us, the people, for all our (many) faults. He can joke, laugh, cry, and also be very angry. He can take us from the material to the spiritual, and be generous about it.

Les Murray once called Dawe 'our great master of applied poetry', and as Dawe said to me in that interview mentioned above, 'Like many critics of particular things, I am half in love with the things I criticise at times; I know the appeal such media phenomena as TV have because I've felt it, too.' And in this, we have the key, just maybe, to why a Dawe poem can get us onside whether we agree with its gist or not. Bruce Dawe's passing is a great loss, but his poetry 'of the suburbs' and further afield, will continue to be relevant.

Part three

Sinews – on Siobhan Hodge's *Justice for Romeo*[19]

Advocacy, elegy and a deep *respect* for horses are the sinews running through this book of poetry. And 'love' – by which I don't mean the false love that Siobhan Hodge notes in her preface as being extended to horses as a kind of 'well-meaning' though mistaken fetishisation and objectification, but rather as a genuine affection for the uniqueness and difference/s of horses. This is no book of anthropomorphic projection, but of seeing and hearing, of sharing life with horses. Though horse life is not contingent on humans, there's been a timeless interaction between horses and humans, sadly mainly with humans exploiting horses. In *Justice for Romeo,* Siobhan Hodge considers the complex nature of human–horse interactions, and especially her own interactions with horses since childhood. It is not about objectification, but self-scrutiny and self-searching as to how Hodge has situated herself in these interactions. In essence, these are dialogues of trust, of call and response, of elation and disappointment, of miscommunication. And further, it is not a romanticised version of human–horse relationships, but a complex and often troubled one.

Through reflections on the distance between depicting the horse in art and the 'inspiration' in quotidian matter-of-factness, the utility of the horse in – say – the world of the ancient Greeks, or of the eighteenth-century English painter of horses, George Stubbs, there is an overwhelming sense of slippage in the poems between the real lives of horses and how we use and see them. Some artists are sensitive to it, giving horses different expressions for different moods; others are so distracted by aesthetics that they move through the horror of corpses, through the anatomies, with a 'scientific eye', and an eye to their art. So, Hodge's poem 'Stubbs' is a powerful challenge to placing aesthetics over life and marks the distance between seeing and compassion. I admire the empathy of this book, but also its hard-nosed critique of human abuse of horses, its confronting the disturbances.

The use of horses for sport, or in war or as transport, and in so many other ways, leads to an expression not only of guilt in this book, but a furious sense of advocacy. Nothing is whispered in speaking back to other humans about the wrongs of exploitation. But there's also the respect and the out-and-out understanding that can be expressed by horse and human. Hodge is able to express this redemptive and enriching spirituality in ways I have encountered in no other poetry.

Throughout the various short, swift and concise sections of the book, there is an intense physicality. Relationship between rider and horse is necessarily physical, and often risky. There are accidents in here – to rider and horse. They are lamented, critiqued, recorded. But what comes of it is the equality between embodiments – the horse's body and the human body are deserving of equal respect, and equal marvel. If the rider goes with the horse, and does not bully

---

19 Siobhan Hodge, *Justice for Romeo* (Cordite Press, 2018).

and cajole, there is the chance of communication that is respectfully and non-invasively physical, as well as, yes, spiritual. What I so respect about Hodge's 'spirituality' as expressed in this work is that it is universal, not constrained by a machine of belief. Hodge has a purpose here – to translate the conditions under which horses, individually and collectively, live when in contact with humans.

One of the most remarkable poems in the collection is 'Przewalski's Pelts' in which we consider – no, more than consider … we engage with the fate of the Mongolian horse as 'breed', but also as individuals, as bodies and souls. So under threat, with their 'rebirth' measured in terms of a couple of remaining horses, they have strangely and somewhat disturbingly thrived in the fallout zone around Chernobyl, which has been designated a nature reserve only because it can't be used for anything else. In recent years, the herd had reached two hundred individuals, but poachers have much diminished the herd. This entry into the fallout zone to profit, to 'murder', reflects on the human condition in dreadful, catastrophic ways. In these horses is hope, as well as agency.

Siobhan Hodge doesn't see herself as holier than thou, though she speaks from great empathy and authority. She also sees herself as complicit – complicit in not being able to stop the slaughter, the use and abuse of 'horse flesh', its consignment to the glue factory when past its profitable days. I say 'its', because its personhood has been denied it – from being seen as living organism to an almost worthless commodity that needs changing into something useful. In a superb trilogy of prose poems, 'Zebra', Hodge takes us on a picture-shooting safari through encounters with zebras: her admiration, her awe, her point of contact, her epiphanies, her distress, our shame. As in so many of the poems, 'skin' and 'hair' are so important – they are the points of contact for horses and people – and it's as skin and hair in the airport when departing that the persona becomes closest to the zebra: 'zebras aren't big sellers alive, after all. Guide has better targets to net. A clearer shot will come later, from the airport. I found you, by Departures, crisp bodies flat and shining under lights between the gates. Tufts and bristles.' The body reduced to 'signage' for tourists – the most brutal of hollow signifiers. I am disturbed by the inherent threat in the 'seeing' (hunting is never far away from 'watching' in the world of trophyism) and Hodge configures this tension perfectly (in terms of the workings of the poem).

One of the remarkable things about Siobhan Hodge's advocacy of horses, uncompromising and partisan as it is, is that she also manages great cultural respect and sensitivity towards human communities. Hers is not an obvious poetry – its pared back, impacted style is so strongly drawn from the fragmentary remains of Sappho's poetry, and a scholarship that has fully comprehended the value of space around a poem – that even 'missing' bits of a poem, the lacunae, are essential to our reading of the world of the past, and in the here and now.

In communicating and communing with horses (as far as a horse will allow!), there are necessarily gaps and spaces, and it's in these than the figurative generativeness of Hodge's verse might be found. Also, her use of the short impacted line allows a riding poem like 'In the Pines', where rider and horse are 'we', to find a way through an often inclement environment, following the path, the journey, acquiring knowledge and dealing together with threat, stating and contemplating both beauty and trauma, involved in a call-and-response relationship between each other, the place, and us, the readers. And the whole time, the intensity and precision of the language draw us into the place, the scenario, the relationship, compelled under and between the pines:

> Collective space in shadow,
> your black coat nips
> encroaching sunset,
> throw the lens astray
> at lines we do not own
> in fallen trees. Soaked
> needles, lost maps and each
> breath shared ...

And we feel the heartbeat under the ribs, the closeness.

I'm frequently fascinated by the shift between (displaced) 'point of view' of horse and human in the interaction. There are times in some of the 'riding' poems, where the horse is being made to perform and we slip into the horse's sense of things, that the work opens genuinely new ways of insight into humans per humans. Yet the horse is always allowed to be itself, not co-opted; the book explores issues of appropriation in so many ways. It's also about the uses of history and the occlusion of humans by other (predatory) humans' activities; it is also the horse-realm as well. Parallel and intersecting worlds. I am still pondering the 'whip' and its tyranny of control, and there seems to be confessions of culpability and guilt as well as accusation in there. The book is a confession and an analysis, a prayer and a recounting.

I – *we* – might also admire that the work analyses a different quality of 'love' and affection and 'sharing' outside the human-to-human, without appropriating the animal into an exploitative situation. To have familial warmth is not to use or abuse or to be entertained, but to be gratified by the existence of the horse. Those people who use animals for financial or physical or whatever benefit, will never see this unless works like this one are written and said. It's a love of familiarity and sharing and respect, of difference and similarity. It's the genuine empathy, compassion, respect, admiration of horses that make this a creative, artistic and moral triumph.

It's also a very clever book, and it needs to be, to articulate the all-too-often unspoken reality of human usage of horses. It's clever in its language-usage, its pinpoint allusions that make us reflect on the language we use around all non-human life, and about what our art actually means when it comes to the living world. It uses rhetoric to upset our/the persona's familiarities and sureties, to contest our safe positions, such as in the poem 'You know', the brilliant and distressing conceit of Romeo and Juliet and the fate of the horse, Romeo, and the failure to appreciate that language is non-human as well; all this emanates from this collection in ways that will, I hope, change the way we talk about human–animal interactions in general and, indeed, human–human interactions. Justice can be done, and achieved.

On Matt Hall's poetry collection, *False Fruits*: habitation and the 'Consonant Feather'[20]

Fruit is the apogee of the pastoral. It's what the work, the waiting, the ritual and the thanks are for. But the making of fruit is costly and even the 'natural' cycle of things will be managed so some factors are privileged over others. In this cycle of post-lyrical poems, Hall questions the form and circumstances of these factors. What are they? In foxlight and in the swell of earth, in the familial connection to place, in the exclusion and recidivism of (be)late(d) presence. What are the rights of creating conditions of fruition?

In tracking presence, we find markers on the trail. They are mythical and totemic; they are every-day and matter-of-fact. They are expected but never prescriptive. As we follow the ley lines, we learn: 'Her throat is clouded with leaves; underneath the black spruce, *bird tracks scrawled through the feathered dust.*' A synecdoche of bodily presence and the signs of (an)other are wound together. A metaphor gives way to description but remains inseparable. Linguistically, there is slippage, but the image is concrete, materialising out of allusion to an earth-spiritual possibility. A 'want to believe' because the signs are there to follow. The poem goes from wrapped line to the succinct embodiment of the lyrical urge:

> sky swelling
> the shuttered leap
> a whittled toy
> rolling
> on the stone floor

This is the settler moment, the lonely object in the lonely house in the lonely construct of settlement. It takes the weight of haunting, not only because of its isolation, the space around it, but because it is a caught (photographed, staged, 'shuttered') moment. The light interrupted from the available expanse of sky outside that is artificial in its appropriation. This is the invader's toy as much as the settler's toy, but it is also part of a quest of reassociation, of belonging because there is a belonging that stretches back through the bird tracks. We have the Indigenous and non-Indigenous in conversation and tension.

And so we are ended in the bracketing final line: the final cut of this arrangement on the disturbed and dilating field of the page:

> The field tussled in the silence of consonant feathers.

---

20 Matthew Hall, *False Fruits* (Cordite Books, 2017).

Loss of breath in making a sound and harmony. The paradox of the consonant and the softfall of the feather. The feather takes a lot of weight and cannot find its vacuum. It has to be heard and seen and we might add it to our tools of comprehension but never own it.

To encounter and re-encounter is motion. And a motion that is exacting. To return and discover again, continuously, can bring only the satisfaction of knowing you have left, and that things can never be as they were. What do you bring back to a place, an indigenous space you are ancestrally part of, but from which you have separated yourself. Is this 'return'? And is 'his' return an inevitable part of 'her' accepting of the field and the field's accepting of her? Can he be the conduit and she retain her agency, autonomy? Does family mean inclusivity? The poem worries at its own edges. As each section of the book accumulates, our middle-ground lyrical enactments and condensations grow 3 ... 4 ... 5 ... 6 lines bracketed, then the split across stanzas. The chasms. The 5 lines ... 4 ... She struggles with the growing belonging:

> The cascade of his rapacious grip, her shadows through the cedarn crown.

She is missing something, something of outside, of other belongings. Of other connections. He tries to draw her to his understanding, his inchoateness. He is struggling with a conviction of understanding, of relationship to land, of the interference of the Western machinery of myth and materiality:

> Beyond the ravine, a dark world pulses through lapsed cathedrals.
>
> inexorable day
> harrowed leaves
> rusting in purgation
> tannins   consonant in rivulets
> descant in the tethered shade
>
> She lives by disconsolate gift, the shrived night, untethered seam, the lassitude of summer.

The house of the self, the family, the birds who are auguries in the literary construct but birds in the moment. The tension of pastoral presentation of a feeling of belonging strained by the alienation of external experience. The lines are trails but they are curtailed by material reality. The domestic is servitude and joy of presence is also:

> the thankless
>
> tasks
> of false fruits

Reverence, labour, rustic performance, curtains and animals and:

> His embrace and shadow, murmurs a child a child, as she aches into branches.

The seasons work away and winter yields its 'last bird'. The cost is high, but the nature of cost is undecided. So the prairies exact their measure, and persistence is a narrative sold to the future. And it is extraction: it is theft, too. A theft that costs the theft of self. The colonial residues that make the ground too furrowed, that we must read through, to follow the consonant feather to its origins, to its stories. The overlays of settlement to be read through and out. The gender entrapment of home and landscape, governance of weather, the emergence of nation (Canada) which costs and costs. There can be no lyric in this most beautifully lyrical lament: the witness is also the victim. And he has invited 'her' into his irresolvable paradox of belonging and exclusion.

On Kim Seung-Hee's *Hope Is Lonely*[21]

"Hope does not grow straight ..."

('Inside of Hope is God's Water Drop')

Kim Seung-Hee's poetry sees traditional Korean forms responding to European, and later American, modernism by opening up to create liberated space, with the tensions between the external image and the interior processing of experience, between the subject and the object, between the idea and its manifestation in our lives, creating a complex and interactive poetics. From the city to the country, from the rural to the industrial, from the meditative to the violent realities of history and contemporary existence, poem after poem confronts and wrestles with what's encountered.

Here is a poet who is constantly struggling with thoughts and fears of death, of self-annihilation, and yet we know hope is close, no matter how despairing a poem becomes. One of my favourite images in this book is from the otherwise grim 'Seoul Melancholy 9':

> birds that penetrate people's sorrows,
> each being a bird
> with a beautiful soul

The poet's distress is for the body and soul of the city as well as for the self fragmenting under stress, and through this, the poet of such introversion becomes a bardic speaker for her community. As we move back and forth through Kim Seung-Hee's poetry, we realise that if hope is there – and it *is* there, in the sun, the body, the shared experience of women, in art and in nature – it is not easy to conjure and not easy to sustain, though sustain it we must, in order to rectify the wrongs.

Kim Seung-Hee seems to me to be a poet of concrete possibilities set against mutable conversations. As Brother Anthony notes, she is a follower of the sun,

---

21   Kim Seung-Hee, *Hope is Lonely* (Arc Publications, 2020).

despite darkness and dread being necessary accompaniments to its glory. This does not mean she is fatalistic, but intensely engaged with the far frontiers of life and death, and if, as the critics note, there is a prevailing sadness, I would argue that it is a necessary constant to make poetry speak out.

In her explorations of the voice of women in contemporary Korean society against the background of Korean history, we encounter writing about the body that reflects its impact on the world *outside the body*. So when in his Translator's Preface Brother Anthony notes the 'centrality' of the 'navel' image of connection to the mother, the 'I'–'we' relationship (that necessarily flows both ways), and the father's daughter becoming the mother's daughter, we might add the changing ways of seeing the reconfiguring of the relationship between a body in servitude and the objects that body is 'forced' to use in domestic life. The cutting board, the plate with the dead fish that is to be carved up, the processes of giving and taking (in terms of gender, a 'done deal' in conservative patriarchal society) segue with the aspirations of art to transcend, to locate, to temporise and to represent.

If this sounds like a confluence of 'East' and 'West' sensibilities, in many ways, given the poet's interest in Greek philosophy and myth, it is not surprising. If 'woman' is aligned with the elemental, she is also part of her community, and ultimately herself – relationships which are anchored in the 'ordinary' reality of everyday objects, tasks and acts, but are in a state of flux. In the poem 'Woman Wrapping the Wind in Clothes' the wind is as elemental as it gets: as artistic construct, it is a variable that the poet as woman can invert, since: 'generation after generation, she robes the wind in clothes'. The singular is collective, and across time the selves connect and work to give structure to 'freedom', the irony being that the wind is a response, rather than a liberty or a choice – it acts as the air pressure directs. With the poem 'Plum Blossom is Mighty' we get to the point of reference we depart from as humans, but in 'Sand Mirror' we are returned to a world of illusions and we ask ourselves who can afford to have visions if there's such a cost?

How real can modern life be – is it, as described in the poem 'Paradise Stop', like the inside of the movie made around us? Maybe the issue of loneliness is exemplified in these lines:

> Solitude being worse than death,
> I remember childhood dreams inside cement.

In the poem 'Avant-gardists', another movie (a Western) expresses the false hope that cannot contain the immensity of contradiction, of the avant-gardist who doesn't have an 'actor's heart', who is a body full of butterflies, who will be sacrificed for challenging the status quo though might find 'respect' after they've gone, like the poet Kim Soo-Young. These are references not only to real suffering but also to a sublimated but devastating reality: that of the 1910–1945 Japanese occupation; the division of Korea along the 38th Parallel; the Korean War; the armistice and the 250km long and 4km wide Demilitarised

Zone, which remains an active 'no-man's land' to this day; the fate of the 1960 Students' Revolution; the dictators; the terror of secret police; and the deep trauma of the 1980 'Gwangju Uprising' and mass-murder of citizens ordered by General Chun Doo Hwan. Also woven into the poem are Kim Seung-Hee's rebellion against the social constraints of the 1950s when she was a small child, her awareness of the contradictions of any avant-gardism (which she approaches both with praise *and* irony), the give and take that runs through her work, and the mournful yoked to the celebratory:

> Avant-gardists are dreadfully fierce though they do not mean to be.
> Because they are so lonesome.
> Like the last scene in a western,
> avant-gardists always blow away like the wind,
> like a faint whistle

Disturbed reassurance is a tonality in Kim Seung-Hee's poetry. Do not think you are safe in the domestic, and do not think the domestic is separate from the world, from nature. In her egg poems (eggs prospectively contain their own navels, which makes for an interesting ontological interiority of self and community on the outside, and other conceptual paradoxes), she is inside the birth, and outside it – the non-birth, the birth, the thwarting, the hope, the ironies. These empathetic but sublaxated poems of 'ordinariness' are philosophical meditative inversions, spoken with total 'mastery'. They blend and move and shift, and create contact points – navels of world. In 'Life in the Egg 7':

> I put a bunch of dandelions wrapped in newspaper into the fridge.
> Inside the fridge the dandelions blossom fully,
> white dandelion seeds grow, scatter, find nowhere to go,
> and in the vegetable box spores of white mould form.
> Every time I open the fridge door
> the spores of white mould left beneath the newspaper as the
>   dandelions rotted
> gradually leak out,
> spread across the kitchen floor,
> get trodden on.
> Foolish dandelions,
> struggle though they may, there are times when they are unable
> to escape from the fridge.

As we move through Kim Seung-Hee's works we get a sense of the interconnectedness of things and ideas, of the reified and the abstract, of the body and soul, intensifying – her poems build into a complex three-dimensional painting of life, and of the self in the life of (many) communities. So piano and river and *Arirang* (a Korean folk song) can blend contrapuntally, merge and toxify, close yet distant and, in the often contradictory 'release' of the essence of place and being. In 'A Thousand *Arirangs*' – '1 Piano in the Breast':

> as if stroking your breast's rusty piano with a hand
> after leaping into the filthy Han River
> where embalming fluid mingles with all kinds of poison, blood, rat-killer,
> and semen,
> then stopping briefly,
> it's hearing far-off a crazy *Arirang* from either side.

I wonder about the pain and stress of sustaining hope, but I know it can be maintained. These are poems of trigger warnings to the self, to be aware, to not let go. I am reminded of Mayakovsky's contradictions between love and disturbed vision in 'A Cloud in Trousers' but tangentially so: Kim Seung-Hee's Korean de-futurism is not waiting for a lover, but moving away from a lover yet remaining divided within ('A Thousand *Arirangs*' – '6 There Is No Book More Lovely than Clay'):

> At the time not realizing it was love,
> squirming, bygone hours,
> I live with a cloud about my neck.
> If the cloud shakes, my whole body flutters.
> My lifeline
> is a line hanging from neck to stomach.
> Life is right.

In his Preface, Brother Anthony notes scarcity of language-work poems in this selection from two of Kim Seung-Hee's recent volumes of poetry, but he assures us that language is perpetually at play. And through these taut translations we do get a sense of the dexterity and extensions of meaning that are a constant: these 'plays' are also aspects of 'hope' in that language might generate a way out, even if the word 'fails'.

Kim Seung-Hee's poetry, as it moves between the actual and conceptual, the concrete and philosophical, works to find ways through. The 'chopping board' is the ultimate metaphor of control and loss, of a paradox that doesn't lessen through repetition. Flowers are a vital force of life in her poetry, connecting earth with sun, and the paradox, and maybe its resolution, are found in vibrant (and disturbed) lines such as in 'Cockscomb Time':

> Flowers clamber up onto the chopping board.
> Hope being preposterous,
> similarly preposterous flowers take their place on the chopping board.

In her surrealism we see a realignment of the imagistic, of the distilled moment, into discursive questioning: her poems are quite radical in their play with 'tradition' in the present. And if travel liberates the mind, it is also a way out of the social constraint of one's personal experience. Kim Seung-Hee seems to search 'away' for hope, for other ways of reflecting on where she comes from, and what a broader 'we' might be in universal terms. But what she is seeking

Beyond ambiguity

is not 'better' but rather the 'unknown', and that unknown is hope. Difference from one's primary lived experience ironically makes hope less lonely. In the poem 'Invitation to a Journey' we read of a visit to America where her daughter lives:

> Drinking an unknown green drink on an unknown street corner,
> going into an unknown bookstore and looking at unknown books,
> then standing with unknown people, each with differently-coloured skin,
> on their way to unknown addresses
> waiting for an unknown bus,
> the freedom of you not knowing them, they not knowing you, is good
> and what is good about the way that freedom is good
> is because you are no more than a scrap of unknown cloud
> with the Hudson River flowing, and that is good.

I find it pertinent that hope resides in the tensions of connection, between different views and maybe 'different' Koreas? Towards the end of this volume, in 'Evening's Party', we have an explosion of tension and contradiction, of the fraught history of personal and public violence, of display and interiority, of loss of control and issues of order, of denial and confrontation. We read, against the whirl of evening, the devastating 'wounded top has no history'; we read about the sick in the hospital of the world, about the continuing hypocrisy, about the anaesthetising, if not healing, of loneliness as we reach across the pain of history whose nexus solidifies in Gwanghwamun – and throughout echoes the voice of the poet Kim Soo-Young:

> So long as it can love, so long as there is a ray of sunlight,
> so long as the evening's bridge is not cut,
> at the time when it has to heal itself and stand up then stand up again,
>   forever,
> the sick top has no tatty history, no rage, no memory.

The spinning top ('Paengi chigi') is a particularly powerful image in the later poems of this collection: keeping upright and moving 'randomly' through the force of the spin, it is a perfect paradox of being. The children spinning their tops become the contradiction of being in the overdetermined place and psychology of social interaction, a sociological poetics. The poem 'A Huge Top' leaves us, in front of the palace gate, with:

> The top is spinning.
> Bright tops are spinning, full of heaven, earth and people.
> As acorns, even squirrels emerge, their bodies shining brightly, the tops
>   are spinning.
> Tops made of trees, of swords, of bones, and light,
> the tops are quietly spinning like dreams.

> A huge, huge top, one I cannot even begin to imagine,
> who can distinguish between dream and dreamer, revolution and
> revolutionary?

Here we see both a closeness to and distance from politics, a philosophical rather than a specific politics, the political complexity of these poems residing in the image of the top.

In writing an introduction to a poet whose land I have only visited through being stranded in an airport many years ago due to a 'crisis', I have tried to connect and converse through many different nodal points (I also have a friend, Dan Disney, a poet and academic who works at the same university as both Kim Seung-Hee and Brother Anthony). Kim Seung-Hee's fascination with the sunflower is vital to me as a way into the affirmations that 'balance', though do not offset, the melancholy; sunflowers are one of the focal points of my life, too, and Ginsberg's 'Sunflower Sutra' is one of my favourite poems.

Kim Seung-Hee's poems speak across lives and out of lives rather than *of* lives, and in this they liberate – women, woman, self, selves, essence from image, life from death. In facing the nuances of an essential poetry and poetics, Brother Anthony's beautiful clarity of line and word allows the complexity of the poems, even with such constant linguistic nuancing and 'détournment', to shine through. This poetry, with its shattering lights, brightens the dark places in multiple and intricate ways. It follows the sun, it is of the sun.

On Philip Neilsen's MS *Wildlife of Berlin*[22]

This is a varied book thematically and stylistically, but also one held together by strong threads – climate change, ecology, animals, specific birds, personal reflection on subjectivity and vulnerability, and a perfectly poised irony that has that rare quality of being both empathetic and critical at once. Philip Neilsen is a known satirist, but one who has always had the ability to self-ironise, and also critique the ills of the human world whilst being so very human in voice. 'He' can both 'tell' and observe, can deploy a complex array of emotions within the one poem. There is real grit in these poems – strong beliefs we might say – but also enough self-ironising reflection mixed with a pathos for the circumstances of daily life. The absurdities, the devastating contradictions of a human world that can't appreciate the implications towards its own health by its mistreatment of animals, and the fraught relationship between the human and 'natural world' are concentrated through Philip Neilsen's obvious sympathies and care for the environment, for ethical human behaviour.

But it's the slip betwixt cup and lip that Philip Neilsen often explores in his poems, and it's in these 'gaps' that the poems generate something beyond what is said, beyond what can be said. They so often have this enigmatic quality. Take

---

22 Philip Neilsen, *Wildlife of Berlin* (University of Western Australia Publishing, 2018) – this piece refers to the manuscript version of the book.

the bird poems of Part 2 – they are crisp, controlled, wry, empathetic with their subjects, but also highly attuned to the literary conceit they inevitably engage with. Take the 'crow' poem: a well-known genre that Neilsen injects with new life and necessity. It's a small and compact piece of brilliance. It also says something about Neilsen's approach to prosodic issues – there's a wonderful knowledge of the spoken line, of natural speech, of letting the line come out of the poem without it become intrusive. This said, it's deceptive, because there's such a measured sense of what the line is.

It's another one of the 'gaps' he develops and considers so well. Further, this control allows him to work variant themes smoothly into a single poem and still create major disruptions. The politics of the 'noisy miner' poems and others are exemplary in this: the deconstruction of the colonial, the 'autobiographical' parallel narratives, the critique of human privileging ... all work together without cancelling each other out. The personal subtexts in this book are intense but also 'offset' by the literary ironist: the university bureaucrat, the philosopher ... the juxtapositions between 'character' and their 'materials' (gardens, brothel etc), make for generative slippages that are wry but also deadly! Such lines as these epitomise Neilsen's glissades:

> will establish an Australian narrative
> within flexible open plan design

Never mind the many hundreds of other sharp lines. Philip Neilsen is one of the most 'extractable' Australian poets – his *smarts* are in his turns of phrase and conceptualising of ideas into pithy, sharply turned units of 'saying' that always have good 'sound quality'. He listens. He replays.

Another thread that enlivens this book is the literary text, or more specifically characters from literary texts, and even writers themselves as 'characters'. His poem on Philip Roth gives a real sense of the way the threads of concern slip in and out of his reading and life experience, become distilled in conjecture and consideration of something outside the him/self. But he's there, segueing in and out of the subject, the 'he' is outside himself but the authorial voice is also implicated. It makes for a lush if dystopic interaction with the 'world' (real or constructed):

> Philip Roth is correcting novel proofs
> when he looks out his French window
> at the silver birches with their triangular leaves
> and there is Alex Portnoy limping alongside him,
> arguing, the two of them together.

The I, the 'he', the slippages of pronouns make this poetry elusive, sometimes distant, sometimes weirdly autobiographical. I love the array of voices that implicate the poet but also show 'him' apart. This is a sophisticated control, manipulation and projection of voice.

Ventriloquism! A critique and irony develops disturbing subtexts when we consider the poems in this light:

> From now I will hunt those who gossip and muck-rake,
> who trade in rumour and innuendo.
> I will update my skill-set
> from psychopath to psychopomp,
> to be a humble guide to the underworld
> in the shape of a long eared owl.

And that's what poems should do, disturb! The satirist is implicated in their most forceful critiques, the deft satirist knows this and works with it. And confronting the directly 'personal', the *self* survives the impact through a cool, collected distance that inflects almost catastrophic impact and damage, almost as if poetry becomes an act of survival:

> My first dead body is when I am ten.
> A buzz below the shimmer
> tells us someone has drowned near the rocks.

There's also a strange relationship between the teacher and student, the writer and reader, between those in different relationships to authority. That authority might be the 'state' (always to be questioned) or maybe a writer or philosopher. I have been wondering a lot about the uneasy presence of Nietzsche in this work, the stress of engagement, the desire for an ontology that will always be corrupted. This is a book full of loss and hopes for redemption, of elegy synched with epiphany, of the rock goddess and illness, of possibility and loss. In many ways, it's an elegy on multiple levels – personal, for friends, loved ones, family, the planet. But there's hope in the poetic gesture, the 'seeing' that might illuminate. All the teaching, all the lessons, all the reports we make, will only create a distance between subjects, create objects in a world so in need of a compassionate subjectivity. How we perform and what we really want to be are at odds: there's a real tension and anxiety at work in many of these poems, which is excitingly unusual given the absolute confidence of delivery. This is a poet who has complete control over his material but the material surprises him as well. Maybe some of the answers I look for are in this stanza:

> Lecturing from the afterlife
> Nietzsche insists we must find a way
> to catch the last moment
> of ripeness before decay.

On Omar Sakr's *The Lost Arabs*

Omar Sakr's volume of poetry, *The Lost Arabs*, is a remarkable and essential work. In a disenfranchised and dislocated country of flesh and spirit, Omar Sakr shows us ways to reclaim, how to hear and maybe hear beyond the 'barking angels', the brutality of dispossession and familial disconnection. But he also offers us various routes through to family, to articulations of justice, to the deepest empathies which come out of stress and loss, and into places where we have to recognise and acknowledge the trauma of communities whose intactness is under constant pressure, and often violent assault. He shows alienation as an imposition of power structures, and he speaks from edges where he knows his own fate and all our fates are determined by conflict over other people's spaces. He writes: 'Like any land I have been fought over with some claiming to love me/more than others, some who are of me and some who are invaders, new comers.'[23]

What 'tonally' highlights in Sakr's poetry is an empathy in irony – the control over his fraught yet beautiful language to show horror and defy the inflictors of that horror with an understanding of the complexity of the journeys that come before us and that are part of who we are. And, equally, there's also irony in empathy – privilege makes the ability to mourn and to 'protect' more viable but more hollow, and privilege is always contested in these pages. The 'American Spring' is the grim counterpoint to the Western construct of the 'Arab Spring', and the frozen sensibilities, the defamiliarised empathies which substitute a Western-colonial consumer hope for another, are laid bare. If 'forgetting has a survival value', Omar Sakr can hear this, but he won't survive it fully, and in not surviving it fully shows us that unless we let language make necessary change there can be no survival at all, that language will be lost. Also, in this singing of language reforming under stress and offering ways through to an understanding, there is the beauty of 'aloneness', which never diminishes community and its myriad intensities and complexities.

This is not an easy journey on which to accompany this remarkable poet, but join him and see how anger can bring compassion, and how compassion can show why there is anger. *The Lost Arabs* offers ways not only into Omar Sakr's personal poetics and psyche, but into a polyphonous sense of community and communities.

On Paul Kelly's 2017 album/CD *Life is Fine*[24]

So we travel from poetry to song, but I have long argued the gap is a small one. The ambiguities between song lyric and poem are generative ones if they exist, and in terms of structuring music around words they do, though not in the impetus of conveying the 'poetic', that is, the relationship between words and impression, between signs and the 'interior' responses regarding external stimuli they evoke. The travelling of music with words, sometimes in disjunction, sometimes slant, sometimes in seemingly complete 'accord', is the

---

23 Omar Sakr, *The Lost Arabs* (University of Queensland Press, 2019), p. 25.
24 I include this review/commentary on the Paul Kelly album because Kelly is part of Australia's literary textual conversation as much as he is of many of its music conversations. In Kelly, the poet and the songwriter meet, making a nodal point that is often collaborative (he works with many musicians and has co-composed albums and songs), and exemplifies the intertextuality of music and spoken text, and also written poetry and sung poetry.

externalising of the properties of the word in music, and music in word. The ambiguity is in the closeness of their forms and also the ability to (seemingly) separate them from each other. Is rhetoric less musical than the lyric? I would argue not. Spoken word accompanied by music is not less musical (or poetic) to my mind than the choir or array of voices *punctus contra punctum* or operating unpolyphonically. Paul Kelly, Australian musician and generational songwriter, is a lover and purveyor of poetry – he sets poems to music as well as writeing his own songs, and he anthologises and discusses poetry regularly. And this brings me to his album of some years ago, *Life is Fine*.

Life is Fine is a *great* album – that is, if we agree such accolades can be applied to a creative project, then it is certainly true of this one. It's so *solid*, and compacted, and yet full of easeful flow and even patience against barriers of tension and confrontation. No technical ragged edges in terms of its construction – not that there's anything wrong with ragged edges, but this album is musically tight and lyrically perfectly co-ordinated – yet it still has elements enough of rawness and 'the occasion' to give a fresh and tuned-in immediacy.

Four of the songs were co-written with Bill Miller, and Kelly is always in collaborative sync with the musicians he works with, sharing a vision. That's what I respect so much about him – his open ear, open mind, and enthusiasm for sharing and discovery. And given that the title and the lyrics of the title song come from African American poet Langston Hughes, the complexity of irony and affirmation might be lost in the cultural transfer/borrowing, but Kelly is a culturally sensitive and respectful artist who listens and connects without appropriation, his music in dialogue with the original text rather than leaning on, taking or extracting. Kelly's is an art of moral integrity as well as a rocking and swinging engagement with the spontaneity of music, and the moment. And he understands the drives of poetry like few other musical performers, singer-songwriters.

If there are ragged edges, they are emotional and creative and fully engaged with; they are in(side) the *self*, battling to find the positive, to keep on top of life – never easy. Those *personal* 'ragged edges' are kept vibrant and dynamic by the superb containment field of the harmonies, of the lead lines, of the shapes of music as a whole. There's a real literary sense of form in this.

What really makes it occasionally grungy and always tough, even in its 'sensitive' personal moments (we might actually believe his love songs!), is the fact that 'trouble' is always close by, that a fall is possible, that the persona knows the threat. We don't know if a crisis will be avoided, we don't know the persona won't 'embrace' it or fall to it, but we go with 'his' hope, we travel the road with him, sail the waters, keep our head above water. We're all okay, too, but only just. Or just maybe. We have to be, we have to try *in the face of*. And *only just* is enough to cling on to – the only quota of optimism we can have. Which, strangely, makes the album a celebration of life, love and survival. In a world of oppression, Kelly offers possible ways out, but all of these are inevitably fraught, zigzagging their way through existence. Langston Hughes knew about oppression big-time, and yet he revivified the word, and in the many threads of the Harlem Renaissance we have confrontation and joy at once, a taking-on of the inequities, injustices and downright wrongs with energy, life, creativity and optimism in the strength of black Americans in the face of segregation. Hughes could also see the fetishisation of black culture by white culture, and wrote texts that resisted marginalisation, that claimed space for themselves and African American people and culture. Listening to Kelly, one can feel assured he knows what all these mean. The implications.

For me, the essence of Kelly's album, and maybe a lot of his work, is that on the edge of collapse we find beauty, we survive, and there's hope. And we flow with the extended metaphor of water generally – 'waving not drowning', but also Odysseus wandering his slow and contested way home. Though this album is really something of an 'epic', it's not an overblown one, never. It's too minimalist for that. A paradox of richness and constraint. Here's an artist adept at the idiom, who speaks to the world in a consciously 'Australian language', and is comfortable doing so. Nothing contrived about it.

We might admire the album's shifts from swinging rhythm to foreboding – the keyboard/s really make that work so well. Luscombe's drums/percussion are constrained, but you feel they might let loose – calm before a storm, which is held back. Instead, they taste of the air after rain (and sound of it). Perfect drumming – never in excess. And the bass lines and keyboards selective and generous at once. The guitar/s *live* between lead and rhythm, between the strum and the pick, and speak as much as the words they are in dialogue with. Liminal stuff! A true conversation of poet and instrument/s.

Let's admire the 'natural' feel of the recording all the more in the context of this controlled sound. There's nothing pat or formulaic about it, and even the Homeric stock epithet of 'rosy-fingered dawn' is given new life – an accomplishment. It lifts onto the screen!

Kelly is a 'master' of the lyrical segue into key, lifting the word to the music and, more vitally, the music to the word. This is the toughest balancing act – maybe only a 'lifelong' practitioner/lyricist/poet/composer can achieve this 'balance'. It's *exciting* to listen to – the lyric in dialogue with the music, the harmonies offsetting. He achieves a contrapuntal drive with a haunting, sometimes frightening beauty ('I Smell Trouble'). And the Bull sisters are in sublime form on *Life is Fine*, and 'their' songs are on playback loops in my head.

A single word sung or spoken in a certain way can do so much: 'petrichor', one of my favourite words, is given life as the *word itself* (Russian formalists' *ostranenie* at work – brilliant!). And Kelly actually gives words *odour* – you can smell and see the texture of the land. This sensory explosion is subtle, building, and actually exciting in an epiphanic way – that's what makes a love song something else ... it's what makes it universal poetry, yet also so personal. That's the key to this album of slippage between self and society – the individual expressed against a collective, greater world. A lyrical vocabulary of encounter in which the texture of strings is strong, forceful and yet forgiving as well. It also beautifully escapes gender-prisons in surprising ways – as we glissade from one verse to another, as we bridge to the outside world.

And yes, *play it loud* (as was suggested to me), which in that paradoxical way also emphasises the quiet moments, the moments of witness and encounter, the seeing of the rising moon together. Every song builds lyrically and musically and remains self-contained while reaching out to others songs on the album, like a book of interconnected stories, like a narrative poem. Something of the epic in this, but broken down, *and* with the delicacy (and intensity) of the seasonal haiku. A polyphonous cultural experience. A musical interlude in a time of crisis. 'Life is fine' – we don't need to jump, even if we are compelled to consider the pressures around us. Resurrection in this, but also the wonder and complexity of spiritual and pragmatic strength. A cycle of songs that respects the space in which it is created – so much rests on the decisions we make. I find it particularly interesting how the persona of the songs doesn't name or know the names of, say, species of birds and trees, but likes to hear them said by someone close. This essence of connection with place is in the vicariousness.

So, maybe it's Paul Kelly's masterpiece, or certainly one of them. I re-hear 'I Smell Trouble' and the album's themes haunt and disturb me all over again. Song after song accumulates – and for me, that's the essence. The album as a *whole*. The many Kelly moments across the years that I cherish are distilled here in one way or another, and then take us elsewhere – from the vocalising spirit of *The Merri Soul Sessions* to the energy embodied in, say, the bluegrass reversionings and surprises of *Foggy Highway* (Paul Kelly & The Stormwater Boys), and all the rest of that wondrous song-writing poem-making that Kelly weaves in and through his music. This is an album of embodiment. And the final song, 'Life is Fine', a setting of lyrics, as noted, by Langston Hughes, takes us into the depths of trauma mediated by the desire and intensity for living: 'I could've died for love/But for livin' I was born.' And Kelly's setting is a reply and a dialogue with the Hughes lyric – Kelly respects and connects, and never misrepresents or makes false claims. Kelly is adept at making music around pre-existing poems – his fusions are generous, comprehending, and, as said, respectful. In loss we confront extremes and we come out of it calling for life!

But don't think for a moment that this album doesn't have moments of levity – it does. As any journey across land or water requires – shifts in tone, the light and the heavy, the aware and the surprised. It's a work that lives outside its packaging, even its form – it reaches into lives via experiences of life. It lives, it rocks, it sings, it critiques, it respects, it surprises, it survives.

The polyphony of voices brought together[25]

The polyphony of voices brought together in this issue of *Westerly* literary journal do not have their own localities, their own emphasis, threatened or

---

25 This is my launch speech for *Westerly* (2018), 63:2, which followed Tracy Ryan's launch speech – so this is part of a duet, but (like Tracy's) is also self-contained. We did a similar thing with Glen Phillips' *In the Hollow of the Land Collected Poems* book launch. Tracy read a launch speech, then I followed. Interconnection, nodal points. Aggregations.

dis-respected through the constructed community that is literary journal publication. In the polyambient nature of location, a consciousness that we speak out of our own experiences of place is set against the consciousness that we *read* other experiences and intensities of place through that same set of personal experiences. In these intersectionalities of ethical-place-concerns and shared and differentiated experience, we are surely reaching towards a more just co-ordinating of respect and belonging. Editors Catherine Noske and Josephine Taylor note in their introduction:

> our engagement with Indigenous authors in this issue has pointed more pressingly to our locatedness on Whadjuk Noongar boodja, *Westerly*'s presence on Country, and the complexities of past and future that involves. This cannot be underestimated in the unending process of understanding self. It is only appropriate, then, that this issue questions and considers the coming into self that writing has always offered. (p. 9)

In this acknowledgement is writ the unresolved fact of dispossession and privileging of a colonial authorising that's intensifying rather than diluting. In Elfie Shiosaki's interview with Julie Dowling, 'Sovereignty, Self- Determination and Speaking Our Freedoms', we hear Julie Dowling say of her mob, 'What they're doing is mapping dispossession in terms of things and how we get treated by local mob.'[26] That's *unmapping* colonialism with its own tools and an undoing of its destructive technologies, its technologies that will yield only desolation.

In Ambelin Kwaymullina's incisive article 'Literature, Resistance, and First Nations Futures: Storytelling from an Australian Indigenous Women's Standpoint in the Twenty-First Century and Beyond', she says of being a futurist storyteller: 'But Indigenous Futurist storytellers do not only address the profound injustices of settler-colonialism. We also look to futures shaped by Indigenous ways of knowing, being and doing.' And goes on to cite Lou Cornum:

> Indigenous futurism seeks to challenge notions of what constitutes advanced technology and consequently advanced civilizations [...] Extractive and exploitative endeavors are just one mark of the settler death drive, which indigenous futurism seeks to overcome by imagining different ways of relating to notions of progress and civilization. Advanced technologies are not finely tuned mechanisms of endless destruction. Advanced technologies should foster and improve human relationships with the non-human world. (np)

Further, thinking over the lines from the introduction to the issue quoted above, and the work of Nicholas Jose, whose novel, *The Red Thread: A Love Story*, is considered and carefully contextualised by scholar Wang Guanglin

---

26 https://westerlymag.com.au/digital_archives/westerly-63-2/.

in the issue, I am reminded of Jose's article on Randolph Stow's *Visitants* in an issue of *Transnational Literature* from 2011, in which he also spoke of 'locatedness'. He wrote: 'For Cawdor [...] His desire is to step outside his own locatedness, and he prides himself on his capacity to do so. It proves damaging all round.'[27]

The relevant bit is 'It proves damaging all round'. When we subsume another's locatedness, even if we are attempting to make connection that is protective and generative, we necessarily occlude, damage, and create false stories of presence. Stories of the self if disconnected from their cause and effect are damaging stories.

Aboriginal stories of location are part of stories that belong to their lines of heritage, and are theirs to tell. Julie Dowling includes this note after her interview: 'The stories contained within this interview may not be reproduced without the story-owner's permission.' It is worth thinking about the issue of ownership here outside and inside the capitalist rubric colonisation imposes on it.

Ownership here is a resistance to theft, to having value added by colonial mechanisms in order to strip away connection to self and presence of its originators – this is what is being resisted in the Aboriginal work in this issue. When the Northam Yorgas offer their remarkable poetry, whose coming into being was facilitated through the participation of wonderfully engaged workshop people, it is offered not as something to take from, but something shared. It is shared (or not) by choice, and the conditions of its sharing are to be respected (as they have been by the workshops' facilitators).

In showing editorial sensitivity to offering a zone of respect for creative and scholarly work of location, the editors are 'curating' but also resisting the curatorial urge to collate and to compartmentalise – their gatherings are to offer to liberate, not isolate, to respect, not constrain.

In his scintillating article, 'Writer as Translator: On Translation and Postmodern Appropriation in Nicholas Jose's *The Red Thread: A Love Story*', Wang Guanglin writes: 'In a logocentric Western philosophy, which prioritises word over image, alphabet over ideogram, all human efforts are very much conditioned by either–or choices, which do not allow translation to experience other kinds of transformations.' The colonialisms of translation are literally deconstructed (Derrida is an active shade in this text), and we might agree with Old Weng, as paraphrased by Wang Guanglin, 'incompleteness is a way to continue people's lives' (p. 64). Which is not to say we are not looking for resolution and completeness regarding injustice, regarding land and cultural theft, but that inside resolution, which we hope is achievable, the self's journey is never finite or limited.

---

27 Nicholas Jose, 'Visitants: Randolph Stow's End Time Novel', *Transnational Literature* (May 2011), 3:2, http://fhrc.flinders.edu.au/transnational/home.html.

It is perhaps pertinent to consider Beibei Chen's article on Ouyang Yu's novel *The English Class*, where he notes of the character Jing:

> Jing is aware of his incompleteness, which causes a crisis of subjectivity at a key point in the text: 'I hate myself so much for being unwhole, for being a traitor to everything I once held dear, for being unable to resist the temptation to fall into delightful peaces [sic], for the delirium that I have courted.' (372)[28]

What all readers have to be vigilant for is the process of how we access and utilise the stories shared with us, especially Indigenous stories and the theft they are told against. Ambelin Kwaymullina notes: 'The need for non-Indigenous writers to step away from (rather than into) the story spaces of Indigenous peoples is an issue that has been raised many times over', and 'But the privileging of the voices of cultural outsiders over cultural insiders remains a live issue across the Australian literary landscape' (p. 148).

This issue is an enactment of principles – the curatorial becomes the collation and exchange within the skilful organising, the juxtaposition of pieces so we read in questioning ways. The self is given its own space to grow within its own community/ies and left intact – in fact, the entire issue challenges invasiveness. The remarkable prose poem project 'curated' by poetry editor Cassandra Atherton confirms how a medium, a 'genre', is never the same in different hands, and that a mode is always an undoing. 'Divination: Linen and Dolphins: From Soft Oracle Machine, a Collaboration with Chris McCabe', by Vahni Capildeo, is a wonderful breaking out of the containment field of formality to bring new departures and proliferating conversations.

And finally, I have to speak for the Fay Zwicky of 1995 and her eternal presence as part of Perth poetry, and the university – her spirit is with us, laugh at this comment as she would. It is relevant and maybe fascinating to note that the words 'ambiguous' and 'ambiguity' (and 'unambiguous') were used nine times in differing contexts by writers in the special IM Fay Zwicky Issue of *Westerly* in 2017 (guest edited by Dennis Haskell[29]), including my own usage in the elegy 'Graphology Endgame 101: IM Fay Zwicky':

> … These are the details of my absence
>
> from your funeral, Fay, the words that will see you
> take leave of a contradictory world for ambiguities
> you revealed in subtexts and allusions, those ancestors

---

28 Beibei Chen (November 2018), 'Bilingualism and cultural translation: on the dilemma of migration in Ouyang Yu's *The English Class*', *Westerly*, 63:2, p. 183.
29 See https://www.westerlymag.com.au/wp-content/uploads/edd/2017/12/IM-Fay-Zwicky.pdf.

you came to later, wondering over youth and ageing,
the nests we weave and the images we nurture
that don't always fit our desires, or troubled dreams,

or allusion or friendships that fade in and out of focus.

And as David McCooey says in the issue (p. 42), '... as is characteristic of Zwicky's openness to ambiguity and complexity, the categories of culture and power are recognised as profoundly imbricated.'

PART FOUR

This section was written to accompany the co-publication of earlier memoirs of Shakir and Ellenbogen in French- and German-language editions (this 'introduction' is unpublished prior to this in English), but also in the context of this work as whole (I discussed the context with George Ellenbogen). Sharing a life, as Shakir and Ellenbogen did, is focalised through a 'disparity' of heritages and histories that would seem in discourse to be in opposition, but are reconciled in their compassion, empathy and willingness to retain their own identities while respecting and in fact sharing each other's, and also the communities they come out of. In some ways, this is the pivotal section of the book, as it moves towards a *giving peace*, searching for mutuality in 'difference', while always tracing the complexities. As I say in the introduction to *Beyond Ambiguity*: 'The section of the "conversations" between Evelyn Shakir and George Ellenbogen in their respective memoirs is pivotal in this attempt. I have long been interested in spaces where, say, Hebrew and Arabic writers can share textuality, and how this reflects on a non-state issue of sharing and co-existence ... I try to consider divisions as acting as *points de repère* rather than separations, and I find such traces in these wonderful memoirs written in English.' Jewish Montreal (with a reaching back into the journey from Europe of the Holocaust), Arab Boston (come out of Lebanon), and the crossing pathways of migration, and an articulating in the world of their 'nows', is generative and resilient, and I attempt to trace this.

Part four

The inherent reciprocities of memoir-making: on the memoirs of Evelyn Shakir and George Ellenbogen

'What did they talk about then, this Arab and this Jew?' asks Evelyn Shakir talking of her father and his friend, Mr Rosenfield. What do these two memoirs *talk about*, between themselves, collected for the first time inside one cover? These memoirs of partners in life for decades, though these memoirs are not about that relationship, not directly. Memoirists in proximity to each other's writing, reading over each other's work, coming out of two very different migrant backgrounds, with families coming from Lebanon to the 'New World', to Boston, from Romania and Poland to the 'New World', to Montreal, Quebec. A woman and a man with their attendant rite de passages of gender fusing with and rebounding against tradition, heritage, always being made anew. Both, in their own ways, continuing a radical journey of change while retaining *proximus* 'identity' as time and the world – old and new – move on. And as awareness of difference grows, as it oscillates between affirmation and alienation, a politics of purpose and connectedness grows.

One of the most vital aspects of both memoirs is the photo – the reproduction of a moment and its shifting contexts. In George Ellenbogen's memoir, *A Stone in My Shoe*[1], we are constantly re-encountering photographs and reconsidering their contexts and meanings to those outside the pictures, and while photos appear also in Evelyn Shakir's memoir[2], it's in a different but still pivotal way. A key point in *Teaching Arabs, Writing Self* comes with her taking a camera to photograph her students in Damascus:

> On the last day of class I brought in a camera. As I look now at the photos, the bright eyes, the frank smiles, the boys in their T-shirts and jeans, the girls in their long sleeves and head scarves, I remember my surprise on arriving in Damascus. Beforehand, insofar as I'd thought about it at all, I'd expected to find what I'd seen in neighbouring Lebanon, most females in Western-style dress. True, a scattering of girls in my class did go bare-headed, but they were exceptions (as was the girl who wore a black veil over her face, exposing only her eyes). The interesting thing was that the mass of girls who had elected to wear the *hijab* were not necessarily following in their mothers' footsteps. As in many parts of the world, a religious revival had swept up the younger generation or, in some cases, caused middle-aged women to dress more conservatively than they had 20 years earlier. (p. 128)

This remarkable passage tells us a great deal about the writer's way of seeing, her pedagogical positioning, her compassion and understanding, and her taking a personal moment and contextualising within a social and religious historicity. The act of photographing is as important as the photo that's looked back over, for it is an act of trust and permission, and permission is highly relevant in any

---

1 *A Stone in My Shoe: In Search of Neighborhood* (Vehicle Press, Montreal, 2013).
2 *Teaching Arabs, Writing Self: Memoirs of an Arab-American Woman* (Olive Branch Press, Massachusetts, 2013).

exchange of trust, such as teaching across cultural difference and religious difference. But this is the wondrous ease and complexity at once of this work – a shared Arab identity fused with religious difference (Evelyn being of her own particularised Christian identification that veered off from the orthodox, to her students being Muslim; but in Lebanon, earlier in the memoir, she is interacting with Druze people, Lebanese Christians, Lebanese Muslims), a shared Arab experience distanced by migration. Acts of separation and reunification are happening constantly, and through her re-engagement with her family's roots in the 'Middle-East', Evelyn finds her way back into community via the act of teaching, and the act of memoirising her experience. A conversation that cascades towards perception of realpolitik. This extract is like a poem in its multi-layering, its possibilities of reading, and its compactness. And in this she shares much with the poetry of her partner, George Ellenbogen.

And of George Ellenbogen's family, we read, 'Although my mother exchanged pleasantries daily with non-Jews, mainly those in my father's garage, she did not seek them out, but in two cases, had relationships with gentiles that were not merely close, but familial' (p. 142). As noted, neither George nor Evelyn really features in the other's memoir (though George makes an unnamed appearance late in Evelyn's, starting just before her illness and growing through and with and outside it as time works things out), as they are stories of different journeys, but they are there with each other in spirit, in a strange sense even before they literally knew each other, great spirits of sharing and peace. This is the humanity of this coalescing of such different stories. We are all there in the overlap, in some way, but outside it too, because neither author would ever impose their stories on another. As Evelyn coaxes her students throughout the Middle East, we must find our own stories and our own ways of telling, and work out how they are permitted (or not) in terms of our own heritages, our own journeys.

These journeys: Evelyn Shakir was of Arab Christian heritage out of Lebanon, tracing her birth-roots out of Boston, a sensitive, inquisitive and role-questioning childhood, really, and her journey as a teacher visiting her heritage place, and other places in the Arab world … and George Ellenbogen, of middle-European Jewish heritage in his Jewish neighbourhood of Montreal, where the street was life, and learning something that came out of this, or digressing from it. At the beginning of *A Stone in My Shoe*, George notes, 'I was finally writing the memoir Evelyn had urged upon me, giving her the Montreal of an earlier time.' And there's something in Evelyn's early declaration of her desire for 'Americaness' as opposed to 'foreignness', and reconciling and embracing. One can be present and return simultaneously. Both memoirs square their circles. And both memoirs attempt in different ways to approach the contradictions of their being afforded the comfort zone when so many others weren't or aren't.

Talking of her Lebanese students, Evelyn recounts: '"Doctor, America is a democracy. Why do they treat the black people so cruelly? Why did they kill the Indians?" No matter which way you turned those questions, there were no answers that did Americans proud' (p. 59). As an American citizen, and American by life experience with displacement and connection of migrant heritage, as most Americans have in their different expressions and journeyings, Evelyn is faced with the dilemma of responsibility for who she is in multiple ways. The passage continues: '"Doctor, do Americans hate Arabs? Do they think everyone of us is a terrorist?" For my students, these were not abstract theories. They all had someone – relative or close friend – in the United States. And some in the class were trying to imagine a life for themselves there' (p. 59).

Don't read these works looking for answers over the conflicts around the state of Israel, because they are not there. Evelyn's teachings in Beirut, Damascus and Bahrain on Fulbrights and as part of visiting academic programmes are re-encounters with the roots of her cultural heritage, which, like all migrant experience, is inflected by the *presence* of *her* birth country. The America and Boston of her entire life till she travelled 'overseas', are always positioned in the context of the tension of Arab relations with Israel, and the belief by many around her that Israel is the enemy. As a non-violent person, she negotiates these tensions, but always looks to justice. George's trajectory is one in which Israel represents to his parents a place of hope and protection for his people, and their visit to Israel[3] from Canada in their later life is a rite de passage of life. He says: 'And the newly created state of Israel was something we viewed with curiosity and wonder, much like discovering a relative in some remote place' (p. 19). And this devastating contextualising of necessity of connection for his parents, through their eyes and eyes of generations:

> Perhaps the pilgrimage to the wall was a way of acknowledging the often sad history of their people, of saying that despite the good fortune that allows us to travel and touch this wall, we remain touched by it, both the wall and the history it represents. In the other photo, they are leaving Yad Vashem, Israel's memorial to the victims of the Nazis. My father is walking ahead, two or three steps at the most, but he and my mother are separated, lost in their own thoughts, linked to their own pain. Both look stricken. As though they had just learned of a catastrophe in the family or been jolted from a deep sleep and battered. Yet they had long been aware of the Holocaust. (p. 140)

3 George made the following comment at this point of reading through my draft of this chapter, and I feel it belongs (as with some later comments) here ... as an organic part of the text, as ongoing memoir: 'Let me share something that's not in the memoir. My bar mitzvah came about just around the time when Israel was recognized as a state and seated at the UN, the coincidence noted by Al Ship (the husband of one of my mother's mah jong friends) at the post bar mitzvah celebration. And I believe it mattered to people of that generation, my parents for example, for whom the Holocaust meant so much. In early adolescence, I was not as touched and marked by it as I was to become. It really *was* a curiosity. Now, much later, I find myself sympathizing with the observation of a Colonel who escaped arrest for refusing to lead his troops into Lebanon explaining to an audience at Brandeis University that Israel had a choice at its inception of being a small democratic state or an imperial power. It chose the first. His contention was that Likud had shanghaied that vision of Israel and reconfigured it with what we see now. And while he acknowledged that he had taken an oath to defend the homeland, the oath did not require him to invade another country and kill its population. (George Ellenbogen, private correspondence with John Kinsella, 15/4/19).

What George knows is a Canada that has travelled the 'historical' route of persecuting of Jews via exclusion and denial of public rights, to a slow 'integration' of acceptance into mainstream Canadian society by the 1940s. He also knows that his neighbourhood was his community, and that with primarily Jewish kids attending *his* schools but with few Jewish teachers, he was defined against and not through the British imperialist residues and the Catholic and Protestant scaffoldings of state. In French-speaking Canada, he and his community spoke and wrote English as their language of integration, and as such remained outsiders in an outsider state. George notes: 'Between chants in the synagogue and anglophilic hymns to the Empire, we scavenged for icons wherever we could and them, hoping for a Jew, but settling for what was available' (p. 16).

The picture of belonging is complex. George also says: 'As a child, it never occurred to me that our neighborhood had not always been as it was. But, in fact, we Jews were relative newcomers, not only to Montreal, but to all of Canada. Cardinal Richelieu's edict in 1627 prohibiting non-Catholics from settling in New France was aimed at Huguenots, but had the effect of excluding Jews as well' (p. 37). The 'newcomers' from Europe during the great wave of Jewish immigration made homes and a repositioned (or another chapter in) *heritage*, creating a new *localised difference* that allowed varying degrees of observance to custom and to religious traditions. 'As children, we drifted with equal casualness into one another's homes, observing the mannerisms and sampling the cuisine of those who came from different regions of Europe' (p. 44).

One of the keys to George's method of memoir-making is to entwine gravitas with levity, threat with hope, and a serious bemusement with the conflicts and hatreds of the world at large. The lead-up to the Second World War, with the battlefields and slaughters so distant, are nonetheless mirrored in his neighbourhood and beyond, and the quotidian is laden with emphasis in this matter-of-factness that presages terrible events. George's familiar, even friendly style, his manner of sharing, breaks down nostalgia into terrifying shadows and consequences, and the more removed these components seem from the life of the street, the more they threaten it:

> Things big and small happened there – my first haircut at Dave's Barber Shop; a parade, menacing in retrospect, of the fascist Bloc Populaire marching through the heart of the Jewish district to protest Canadian participation in World War II, which they viewed as an intrigue of Anglo adventurism financed by inter-national Jewry. Essentially, Rachel Street was the estuary that led to a larger world. (p. 47)

And Evelyn Shakir *of Boston* travelling an hour on the streetcar from West Roxbury to Revere Beach on the northeast outskirts, where her Uncle co-owned (49 percent she later discovered, not an equal interest), *The Cyclone*, the massive rollercoaster that defined that beach area and rooted her childhood in wonder and even fear (the Uncle was a forbidding and even 'threatening' character).

The Cyclone becomes a symbol of the strange opportunities of a 'newness' proffered by migration, an almost radical difference from old, 'left behind' patterns, but also an extension of the leisure aspirations of the New World, especially of the America of the 1940s and 1950s, and its commercial-consumer answers to the overdetermined relationship between 'work' and 'freedom'. The migrants brought their own commercial aspirations with them in their reaching out for a better life, for success, and these aspirations segued with the aspirations of the very idea of an 'America' (and, indeed, a 'Canada'). Pride and difference out of the realisation of the success or failure of these aspirations making broader community. So, despite very different belongings, the Middle East and Eastern Europe, these memoirs speak to us similar experiences. Evelyn's mother ran a small clothes-making factory In Boston, George's mother was a seamstress working at home in Montreal. Evelyn's father worked regular hours with his own complexities; George's father eventually found his vocation in working metal and, though going through ups and downs in business fortune, eventually ran a successful panel-beating business. George would have loved to have had his father's skill, but turns out to be no Hephaestus![4]

We are always conscious of *extensions* of small-business capitalist America and Canada, raising children who would find their way to literature, and in George's case, the writing of poetry. That link between use of the hands and use of the tongue, all of it in developmental flux, urging inwards and outwards. Read together, these memoirs give embodiment and hope to Derrida's complexity of the human condition, of living in peace with difference and finding *just* answers in this peace. And that's what I am doing here amongst these highly personal stories, these journeys – I meet them, as all readers will, at the crossroads with its risks and its promises. At this point as they cross each other, I find directions of hope, and none of endgame.

It's not only a matter of the communities we grow up in, but how we inform and are part (or not) of our own communities. What keeps us to them, drives us away from them, draws us back? We will always have relationships with where we come from – near and far in place and in time. Of these palimpsesting overlaying stories that make large narratives, journeys of humanity that must be reconciled and celebrated. George writes:

> What I ended with was a discovery of neighborhood rituals that sustained me, that sustain millions. Evelyn was probably as surprised as I was at the emergence of this focus. But she certainly recognized it: it had, after all, been the focus of her own work on the Arab American community. Unbeknown to us, we had witnessed

---

4 George: 'Looking back, John, it strikes me that both Evelyn's parents and mine were crafts people who made things and their offspring lacked those skills … except that they made in other ways, Evelyn and myself with words, my brother with paints, woodcuts, musical notes. As a child in the old country my father was apprenticed out to a tinsmith, and when he arrived in Canada, he had already mastered that trade. It was his good fortune to be able to apply it to an activity (auto repair) that was in demand.' (George Ellenbogen, private correspondence with John Kinsella, 15/4/19).

our work, though written under the same roof, follow different channels, one Arab American, the other Montreal Jewish; but when they emerged, after flowing through their own subterranean passages, they revealed the same preoccupations, concerns, and aspirations, and, like us, had come to their own special relationship, the relationship that unites disparate neighborhoods and individuals, that of trust and acceptance. (p. 12)

And the painting of neighbourhoods is rich in both memoirists. For George, sport and the rituals of sports which correlate to secularised religious-cultural ritual in a shared space of nation ('And yet those heroes were there. As we moved through high school, the ones we acknowledged most readily were athletes' (p. 114)) are pivotal: games, stories, the 'symbol' of Mount Royal, the St Lawrence River, all beyond his street, but within tram reach. There's a constant search in 'George's Canada' for those he and his friends might identify with, and sports broke down barriers between black and white, Jew and gentile. But there was always the desire to be directly part of something, to have heroes one understood: 'Between periods, eager to find a Jewish player, we would study each name on the Canadians' roster. Maurice "Rocket" Richard? No, there was no way that the French "Maurice" could be construed as a Jewish "Morris"' (p. 117).

A characteristic of George's memoir, as with Evelyn's, is to present occasions/scenes that express deeply felt desires and hopes whilst retaining a critical distance. In doing this, he creates a form of reality-check of broader humanity in which one's community and origins are never belittled or devalued, but are highlighted against the often very different perceptions of the world-at-large. Such slippages are highlighted, and sometimes even cherished through gentle irony:

> Looking back, I puzzle at this compulsion to extract a Jewish constellation from the sports world. After all, as our elders often pointed out to us, Jews had made a mark in music, in philosophy, in the sciences, and in letters, providing the assurance that we had been given some share of the world's wisdom and talent. Yet our hunger for Jewish sports heroes persisted. (p. 118)

Always focussed/focussing back on *his street*, even when the family summer-vacationed in the Laurentians at Lesage, Quebec, on the Leblanc's farm ('The openness of the fields, the orchestra of barnyard sounds and nocturnal chat of cicadas spoke to me of endlessness'), and where George is confronted by the killing of a pig ... to his later stays at the family place on the lake in the mountains, where unusual seclusion-searching neighbours helped make his transition between home and the immanence of a new life beyond immediate family. Some of the most astonishing writing in George's memoir relates to the family holiday cottage on the lake at Nantel. A wooden house on the lake and mountains around, lovingly described – retreat for father on weekends after work, and the materials of nature poetry versus urbanity for the emerging poet.

Pivotal is this line of the memoir, for it brings the breadth to the lyrical conversationalism that would become a marker of George's verse: 'I realized that I was in a country with no neighborhood' (p. 152).

The killing of the pig comes as an epiphany to the boy George, but also, retrospectively, looking back inside and outside photos, to a failure of nostalgia (which makes sense for George, but less so as time goes on) and the anxieties that arise from retrospection and retrieval of earlier experiences in terms of how they make us who we are in the 'here and now': 'As the Leblanc family hovered like a team of surgeons, it responded with squeals which were as close to a human sound as I have ever heard coming from an animal' (p. 83) and 'It was our way of learning that even summer idylls come to an end and that the days of summer finally have their nightfalls and their frosts' (p. 83).[5]

In many ways, the pig-killing becomes a metaphor for an emergence out of the security of neighbourhood engendered by George's parents, and other folk of his childhood community – a form of confrontation with the uncertainty and trauma of where and why they migrated, of who they are in this 'new place', which for George is entirely his home place. Heritage makes us, but where we are born and walk and talk and learn has a hold on us that can never be entirely shaken, even if we desire to do so.

And even the neighbourhood exists in a greater local world, and that can be wondrous and enticing, as well: 'From the [Mt Royal] lookout, the city was vast; its twinkling eyes acknowledged the possibility of hurtling ourselves through braids of darkness into whatever possibilities we could find down there. To a child about to step into his teens, the choices were both limited and large' (p. 52). And, therefore, he sees a loss of community in the abandonment of neighbourhood for suburb: 'They called this suburban death "moving up' (p. 84).

'Connection' is everything in terms of making the *here and now* viable, of feeling part of something: of place, cultures, language, history, crisis, deep loss, survival, routes through despair, engagement with joy and celebration. And so when someone meets someone else with family connections, say to a town in Lebanon, or a shtetl in Romania, it is a homecoming in a new home. The sense of permanence comes ironically out of the vicarious, in the same way that George anchors his sense of connection to the uncertainty of photographs; because something is always happening outside the frame at the moment of taking, and looking back, we fill in the details of time passed, with the Proustian intensity of time experienced by ourselves.

George will always be at the *beginning* of his experience with the end of his contemplation: 'Looking back to that old neighborhood preserved in my photo albums, I continue to seek out adventures, anything of the high mimetic that I can scrape from my parents' experience. What I find is that these experiences

---

5 George: 'As I see it, that and the death of a classmate are my first vivid introductions to mortality ... though that incident might well have made impacts that I'm not aware of.' (George Ellenbogen, private correspondence with John Kinsella, 15/4/19).

are never three dimensional, more like chips of paint that remind me of but never replicate the day to day world of my childhood and adolescence.' Memoir seeks to lessen the distance between our own experience and the experiences of those around us. Family and neighbourhood are focalisations of a self that will always depart in some way.

Both memoirists are writers of deft beauty. George's weaving of motifs such as the barber as conduit for history and locality, for humorous anecdote that makes life liveable, and as vehicle for serious ethical consideration; Evelyn's astonishing evocations of Revere beach and the surprise, the suddenness that goes outside the narrative of self as central and the sexual innuendoes, suppressions and fabrications of co-existence 'You were flirting with boys and shaking your little behind' and the boys trying to spy, and the rollercoaster racketing overhead for 20 cents a ride, and the women pushing their breasts into bathing tops heading down to the sea, and the forbidden and taboo of culture and teenage years, and the echo late in the book when breast cancer and mastectomy shift life and yet don't, which is the gift of the text as one of confrontation and recovery. What I so admire in Evelyn's work is the affirmation of women, veiled and unveiled, and a search for body and truth through language, learning and the implications of family, from birth to her mother distant and unwell and questioning memory.

And in many ways, the relationship between mother and daughter, between mothers and daughters, binds even when it frays. Evelyn's contextualising of memory through her mother's life and changes in her relationship to the material – to the exterior world – is an intense expression of unspoken and strangely shared interiority. Distance makes closer as much as closeness can bring distance. The daughter will always be judged, but the mother will come to rely on the daughter. And the daughter is always trying to find a route through the contradictions of journeying *and* being 'called' back home.

As Evelyn works through her own illness, the massive generosity involved in writing *shared existences* resonates out of the work. The domestic scene or locale is often where we look back over the stories of the journeys we have taken together, or where we discuss journeys taken alone, where we recount and share experience that then feeds into the lives of family, partners, colleagues, friends, and maybe the broader community. In the kitchen or lounge (even in the meeting rooms at work), experience coalesces and 'settles' into something that can be reflected on, possibly shared and even enjoyed 'together'.

But so often 'homes' are the repositories of *other* people's stories as well, especially those of deceased family. In the quote that follows, the writing is stunning and deeply moving, but not only for the obvious reasons (*style!*), but because of its almost bizarre humour and 'standing up' to those deeply loved. The reader is immediately drawn into a complex matrix of love, family, belonging, departure with its residues, and the exposure of the interior self to the outside world. I see this as a gift (Derrida, again?), this 'no bullshit' directness, this *just being* as it is (and was) – no lushness, no pointless nostalgia, and yet it stuns with the sinews that bind to the point where the lost mother's room – remaining as it was in life, *in medias res* – defies time. Preserved out of neglect rather than nostalgia or emotional pain, it nonetheless solidifies the pain of time's passing. We read of a room caught in the gender significations of a generation, of how a mother raised her son (and daughter), and how her daughter does or doesn't fit in the truths of heritage and their many slippages. Again, it's almost prose poetry in its compaction:

> Still, the public rooms in my house – living room, dining room, and even kitchen – are, by sane standards, presentable enough. The face I show the world. Upstairs, behind closed doors, it's quite another story. Upstairs and down – sounds like the makings of an inverted allegory. My mother didn't fool with such hocus-pocus. She just told me I was lazy.
>
> What would she say if she knew that, eight years after her death, her bedroom is still as she left it. A skirt on the sewing machine, waiting to be mended. Underthings in the hamper. Nylons bunched in her everyday shoes by the bed. She and my brother shared that house, and he still lives there. But, of course, he'd never think of sorting through or putting things to right. Woman's work, he tells me. I guess he's right. (p. 166)

Both Evelyn Shakir and George Ellenbogen are writers searching for their collectivised and particularised humanity through their travels and dislocations, always thinking back towards home in their absences. George, travelling to Poland later in life attempts to reconstruct his mother's past, her first twelve years where later under Nazism only a few of the Jewish community were to survive the Shoah. He says, 'He [Felix Karpman, one of the few surviving Jews] walks briskly, pointing out buildings, commenting to Eva until his voice blurs into a soporific hum, but what she translates prods me into my mother's world' (p. 131). His mother's voice is constant and informs his own childhood. And Eva speaks the history that he binds so superbly through his memoir, and his poetry (here, specifically, and taken on the whole, as a body of work) comes out of a necessity of articulating his responsibility of the individual out of community. George tracks the failure of 'modernity' (in all its manifestations!) to counter the evil to prevent it ever happening again:

> I turn to leave her [i.e. Eva] a private moment and notice on a wall behind me a poster advertising an Arnold Shwarzenegger movie with the caption 'Soon the hunt will begin.' I am transfixed by the blank pitilessness on that face, its serenity of pure destruction. (p. 132)

'Postmodernism' can often (though not always) become a diversion or distraction from the reality of the horror, and cannot ultimately answer the need which has to be addressed in so many different ways through so many affected voices. George turns to the lyric for hope, as it is personal and universal at once, it opens the moment and can contain history, though the lyric can also fail and be misused – George's work in mixing a rhetorical consideration of events with the lyrical moment attempts to confront this system's failure of language, the very thing that left Celan with fragments in the face of unresolvable horror.

George writes of the Nazis later turning gravestones of Jews in his mother's village into road surfaces. One of the most astonishing and moving pieces of poetry merging into prose while remaining intact as 'art', is to be found in this traumatic and magnificent passage from *A Stone in My Shoe*:

> They blaze like shattered
> diamonds on emerald
> soft as cloth or meadow,
>
> a gift for anyone
> who leaves the road
> and walks among stones
> that have found their soil
> but will not remain silent.
>
> As far back as I remember, it was my mother's voice that broke the silence in our flat. Perhaps in Gora Kalwaria her voice might have been muted by the poverty of table scraps, the fear of shattering glass in a synagogue, and, later, in Montreal, the humiliation of sitting in a classroom with English, her new language, spoken so deftly by the other children, turning in her mouth to ugly bulbous sounds. Later on she noted, with pride, some few moments of assertion in her childhood – organizing plays as well as a home lending library – although these opportunities had been limited. But the compulsion to arrange the space around her, whether moral or aesthetic, grew as she grew into adulthood.
>
> Having endured anti-Semitism in her native town, she had a sense of when she could and could not act, of where the line was drawn. But if provoked she would cross it. (p. 135)

This ability of shifting between modes of expression has marked George's creative work as it indeed has marked Evelyn's fine fictionising and critical-interview work of Lebanese women in America: to lift out of oppression, to assert humanity against tyranny – micro and macro – unites these two as writers working across different forms and genres, and tonalities of language. Evelyn's feminism is fused with the act of searching, and with the act of recording other women's experiences. It is a sharing, always, but it is also a claiming of geographies of story-telling and a means of teaching out of female experience.

In *Feminism and Geography: The Limits of Geographical Knowledge*[6] Gillian Rose writes, 'Concepts of place and space are implicitly gendered in geographical discourse. *Place* is understood by humanistic geographers in terms of maternal Woman – nurturing, natural, but forever lost. In stark contrast, the discourse of time-geography depends on a transparent *space*, which

---

6 Gillian Rose, *Feminism and Geography: The Limits of Geographical Knowledge* (Polity Press, 1993).

refers only to the public space of Western hegemonic masculinities. What both place and space have in common, however, is the exclusion of women (among others) from the geographical through certain masculinized understandings of geography' (p. 62). Remembering this was written almost thirty years ago, its essence remains essentially 'true', and moving in and out of Western zones of conceptualising space and place, Evelyn places herself not at the centre, but as a participant observer trying to work with blocked toilets, volatile political situations, students who have so many personal concerns that in Western understanding are often lumped into specific types of aspiration. She is also in the Middle East on American capitalist funding and through Americanising educational extensions, which arose out of masculine conceptions of space. What she can or cannot access as a woman within externally masculinised spaces is explored through her speaking of women while writing of place. Her reclaiming of the conversations of women in spaces (usually, if not always, in the context and time) 'designed' by men, is remarkable and generative. A light but sharp irony is never far from her lips, even if expressed in a very short sentence fragment that doesn't quite say it all.

There is an incredible moment later in the same chapter in *Stone in My Shoe* where George talks of his mother resisting the bigotry of a policeman towards a peddler, leaping from her sewing machine – the domestic work and labour of income always expressing from inside the house into the street, the neighbourhood and collective responsibility: 'She dropped the fabric in her hand and tripped quickly down the porch stairs. She was haranguing the policeman before she reached him' (p. 136). Mothers!

Poetry is a binding language for both memoirists, be it the language of D. H. Lawrence in Evelyn's PhD thesis, or via the poems composed by George, who writes: 'Montreal remains a pilgrimage point that I move to sometimes with hesitation, more often impetuously, like a lover. To make the asphalt recede more quickly on my northward drive from Boston, I occasionally sing or recite poems.' (p. 86). And the link between locales of past and present is focalised through their own constantly adapting form of 'visionary dreariness' through poetry and poetic subtexts (as noted, I feel Evelyn's prose is deeply imbued with the cadence of poetry, and also speech from many different cultural spaces). The idea of poetry serves as a possible intermediary across time and place. Poetry is at least partly the border of the pilgrimage in both memoirs that connects the past, migration and their journeys of (and to) the present.

Both memoirists need to follow the echoes of the responsibility of belonging. In their 'settlings' of life in memoir form, they are still wrestling with the many moving/working parts of the migrant story, of their own birth countries (Canada for George, America for Evelyn), and their shared life together in Boston (and other places in the world). In searching out origins of family and considering the motives for earlier generations' migration, answers are searched for; some are horrendously obvious such as persecution, others are tied to hope and opportunity, and others are about restitution and giving back at home and away at other points of *homeness*.

And a large part of this is the movement from childhood to adolescence to adulthood and what is *allowed*/sanctioned by family, and what is not. Constraints on girls which boys don't feel (or often even manage to sense), cultural constraints that *are* different but that don't *feel* different in the broadest sense of *just* being children, expectations of patterns and behaviours set up by family and community, but also by the self.

Evelyn *stepped out* in more overt ways, really, but George also had his own trajectory *away*. All involved which rituals to break and which to keep – in terms of religion, food, community, everything. There is the (mutual) lament of loss and change, and such memoir-making can, if only in part, help restore and enrich. And there's the memoirists' struggle to talk *between* memory and reality, such as with this articulation of a loss that seemed to go deeper in time (but is a loss, nonetheless) for George: 'Only later did I realize that I had been deluded; the synagogue, in fact, was no more than thirty years old' (p. 98).

George uses a technique of personal reflection going into local cultural historicising then drawing the lens out to consider details that are extra-cultural and also entirely outside his own cultural experience. This 'growth' of knowledge and encounter is essential to who he is and what he writes of himself. (And this is true of Evelyn as well.) George notes cultural and religious markers to pin narrative but as a 'daydreaming' (big part of his schooling!) poet of the streets (and sometimes the country), departs from them (as) suddenly and reconstructs the individual against the backgrounds of family, community, religion and personal experience to make the self: 'In truth, my emergence from childhood into adolescence did not come from anything so sudden as a bar mitzvah' (p. 101).

For George, the key is to always look into *other* worlds[7] (as Evelyn looks into other worlds that make who she is *whole*, by filling in the 'blanks' created by migration). He is saturated in 'his' world/s, but always open to new experiences, to build on his knowledge:

> My walk to Baron Byng High at age twelve had introduced me to another world: crossing Rachel Street was like crossing the Jordan into a new geography with new longitudes and latitudes, much to be discovered. My daydreaming leapt to those explorers introduced in elementary school, the bearded coureurs de bois, Radisson and Groseilliers, portaging through woods and down rapids into the Canadian

---

7 George notes: 'Yes, that's very much the case, John. It's odd that during the 6 months I spent in the Arctic in 1956, I never wrote about that dramatic setting with its closing darkness, its stiffening cold … Only now do I want to look back at it because I feel that it's had a shaping effect on me. I think maybe the section on Vuillard in *A Stone in My Shoe* works that way. When we look far back into the past where it's all misty, the lenses we see through are specific images, shards of experience that give us shaping images, the beginning of narrative. When I return to those Arctic months it might be Jack McMahon's teeth frozen in a glass of water or running to escape the incoming tide at Frobisher Bay that opens up that chapter of my life' (George Ellenbogen, private correspondence with John Kinsella, 15/4/19).

interior. My old neighborhood leaned against a darkness I had rarely penetrated as a child. (p. 101)

Evelyn does similar via recounting her students' responses to questions and assignments, and the cultural dynamics of classrooms, and especially so in talking of social life and living in, say, Damascus in a flat (as opposed to the flashy hotel of Bahrain which is always a distracted experience). In Damascus, she is surrounded by the Assad oppression, and the array of external oppressions (Israel in the Golan Heights, Syria claiming Lebanon as part of Greater Syria and the Lebanese resisting such colonial claims), while trying to be a conduit for educational freedom and integrity – ignored by colleagues, and finding connection through the cabbie, local food vendors, where difference is also emphasised.

In George's childhood neighbourhood/community, Jewish communism was not radical as much as part of discourse, and yet the get-ahead of migrant experience and gradual assimilation away from the horrors of Europe and the Nazis meant a different way of dealing with the 'complexities' of assimilation bullying. Capitalism underpins the collective dream of nation and it is what difference tunes in and out of: "'I'll tell you what capitalism's given you," raged Mr. McPherson to a class of skeptical students. "It's given you your radios and television sets" (which struck me as an odd thing to say since no one I knew owned a tv)' (p. 108). Radicalism is inevitably diluted by the fact that 'participation', 'integration' and 'belonging' lead to a broader social acceptance (and less bullying). From 'rites' to the 'rights' of peaceful existence and even co-existence, we arrive at a strange parallelism between communities: 'For all our flirtation with radicalism, however, we were smitten, cowed by much of what we saw in British culture, the very language of *As You Like It*, read in the ninth grade, with its power and grace, its distance and proximity' (p. 108).

The salient point is found in the antithesis to who George must become ... non-compliance is encoded in so many ways – and often in contradictory ways (immigrant heritage, Jewish community, demands of the British empire and English, French colonialism and so on): 'That distant world had issued an invitation. If we worked hard, played hard, we too could shed the last of our immigrant traces and take our place with other colonials in the expansiveness of the empire' (p. 109).

And it goes right down to issues of permission, compliance and the ability to shape one's humanity within structures that might well seek to exclude and oppress via laws designed to suit the majority, the centres of power: 'Lawyers and their official sheets of paper always held a terror for him, as they did for other immigrants, who saw them as the invisible hands of a government raised against their aspirations' (p. 130).

The migrant father who worked his way from central Europe over land and then shovelling coal in a steamer from Liverpool to Canada, is always vulnerable to cultural quarantines that contradict the colonial world's desire for labour, to use and not give rights:

My father had not forgotten that he was an alien presence with no passport, no official papers. Questioned by the Royal Canadian Mounted Police about his credentials, which were bought, he wouldn't be shaken. But they left unsatisfied, threatening to return. For him authorities in uniform were never the representatives of law and order, but enemies, not to be trusted. He'd keep his own council. (p. 131)

It's hard ever to recover and assert from such a position, but gradually George's father, strengthened by having his wife at his side, did, as did she. A team – and family teams are much of what both memoirs are about; early family but also extended family of heritage and what one does and doesn't do with those connections. George was imbued with this, and Evelyn also went and retrieved a collective history from its origins: a heritage. Together, maybe, these memoirs address the paradox, but we must read them intertextually. One essentially European, the other essentially Middle-Eastern, both migrant, both in their own ways part of colonialisms, and both undoing colonial binaries. They can't offer resolutions, but they can offer pathways to comprehension without bigotry.

Each memoirist presents culturality of identity in the context of where they live in the 'now', as well as the past – for the 'here and now' is the pluralism of migrant worlds. George writes:

The Haggadah, reminder of earlier hardships, had little meaning for me then. Even afterwards, as the epochs between the Exodus and the Holocaust turned from incomprehensible shreds into a single tapestry of wandering and persecution, the crowded table at Passover with plates shuffling in slow motion to an orchestra of laughter and chatter reminded me not so much of piety as of conviviality, of the essentials of the comic spirit, of the comforts that human beings could bring to one another. (p. 61)

But equally, heritage is the matter-of-factness of the individual in community with their own concerns, pressures, worries, trivial details to sort through, which can become overwhelming, and consequential for themselves, their family and the community itself. Evelyn's mother was a strong advocate for Arab women where she lived, and the greater community, and this is entwined with the millions of fragments and threads that make up raising children, each different, and each on their own trajectory, with Evelyn's maybe even more divergent than her mother might expect. But then her mother was divergent in so many ways herself, but always came back to what was core for her:

Though, like most Arabs, my mother Hannah, loved poetry, aphorism, and elegant turns of phrase, she had little inclination toward learning in the abstract. Her deepest admiration was reserved for people who could do useful things – tailor a jacket, hang wallpaper, unjam a window, change a flat. She was handy herself. (p. 19)

As to how we see and perceive of ourselves growing up – try the moment where Evelyn recalls her *Cyclone* uncle having a go at her for being 'spoilt'. The 'texture' of life, as George calls it in terms of family togetherness and those occasions that suddenly depart from the norm, and out of this, memoir becomes the embodiment of the languages and images of our shared experience. George writes: 'Such images and memories continue to grip my imagination; they promise more than a treasury of anecdotes to be served up at a dinner party. Only recently have I begun to understand what those images provide, specifically how they highlight the way in which childhood and neighborhood survive in my memory' (p. 85).

We become the collective of our family's past, and a relative's singing (in George's case), the synthesis of art and music and one's past, the 'Proustian' evocations from childhood that help us know who we are and what our ethical responsibilities are, become the formation of our consciences.

The *photos* are still with us. Both memoirs carry photos in dialogue, but George's is a *direct* conversation, a wrestling with what's not in them as much as what is. Evelyn uses the successes and failings of teaching as her photo-equivalent, in which what is not drawn out in a lesson or a response is as much what she's addressing as what is there to be heard and seen. There is a particularly apt passage in George's memoir where he lifts the portraits of a photo into the realm of being – an existential moment that's ironically shared: 'In a photo of my father, Motl, and Meyer, taken in the late 1940s on a park bench near my Uncle Meyer's apartment in the Bronx, I see something less than titanic. Scoured by their North American experience, they have been resculpted as mere humans' (p. 127).

Late in *A Stone in My Shoe*, there's a wonderful drawing together of life and text:

> Whenever I taught the Anglo Saxon poem, 'The Wanderer,' in which the wanderer is conveyed by the Anglo-Saxon word 'eardstepa,' ('earthstepper'), I was reminded of my brother who had chosen to walk his own paths, to sketch and photograph them, and to speak about them to those eager to listen to someone who lived in two worlds. (p. 163)

In making a place in a world that lives inside and outside the records of being we keep – of our own lives and those around us – he makes decisions on what to tell and what to keep to himself. And yet, he is (also) speaking with Evelyn, and she will hear dramatic moments of challenge such as: 'With the first bite, I had crossed a line. Esau, we are instructed, sold his birthright for a mess of pottage, basic food, crushed cooked lentils with onions and garlic; in the dead of winter I sold mine for a breaded pork cutlet. I have yet to sort out the outcome of this exchange.' (p. 168)

The 'crossing' of a dietary taboo and a leaving of neighbourhood are an enforced rite de passage with self-cultural loss consequences – a bothering of conscience over a lifetime, a *fitting into*, but with questioning. The pig death resonates outside lyric and ritual as conscience.

Beyond ambiguity

In considering cultural determinism and the stereotypes manufactured around communities, but also the realities of what communities are, both memoirists struggle with interiors and exteriors, with 'ambiguity' and 'transparency', with levity and intensity at once. I could ask George what he makes of Evelyn's first wonderfully self-deflating line, her opening gambit: 'It's my experience that Arabs and psychiatrists are natural enemies', but I won't, because I know the laughs and discomforts around this line will have been gone over many time in their house, their lives, their shared habits of warmth and mutual respect, these inherent reciprocities of memoir-making, and their shared acts of expression.

PART FIVE

On an Innovative Poet's Book, Never Published – Asked to write an introduction to a new book of poetry by Scott-Patrick Mitchell that never appeared, I wondered about the life of such texts (the book itself, the intro apropos of a 'hidden text'). Within this book, this short chapter is an example of the evasiveness of critical text-making, where its referent is 'lost' or changes into something else (Scott-Patrick Mitchell's poems would find different lives in different contexts). So the book itself becomes ambiguous, as all physical manifestations of texts are vulnerable to deletion, erasure, to loss in some form. In the first volume of this trilogy, I discussed the erasure of digital files of record I called 'Net Death', and in some ways this echoes that. But it's different – the loss is only partial in the immediate, and the text written remains a moment of engagement that says something, I think, about textual practice. The direct relevance to the argument of this book resides in the following quote: 'Love and desire, lust and consummation, are not about imposition. Again and again, these are poems of rights, poems of language's possibility to extend outside the status quo, to particularise and universalise at once, over and over, but to know respect and intactness of self and community.' Scott-Patrick Mitchell (SPM) identifies as non-binary, and it should be said clearly here that this does not necessarily accord with 'ambiguity'. The defining of non-binary as 'ambiguous' is completely at odds with the affirming decision-making behind identity. Such 'definitions' are beyond ambiguity, and only those who see a binary in gender will construct a discourse. In their poetry, Mitchell deals with ambiguity of language and even situations and interfaces with world, but this is not via an ambiguity of identity. Sexuality and desire are central to the poet's poetics, but they are not fixed by even the language they use.

On an innovative poet's book, never published: introduction to Scott Patrick-Mitchell's *Vade Mecum*[1]

We have: eros, psyche, 'the mountain, the valley, the river, the tree'. We have self, we have process and other selves, we have nature. We have language, loss, and intense desire to heal. 'Desire' is a word in the dictionary we've missed really coming to grips with. It's so much more expansive than definition allows – SPM expands our understanding, the possibilities. So much of this is shadowed in this text we perform in our own ways, spaces.

Moisture, stars, The Lord's Prayer rewired and defused, a guide to ways of expressing love and the right to speak it. Healing, the medicinal, reassurance, affirmation in the face of a tense world and its ironies, bodily alchemy, the human as the cat's familiar, the beauty of abjection, fluidity and the friendly face of (nonetheless) sharp satire. SPM delights in recontextualising language, taking a nineteenth-century cliché as an erotic and semantic ploy – 'dew' is the pun par excellence, sincere and disarming.

'a salem love poem' interplays convention and filmic representations of 'American' self-originating stories, which base themselves on the anxiety of displacing the native American belongings with new world ghostings, of witches escaped from the old world to destabilise the colonial presence. In such slippages are SPM's voicings – their bricolage of presence, made up of all they watch and experience, those semiotic feedings of a wired-in life that is cybernetic, and feeling the angst and pain of love's pleasures and failings. Burnt offerings, swords to ploughshares, witches as victimised, the colonial imposition – at stake, the self-given in a risky world of no clear meanings, where text is the pattern we make for ourselves to state innocence and culpability woven together. How can a love poem declare itself in the contradictions?

SPM is not going to play ball with a dick pic. They might not send it to the mother of the offender (fair move after warnings have been issued and little choice is left!), but they are going to tackle any imposition with what it deserves. They are conscious of boundaries, and they are going to differentiate between the rights of text to go where it will, and the rights of the self to declare what is appropriate or not. What goes, and what doesn't, is in flux, but 'no' means no, as it always should. There's a highly attuned sensibility when personal and

---

1 This has an interesting textual history, I think. I was asked by the author if I would introduce their new book of poetry and after reading the manuscript, and knowing SPM's work well, agreed to do so. After I finished, the publisher collapsed, and in agreement with SPM I blog published the piece. I am interested in the life this piece gives the work as something other than the work – it seeks to genuinely and appropriately and respectfully 'represent' it, but it also exists as an ambiguity of context. Gathered and offered as a nodal point herein, it moves beyond that ambiguity – the interstices and crossovers, the 'in situ conversations' with other works about textuality, authorship, presence and absence, and acts of reading bring it into a different kind of enactment and enacting. I hope.

political rights are contesting for space in a consuming, capitalised world. The right of presence, to share without constraint, doesn't mean the right to objectify and to take away from intactness. Desire and imposition are not yoked in sexual discourse:

> words like stretch & choke
> spill freely from this bloke
> as he objectifies me into the
> object i will never be

Love and desire, lust and consummation, are not about imposition. Again and again, these are poems of rights, poems of language's possibility to extend outside the status quo, to particularise and universalise at once, over and over, but to know respect and intactness of self and community. Complex conversations that need to be had, through puns, play and concise expression. This is a poetry that knows – that is unrestrained in the references it feeds on and feeds out, will revalue 'tired terms', and invigorate the unexpected as well – a vibrant even playing-field of wit. We are we, and us is I, and yet unappreciated as a self the pursuer wants us to perform, to role-play for them, but forgetting we too have roles *and* subjectivity. Now, there's a generous willingness to play along, as desire says so, and love definitely insists, but not at the loss of self-respect or rights to be loved as well. It's not simple, ever, but it can be rendered in the beautiful, in the gesture of the love poem. A dawn moment, an aubade that is love of the world as well. Again, mutual and proliferating respect.

Such a desire for living, to be alive, and to share that. In the containment of the poem is the proliferating largesse, the welcoming on the journey – intimate companionship. Polysemous love and desire out of an invigorating view of body and spirit, in which the trans is the normative and a worldview grows and expands as inclusive is what is and what has been hidden by the repressive control mechanisms of states, and their tooled-up iron maidens of gender, sexuality identity control. This is a book of liberty and freedom with awareness running in-sync with a desire of just outcomes.

Elegy – the loss of a sister anchors us to the narrative of life as performance, as crisis, as vulnerability. What is left after loss? It's powerful because it isn't easy, none of it.

Celebrity is local, not mass, poetry is the breath, as Yoko says to SPM in the twittersphere, but even more than the unspeakable, it's the unbreathable – which is pain but also a desire for what's best and loving and durable in the poem's compactness, with levers of pleasure and intense sadness working therein. We are loved by SPM in this, and we need to love them back. We can, you know. And in such respectful and varied and varying ways. So many degrees of encounter and so many words we still need to conjure, just to make do. The wet of death, the wet of love, the saline solution that conducts the currents across states of being. We share in our differences; we make the larger thought patterns in speaking, in breathing others' breath.

Beyond ambiguity

Our chant communication, our 'post-verbal' poetry is also a delving into the choate, the inchoate, the pre-speech. Not post-structuralist only, but a conversation across the linguistic tree, its branchings. And so what do we give and receive outside prosody, outside the organisation of a poem? The mouth moves, and the eyes see inwards – there are no physical or psychic 'impairments'. All differences are gains. The lexical is just one path. Other paths, so many others, are vibrant within these containment fields of language that let go, let go, let us in. Share. Osmotic. Where Kurt Schwitters saw his vowels go outwards and echo, a resonance that might have to come, that has happened, is *doing*. Beyond. Deep pragmatics of needing a poetics of inclusive beyond. These are our poems, too. In the teaching and receiving, receiving and teaching, the mentoring and being mentored, in the open collaboration. In the cipher, the 'shaman', the medium. We are here, too.

And in the fake-news world, the Lincoln residues. But this is non-violence, only the violence refracted through the performative act of power. The tyranny that wills its violence. The theatre is not real, though Lincoln fell. The metaphor for violence is horrifying enough. Peace. Pacifist language must step in, calm the choir, the hecklers, the hawkers of hate speech. But the terrible possibility of violence is there – violence making violence. And that's terrifying.

But the poem *enacting* is costly and difficult, and people don't always get it, even close people. Yet people need poems for *them*, and poems must be written for them – it's compulsion, need, and much more … ineffable:

> being a poet is like being an addict
> because your sister will send you
> text messages that read you fucking
> junkie poet cunt, why don't you go
> & get a real job & she doesn't know
> that you do indeed have one: your
> job being to open the souls of every
> person you meet to the mightiness
> of the unknown, a thing you can
> achieve if you have that singular
> right perfect poem

Being an unromantic romantic can be devastating, and shares qualities of and with addiction/s.

Orthography is survival in a violent world, not only a mirror. Loan poem, learning to read, rehabilitation of definitions, the list and its echoes.

This book is to the memory, to the body, to the being of sister. Sister lost cannot be rebuilt but the breath is present and moving and still ~~there~~. Elegy is conceptual sprung rhythm. We have, in 'the white lilly', the matter-of-factness of it, the loss … the need to write the poem, to write the poem for them, those who have lost life, for life itself. The poem resonating for her – recuperative in some ways, but also:

> when you lose a sister
> to cancer, you sometimes
> wish you could remove a rib
> rebuild her into being, but ya
> bloodwork don't match, even
> though, when you use that
> face app, to find out what
> you would look like as a
> woman, her face pouts back

There is disturbance out of loss – desire becomes distressing and its path to redemption is troubled, self-punishing. The sense of self collapsing is thwarted by redefining the self in the world outside the body, the flesh, the psyche. An anxiety over death is a search for reason, a need for 'elegance', as if form has some way of holding back loss, emptiness. A process of rebuilding, of manoeuvring out of the way of the 'fuck off we're full' horror of right-wing bigots.

There is *nature*, and it is outside the self, though to merge with it is redemption, too. Yes, yes ... Lake Monger, the moorhens, the swans, what the line actually takes us to. Cough of an ibis, secular resurrection of suburban – the 'bird poem' as encounter with so many threads of enculturation, and of bird itself. *Yes*, nature is rising in the breath as it was always there and always will be, and we need to stand against the exploiters and protect the spaces where the bulldozers go. *Yes*, you and I and we and they sang to the bulldozers – we were there, all of us. I know the mantra, so do you, and so does SPM. Concern is part of it, being active and out there and speaking our breath is essential. Self is nature, too. We owe it. We owe culture. We need to listen and touch and see and sense and make poems as we can, any way we can. And wet is water and it has a structure and ecology, and *makes*. This is city speaking. This is city more than buildings. This is city community people nature and buildings. This is Perth, this poem book. This making. This respect. Listen. Breathe.

PART SIX

This section is divided into four sub-sections and is concerned with collaboration in activism, writing, community and common purpose. I worked with Swiss sociologist, novelist, poet, sculptor and artist, Urs Jaeggi from the mid-1990s, and here are parts of collaborations with discussions around their making and enactment. There is also a consideration of ambiguity ('textural ambiguity' – with its text/texture 'plays') in the making of poems on photographs, and in photographs themselves in 'On Textures of Ambiguity – a collaborative exhibition of poems and photographs [of Will Yeoman]', in which the subtexts of this book come into relief: 'I am fascinated by the way *apparent* ambiguities come about from not being able to position an 'object' in relation to other 'objects', to set something seen in the broader context of seeing – to show the other co-ordinates around a single point; the inability to show the GPS co-ordinates, so to speak, might actually tell us more about the locally specific than the vista image, the points of reference, the photograph of the broader landscape'. The act of displaying and exhibiting has been a theme across this Poetics Trilogy, with the curatorial act always in question. And a late addition to the book because though I have been working on a cycle of poetry books with Kwame Dawes over the last eight years, I have not written about our interaction across this trilogy of critical works. Included herein is a short piece about *Tangling with the Epic* (Peepal Tree, 2019), which investigates the politics and mechanics of the Spenserian stanza (and was originally delivered as part of a joint online keynote with Kwame for the *Points of Interest: Early Modern Punctuation, On and Off the Page* conference, Cambridge University, 2021). From collaborating with another writer/artist, the section moves into more personal poetics considerations regarding activism. Throughout the trilogy, I have used my own poems as ongoing 'windows' into practice, with specific usage in tension with the ambiguities of the language arrangement, the prosody, of the texts. And we 'resolve' into the contradiction of supporting a cause while objecting to some of its methods (as failing, to my mind, to take in some of the contradictions in a specific 'protest' action). The section, and the book (other than the conclusion which address all three volumes of the *Poetics*), concludes with communal statements of participatory activist poetics.

PART SIX (A)

Working with Urs Jaeggi[1]

I worked with Urs Jaeggi on a variety of text(ual)-visual-poetry collaborations from when I first met him in Fremantle, Western Australia, while attending the 1995 International PEN 62nd World Congress. When I moved to Cambridge with family in 1996, I got to see Urs every now and again as I often travelled to Germany. He and I read together in Berlin and Hamburg and created a book via fax machine entitled *D & G* that has since been lost. There were a number of paper versions of *D & G* circulating around the turn of the century, but none of them seems to have survived. A section of the book was published in *Chain* magazine in the late 1990s, and I am trying to find my copy so I can scan and place some of our work from that issue on http://poetsvegananarchistpacifist.blogspot.com/.

Following on from *D & G*, Urs and I collaborated on a number of other works via email, with fractions and fragments being published here and there over the years (e.g. in *Vlak* magazine). Most recently, we worked on 'drawings and poems', whereby I respond to series of drawings sent as attachments by Urs. This is the reverse of a process we employed in around 2006/7/8 when I sent Urs my *Divine Comedy* 'distractions' and he 'illustrated' and sent back. Those drawings never found their way into the English-language editions of the work (WW Norton and University of Queensland Press), but a few did find their way into the selection by the Italian publisher Raffaelli Editore, with translations in Italian by Maria Cristina Biggio in 2013. I have scanned some pages and will include in a future blog post.

What I present here are some snippets from our most recent work together,[2] and I intend to add to this over future blog postings. Collaboration has been a vital part of my creative working life, and is really what I am most interested in, and of most value. As well as working with Urs for over twenty years, I have also had the good fortune to work creatively with Louis Armand, Pam Brown, Kwame Dawes, Toby Fitch, Dorothy Hewett, Frieda Hughes, Wendy Jenkins, Paul Kane, Gordon Kerry, Niall Lucy, Rod Mengham, Drew Milne, Thurston Moore, Charmaine Papertalk-Green, Barry Phipps, James Quinton, Tracy Ryan, Mona Ryder, Susan Schultz, Russell West-Pavlov, Karl Wiebke and others, and I feel privileged in these interactions.

I begin with a letter and poem written in celebration of Urs's 80th birthday, and included in a primarily German-language volume celebrating the brilliance

---

1 My friend and collaborator of many years, Urs passed away in Berlin in February 2021 when this book was in the publication process. My memorial to Urs can be found at: https://poetsvegananarchistpacifist.blogspot.com/2021/03/in-memoriam-urs-jaeggi-1931-2021.html.

2 Post my writing this and not long before Urs passed, we co-wrote a notebook work in person over an afternoon at the James Joyce Foundation in Zurich entitled 'Reverence' – our final collaboration. See: http://poetsvegananarchistpacifist.blogspot.com/2020/02/reverence-part-one-further.html.

Beyond ambiguity

of this Swiss-born sociologist, cultural and social activist, novelist, poet, visual artist, sculptor and much more.

***

Happy birthday, Urs. I thank you for your friendship and for sharing your work with me over the years. Working with you on various collaborations, including *D & G* and most recently the *Tractortatus* texts, has been an ongoing revelation about the possibilities of art and language. You are the embodiment of the Renaissance artist and thinker – all is in your ken – but in a truly contemporary way.

Here is a poem based on a few factors: visiting your apartment in Berlin in the mid-1990s; the painting used as the cover image for *Salt* magazine number 8 (1996); and very distantly, your wonderful poem-text 'Miles', published in the same issue of *Salt*.

I often think of our performances together in Berlin and Hamburg. You are the liberator of the word!

Pause

   for Urs Jaeggi's 80th Birthday
In the room *the room*
you offered the staying
place the rocking-horse
room where night-fright
made no horror and no
shadows just the zoo-light
carried in from wanderings
about the wall machine
down ergo silence of cabinet
of sketches expressing
shudders and stillness
an ergonomics of presence
where comfort allies
with friendship and intensity
with sincerity and circles
wavering circles and souls
stepping down and out
through window and image-bank
in book-frame and covering
voices with plausible trance
or entrance – *thankyou*
for the cover the glint
and gleaning of salt
and movie-time rescue
like risk like announcement
overtalking to echo
through theatre and audience,
failsafe nor forget-me-not rhizomes

Part six

tunnelling streetworks
cloistered or blossoming in window
of multilingual fruitfulness,
no imprisonment in artifice
or maybe *freedom* in artifice
but not 'officialese' (you made
your escape! you sculpted
plastic form office throne
choke of narrative, storyline
fame left on the altar),
degrees of ranks blown
in by Peter the Great
and no notice taken
or left freehold resurrection
poem of provinces – dead
souls – no, no estates
made from transfer or silence:
third persons telling their tales,
folk tales and heritages,
red and blue witches,
sagas   epics   prophecies
I heard Khlebnikov asleep
reciting asleep I was awake
asleep near the rocking-horse
childhood recognition of apocrypha
I was part of we all were you'd think
or you were too and I detailed
the twists and scrunches
of paper that made up
your eternal poem your
challenge to rock the horse
to rock the boat
to rock the monastery
of learning and blight,
chronicle   recital   ode
paint hunger form
catacoustics
of inner-city apartment
as generous as caverns
and sky, '(dritte Lektion)'
in the mineshafts of wonder,
investigation, breakthroughs,
sticking-your-neck-out
loyalty of palette is body
of palette is opening colour
outside its spectrum
without the inducements
of colour, refraction, spectra,
prism analogies, dispersion,

Beyond ambiguity

    diffractions the clamour
    for laws we never want,
    we pass without pause:
    sharing is silence and noise
    and the joy of knowing.
    Bonding and making,
    rooms to fill and empty,
    all made in the shades
    of living contrapposto.

        with very best wishes,
        from John Kinsella

And some drawings and poems (i.e. Urs Jaeggi's drawings followed by my poem-responses):

Figure 3 Drawing: ink on paper by Urs Jaeggi.

```
      V          V        V    V      V                                    V
      e          e        e    e      e                                    e
     rollicking theory as any other answer might seriously come out of Frankfurt
     H t         t        t    t      t                                    t
     egel        e        e    e      Freud                                e
      b          b        b    b      b                                    b
      r          r        r    r      r                                    r
     Marx        a        a    a      a                                    a
      e          e        e    e      deposits                             share
                                                                           o
                                                                           u
                                                                           s
                                                                           e
```

Part six

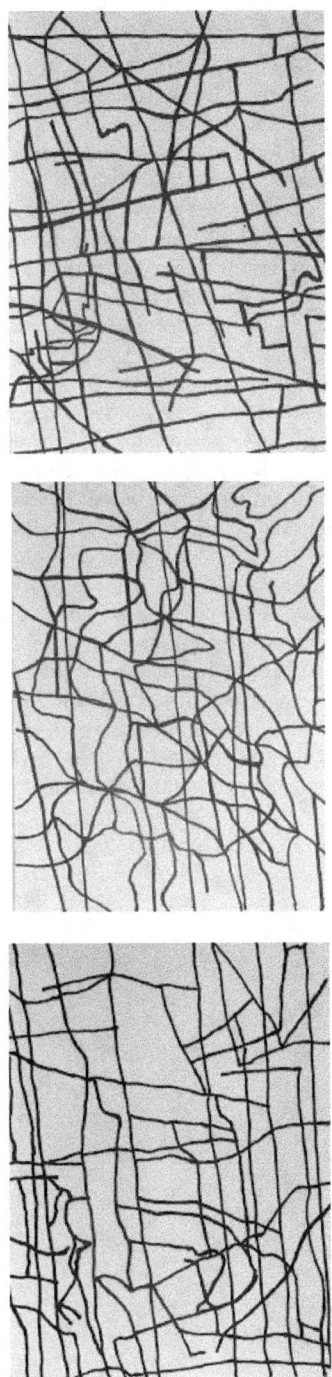

Figures 4–6 Drawings: ink on paper by Urs Jaeggi.

Three Labyrinthine Transcriptions

Shlimazel leads us here *which is nowhere* as the saying goes as the thread bares along the frayed edges to enweave the weft inward, lattice-like, amazed or unamazed leaves you the same path choices which forks unalike in end results and so through the long grass — dead, dry, underwritten by a green that can't get going — to find the boulders where all shy species congregate wondering why they're with each other being equally shy in such company of shyness, and then a noise! and gone! scattering in all directions with their own patterns and a generative chaos of survival a fractal desire for preservation and there *we* are lumbering up to survey and noting tracks in the odd bit of exposed dirt and then a small pile of scats maybe echidna cylinders full of ants or maybe possum scats with vegetation still digesting into earth, as so many trails cross as so many trails are reused as so many trails source food and water by differing codes of access and definition the leaves of one shrub being enough to sustain moisture levels in one creature but a devastation of thirst to another and so the ants make for their funnels and colonies connect and mirroring below ground the honeydew feeders & the blue butterflies no drones overhead but yes, heat signatures brilliant in the black ink of our templates, the charcoal of our fires the capillaries we affirmably label as rhizomes through an underworld we are certain to leave to reach up into the thinning canopy where wandoo crown decline weeps dead leaves weeps constellations we fly past on boosts of light that have eaten earth the planet earth still alive for all its encounters with asteroids.

Part six

Figure 7 Drawing: ink on paper by Urs Jaeggi.

Confrontation

When the boomers
confronted
on the second tier
below the house,
we described it as a dance. None of us have danced recently,
nor attended a dance, or thought much about dance,
but it's inherent, isn't it? We pluck memories
like fur from the coats
of rivals we don't have, or don't want. We are not
violent. But the old boomer – scarred, dominant –
hangs on to his mob for another season –
three rivals, almost but *not quite*
as large, wrestling for supremacy.
All lived to tell tails
they balanced on, 'boxing'
and tipping opponents
until first and second round losers demurred
to watch from down low
the final tilt, the *pas de deux*
that defines the sociology
of the present, and what will be
for a time, a cycle.

And from earlier in the latest collaborative cycle:

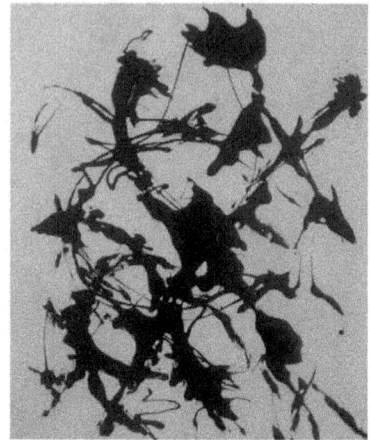

Figure 8 Drawing: ink on paper by Urs Jaeggi.

Intentions

I intend to travel beyond the spectrum.
I intend to recast lines and mergings.
I intend to open the doors and windows when it's storming.
I intend to let language escape into geography.
I intend to let geography escape into language.
I intend to awake the sleeping.
I intend to wind the chronometer backwards.
I intend to stir the wind against gravity.
I intend to colour all reproductive parts of the flower.

Part six

Figure 9 Drawing: ink on paper by Urs Jaeggi.

Closing Bell

Passodoble shock to casternet
Psyche's blastdoors, to confront
a mirrorcall, a despicable wall
of Self stretched to profit ideology.

We see into your *pas de deux*,
your rough riding aubades
to make a myth fit phrenology.
We sense a universal and tranquil pool

beyond your aqueous humour,
beyond the closing bell.

Beyond ambiguity

Figure 10 Drawing: ink on paper by Urs Jaeggi.

Kiss

Repossessions of peace
counts empire-standard,
clauses claws & shadows
philology of body type
facing departures.
Nip the randomness.
Take the chance.
Reading & expression =
stones hauled so far
upright.

Part six

Figure 11 Drawing: ink on paper by Urs Jaeggi.

Ruins

Struggling over the ruins
as a black rain swirled,
they wiped their eyes
to better see the spirits
rising from spent palaces,
granaries, and tombs.

Beyond ambiguity

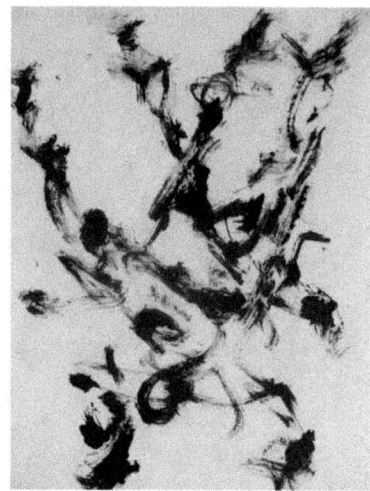

Figure 12 Drawing: ink on paper by Urs Jaeggi.

Greetings from Mexico Received

'Froto mis párpados:
el cielo anda en la tierra'
    Octavia Paz, 'Madrugada Al Raso'
My brother-in-law
travels frequently to Mexico.
He sees the dawn over mountains,
he sees fresh light silhouetting
timeless ghosts in the streets, the trees.
He sees far beyond any wall,
and on The Day of the Dead
he sends us greetings
and we share, too.

On *Textures of Ambiguity*

Exhibition (Feb–March, 2020, in York at Gallery 152)

    photographs by William Yeoman
    poetry by John Kinsella

Preparations for this exhibition were in process over a number of years. The first discussions took place via email in late 2015 and early 2016 and gathered pace in New Norcia in July of that year, where Will and I coincided and both noticed a large ancient log prone and cut down near the open, grassed camping area. Even at that stage the collaboration was about texture and consequence. Talking with Will later on, we found that we both have a strong interest in how a photo of a detail can create an impression of ambiguity of and about place. And what specifically interests me in this is a kind of inversion – how ambiguity can enhance an understanding of place, even a very specific location. We might not be able to discern precisely what the photo is showing us, but if we know where it was taken, then the 'textures' of the detail, the 'up close' moment, might become a kind of portal to understanding.

    I am fascinated by the way *apparent* ambiguities come about from not being able to position an 'object' in relation to other 'objects', to set something seen in the broader context of seeing – to show the other co-ordinates around a single point; the not being able to show the GPS co-ordinates, so to speak, might actually tell us more about the locally specific than the vista image, the points of reference, the photograph of the broader landscape. If it is in fact 'all in the detail', then all that's not in the detail is also part of that detail – we can learn about the context of what we're seeing by imagining what its context *might* in fact be. Even a bird's eye view might be on something very specific, honed and homed in on to separate it off for a moment before bringing it back into context, into its place of connection and belonging. Connections don't cease in the moment of isolating.

    As we worked primarily on Noongar boodja, the specificity of what Will has photographed and what I have written 'on' is deeply relevant, even when the viewer is presented with 'ambiguity' of specificity. We name-identify the general colonial locations ('York', 'New Norcia', 'Toodyay', 'Northam'), but that doesn't mean these images aren't acknowledging or reaching towards their traditional Noongar namings, their layers of history and language as country. They *are* making such an acknowledgement, but hopefully in a respectful and non-appropriative way.

    The 'ambiguity' is also an act of respect in seeing and not claiming, in being part of a moment, preserving it as an image, but not taking it from where it belongs. And in my poems around these images I have tried to encapsulate that way of reading and speaking. Ambiguity is doubt, but it is also other possibilities, other ways of seeing. Ambiguity is also about being faced with indecision about possible outcomes, but not being pinned down. It in itself has many textures and our senses are attuned to working a way through ambiguity. It's also an ambiguity of textures – looking at a photo image, you can feel the surfaces reaching out to you and you can imagine how they might feel.

But it's look, don't touch; or is it? What we have before us in the photographs, and even in the poems written on to walls, are simulacrums of real moments in context – the textures have been emphasised by being 'caught in their moment', but though removed from place for display and encounter, they are still about intactness in where they were taken, and in what they are outside the image. They retain their real texture, and have the texture of 'art' as well. There are so many ironies in this when one considers, say, a track to a mine or quarry that's wrecking country, a massive felled tree with saw cuts that went only so far before being abandoned. There's the uncanny, the displaced, the traumatised, and the strange out of place sense of 'touch' – the photo bringing on associations that trigger other sensations, other hopes, other redresses. And the locale of display – the old walls, the crumbling plaster, the irregularities of surface … there's the ambiguous and specific relationships between photos, poems and the colonial residues and the stone of the place upon which they are being displayed. It, too, is a dislocation of country we are trying to address, but letting the juxtapositions speak for themselves as well.

For me, seeing plastic and metal chairs against a painted wall is a trigger to form, to light and shade, between the casual and precise. I see the textures and they are shifting even in the fixed state of the photo. Those shadows won't stay there, and the chairs will be sat in, moved, rained on, deteriorate in the weather. The poem runs with those textures of ambiguity and goes many places, into many locales, but always respecting origins in the local.

There's a personal relevance in Will including three images taken outside the wheatbelt – from Melbourne, Manchester and London – that I also feel a connection with as places I have spent time in, contemplated through degrees of personal and cultural separation … these are textures of place I can see in my head, and have encountered. And they have strange threads into and out of the wheatbelt that the poems try to consider: colonial, migratory, 'export' and 'import', communications, post-coloniality, and also as an emphasis on a hope for a decolonising. And they are 'place' in themselves, separate and yet connected, likely in the main thinking themselves autonomous of us here (where *is* this *here* for the majority of people 'there' thinking about the nature of their place, the place they are passing through, the place they feel varying degrees of connection to?). But none of us is completely autonomous of other 'heres' – they are themselves made up of so many movements, so many journeys, so many dislocations, so many belongings and exclusions. They are themselves, and not, and more, and will be something else again and again. And yet, boodja is boodja and will always be boodja. I note this again. And again.

The local is part of the biosphere. I am a believer in absolute respect and intactness of the local – but conversations with other 'locals' and between localities is essential. Where we live in the wheatbelt is on Ballardong land, but close to the 'boundary' of where Whadjuk and Yued country intersect. A place of specificity and transition. In consulting with Elders over the years, and recently again, I have confirmed the boundaries and I know on whose land we are, but it's also a place of conversations about boundaries. I pay my respects and acknowledgements, and know in such contexts the threads that reach in and out of this exhibition pass through country.

Years ago, in York, I wrote this poem that was part of a book called *Shades of the Sublime & Beautiful*,[3] and when seeing Will's first batch of (New Norcia) poems for this collaboration, I thought, yes, this is it – he is investigating what texture means, what its implications for artist and viewer might be. And though it is anachronistic to this collaboration, it also seems prescient to me, in the context:

Textures of the Wheatbelt

Hessian waterbag cool in shade-house
swings with resistance, a cooling action
of flow that would slow flight down,
interfere with logic, a textural
draught, a rough divvying up of cloth
and air and water tilted against a burnished horizon,
stems of Paterson's Curse inflicting glass needles
like beacons, to rub against the angle of entry
like cropping out of season, or setting
a rabbit-trap off with a bare foot or sandal;
the shed strips of rough grey outer bark
of the York gum tune the green-grey
glide of undercurrents, the underneaths
out of sun and weathering winds,
gripping barbed wire to pin it down
and climb over to catch the flickback and skin-jag
and to wonder why you deserve such ill luck:
it's a matter of physics; an exfoliation of rust
is sharp and withering, crumbling cut,
all damage in bind-a-twine ripping over skin,
through clenched hands as bale slips sideways
and spills in segments, a burning as fire
and satin and density of colour,
red welts rising against the pliers' cut,
so much plant fibre and wire, blood slicks
like oil and water mixed against chemistry,
a science of bone finery and sharpness,
sinew and sever, a feathery drift of ash

---

3   John Kinsella, *Shades of the Sublime & Beautiful* (Fremantle Press and Picador, 2008).

> made ash again where fires are burnt often,
> where steel is extreme even through gloves,
> and a clod of loamy earth sticks just right,
> too much in heavy clay, too little in sand
> welling out vast planes, low scrub gone,
> a white scrunch echoing rims of brackish water,
> wings and carapaces irritant and emollient
> on harvest windscreens, grain-dust working
> pores best described as agnostic
> in their receipt of itch.

In most cases, Will has provided a choice/selection of photos on agreed upon locations and I have 'responded', but there are a couple of exceptions. Firstly, the 'corella' sequence was written in York in 2006 (actually in an office I had above the York post office!), and to which I have added a new part (10) – I wanted something to connect a not distant past to this present – to speak from York to Jam Tree Gully (north-east of Toodyay). It connects with the photo by Will subliminally as well as overtly in its being 'updated'.

The other exception is an image I had in my head from my walks around Toodyay that reminded me of a series of drawings by Urs Jaeggi – an image come out of a *texture*, out of walking a path with its strange ambiguities of 'maze' and 'path' (it is literally a repaired walk path). This image brought to mind Will's practice, and his ability to intensely capture the specific, the particular – that paradox of precision and ambiguity expressed in the composition of texture, the sense of 'feel' one of his photos can emanate.

So, a poem came before the image (the reverse of our usual process in this): down in Toodyay town there's a repaired bitumen path that runs along the non-Main Street side of the river (it starts just down from the school and goes all the way to the road leading down towards Toodyay/Newcastle bridge emerging near Mt Anderson road). It's a crazy array of repairs that look like Urs Jaeggi ink works which I have written 'about' before but now see new points of entry from 'afar'.[4]

The poem connects my experience with Urs Jaeggi's drawing textures, and lives in expectation of Will's interpretation of the space-place. It is a poem of anticipation, but also a poem about the irony of anticipating in a space where so much knowledge exists, so much awareness of overlay and imposition and consequence.

So, textures of ambiguity is as much about precision and accountability as it is about evasiveness and universality. We could also concurrently talk about textures of paradox, and even textualities of paradox and ambiguity. It's all

---

4 See http://poetsvegananarchistpacifist.blogspot.com/2017/07/working-with-urs-jaeggi-1.html.

working together – pulling away, coming back, concentrating. When I look at Will's photos I almost fall into them, and take all the moments of encounter I've had with 'similar' ways of seeing and (re)create my own experience. But that experience is never separated from responsibility in presence. And the fact we are photographing and writing Noongar boodja is the non-ambiguous point of reference from which we attempt to make some kind of comment about where we can connect, and also where we disconnect and shouldn't connect. It's not all available even for artistic interpretation!

For my part, these poems interconnect with other long-term creative and critical writing threads – I have been writing 'graphology poems' (reflecting on the nature of handwriting and orthography and place) for almost twenty-five years, so I wanted to connect this collaboration with that ongoing process; and then there's my interest in 'ambiguity' as a thing in itself come from creative-critical practice over recent years. I like to work in spatialities where difference meets, where difference might create new conversations through crossover and illuminating in and out of the shadows, which I celebrate. And in this, I think I celebrate the textures of ambiguity with Will Yeoman and his intense up-close photography. The following pages carry a few of Will Yeoman's photographs (originally in colour) and my accompanying poems.

Figure 13 London (2016), by William Yeoman.

Graphology Kaleidoscope: late addition after being immersed in the *Olafur Eliasson: In Real Life* (2019) exhibition at Tate Modern, London, and thinking over Will Yeoman's textural photograph, *London* (2016)

Spall of light set
solid form as instant

versions of us either
translated into range

& array of kaleidoscope
or polycentral ambiguity

of pattern disruptor –
colour touch test, *grip*

surface right angle fall as film
wavelengths materials:

surface, pigment, solidified
flow – *seen*, it's hard to see

any another way intact, motion
after-effect you might want

to cling to and climb – claw –
as contrary and prickling – abrasive smooth –

'slice of light' dished up
from the sharp sign

of the 'professional
services network'

bringing *London* into homes
as the prophet who insists

we were warned *the sky is falling in
and now it is* says all he has to say

one foot on wet graffiti
another on the riverwall – sharp angle –

St Paul's still scrubbing
at the stains of *Occupy*

mirroring its feet, lapping
glitter ball light as movement personified –

Figure 14 Fremantle (2016), by William Yeoman.

so, yes, light *is* movement
light was movement …

shape shapes shape as we paint,
adhere dissolve splinter

impersonate and illustrate
against the force majeure

of municipal illustration,
all epigones of source,

retreating glaciers
and the burning

of Australia, too.' It's in
the modelling, the kaleidoscope.

On Will Yeoman's *Fremantle* (2016) and Thinking Back Thirty Years Ago to Sleeping Rough in Fremantle

Heat and moisture and salt off the ocean
are the walls we inhabit the littoral the typos
of dwelling the breakdown of wash against
the niches of growth the undersea gardens
wavering as dressings to each awakening
crack and mildew or oil spill in flume or
spawn under a dark moon as conjunctions
between clauses of revenant suns – who lived
here before when the damp got in and what
rusts as deep-sea storms come in freighted
with cargo the port processed? Maybe it's something
at least semi-permanent via a wall's breakdown,
down into limestone the pH of navigation
plotted from shores from landing and embarking
and all those street moments when shelter
for me on a drier night was cardboard slanted
against such a wall, unwashed in the charts
and memorials the shell-polishing brine
that covers nothing up. Maps beyond
restoration, acts of recovery – this port,
this rivermouth, this climb back up to Scarp –
channels, depths needing shallows, satellite
view before satellites aided the maritime.

Beyond ambiguity

Figure 15 York 1 (2016), by William Yeoman.

Villanelle of Bottle Tree Pods and Cemetery (Will Yeoman, York Cemetery Photo)

Fruit that partially relates as fallen
there's little choice but be taken up by birds
or find ground to set root a new generation.

This crisis of the seed and the burial garden,
the spirit's hold-all that protects its words,
fruit that partially relates as fallen.

As kids, not knowing where they came from, we'd turn
them carefully in case some itch was deferred,
or find ground to set root a new generation.

We didn't know where the dead and the sun
met where they spoke and we did not speak in the shade,
fruit that partially relates as fallen.

Where things come to rest, some older person
told us, shaking the leaves and the pods
so we'd find ground to think a new generation.

Those shaped stones, headstones grown,
but it was the blue metal the gravel the soil over-turned –
Fruit that partially relates as fallen
to find ground to set root a new generation.

Beyond ambiguity

Figure 16 York 2 (2016), by William Yeoman.

On York Court House Wall [Photo by Will Yeoman]: Court as a Hill

for Cassie and Charmaine

It is for Aboriginal poets to talk
of where this stone comes from
and what holes it left behind
and what holes it was forced
to make sliced and diced stood
end to end to raise up to shape
a hill of discontent to progress
stone to *stones* to blocks to mortar
and keep the spirit level to hand,
each layer of dust and particulate,
each layer of warm hand to cool
wall against an outside that threatens
eased into place, layered as 'history'.

PART SIX (B)

On my own, my language is not alone

Derrida writes, as mediated by Spivak's English translation, 'Writing would thus have the exteriority that one attributes to utensils, to what is even an imperfect tool and a dangerous, almost maleficent, technique. One understands better why, instead of treating this exterior figuration in an appendix or marginally, Saussure devotes so laborious a chapter to it almost at the beginning of the *Course*.'[5] And in making a poetics of one's own poetry, and the practice of activism that emanates out of it and oscillates around it, is to draw all the interruptions and divergences of language as you have it at any given time.

Every day I talk with Tracy about mutual sources regarding how we speak together – television shows we watched growing up, songs we heard on the radio, books we read, movies we saw at the drive-ins or cinema, living in the same part of the world under the same conditions, being part of an ongoing colonial dispossessing though not understanding this till we were older children and even then in increments. Lots of overlap in content, but also in discontent. So, unable to express the problems of presence as we barely understood, we developed our own languages. Languages with much in common, but different. There were the signs we read through, but they became figurative and though meaningful to us, maybe abstract, even ambiguous, to others.

But, really, I am speaking for myself here, and thinking over how we both first heard the song 'Puff the Magic Dragon' and its twists and turns in our own perceptions and meanings from childhood to now. I write a poem in a conundrum of external and internal tension: of signs and symbols. I resist completion, and yet move towards completion. This volume is the third in a trilogy of poetics volumes, and yet it has anchor cables and flapping strings of thread – caught in southerly and easterly winds ... one bringing the cool, another heat, then switching as the planet shifts. In the climate corrosion I have been recording in my poetry since 1978 when I was fifteen, the sense of the symbol and the sign erode language – for me – to words displayed on a screen in my head that can't emerge because no sounds attach to them. I have recently 'signed off' on my 'Jam Tree Gully' poems cycle of the last ten years, and I am signing of on this act of giving middle vision to the peripheral, of focussing on marginalia and ephemera to an existence defined by writing, literal handwriting and typing on an old manual typewriter. Then converted to digital form, but eschewing with embarrassment and self-condemnation. The mapping of the words of the tree in the field of the will and testament of being?

Here's the paradox of recognising the absurdity of a fear of contamination and yet trying to articulate the impossibility of contamination merely existing as

---

5 Jacques Derrida, *Of Grammatology* (trans. Gayatri Chakravorty Spivak; Johns Hopkins University Press, 1997), p. 34.

abstraction. In part, that's why Derrida fails in his exposé of nuclear weapons[6] by not confronting the nuclear empowering of the French energy industry. That's why irony and contamination, metaphor and brute reality of the mass noun with the figurative ambiguities and possibilities extracted. That's where I swirl in my poems, lost in their spirals of affirmation and witness, looking for ways to move beyond the ambiguities.

Rocks can burn, too: and there's nothing ambiguous about it

We are spending our day watching the hill-tops and horizons – being on a hillside there are various horizons – because of extreme heat and high easterly winds. We are talking of extremes never experienced in this area in early November according to 'records'. Yesterday, we had a 'defend or leave' order because of a fire just down the road, and another simultaneously, just over the NBN tower hill (that the highest point should get this moniker is a disgrace and a sign of the ongoing colonialism we are embedded in, for all our refusal, for all our unambiguous objections and desire for restoration of Noongar rights without knowing how to enact it from a personal point of view, still dealing with a mortgage, still dealing with unbelonging and belonging).

I had left Jam Tree Gully at 3pm to collect Tim from his school bus drop 60k away, and as I was heading down Toodyay-Bindi Bindi Road I thought I could smell smoke. Then I saw the helicopter coming in fast and instantly knew I had to turn around and head back to Tracy, on her own at Jam Tree Gully. We keep only one car for ecological reasons – a small 4-cylinder car – and even that we know is wrong. But we are isolated and there's no public transport. So one car, and in fire season we have to go out together and it constrains us to each other in ways some would find hard to cope with. Liberty is relative in some ways – it certainly isn't a choice, but an obligation.

But early November is usually still 'safe', though we were cautious and checked emergency updates and scanned the horizons and took all our usual fire plan cautions. The firebreaks had been done (*never* sprayed with herbicides), and the grass cutting finished after days and days of work, and routes of escape worked out. [I just stopped writing this because another fire alarm came in – turns out to be the southern site just a kilometre from us ... we're on alert and maybe have to leave again ... again, as you'll see ...].

So, I turned around on seeing the helicopter and came straight back as Tracy knew I would and she was ready to go, having also been alerted by the helicopter, and we left immediately with only essential personal papers in hand – everything else abandoned. The firefighters managed to get it under control and after collecting Tim we were able to return home.

Now it looks like we might have to leave again. In the local paper one of the reactionaries who speaks their mind in this region talks about 'Climategate' and

---

6 Drew Milne & John Kinsella (2017) 'Nuclear theory degree zero, with two cheers for Derrida', *Angelaki*, 22:3, 1–16, DOI: 10.1080/0969725X.2017.1387358.

lives in their full rural bunker-mentality denial. This is the reality of here. I just heard Bob Dylan singing in my head, 'I'd go through a blazing fire, darling, if you were on the other side.' Well, you can't quote music lyrics without permission nightmares, but I am risking this because I don't think Dylan would object as I write it while my family and I remain anxious we might have to leave again and see 'all we have' burnt to the ground. It's not a materiality, a 'things' issue, it's a somewhere to sleep, somewhere to eat issue.

I don't believe in property or ownership, and I believe this stolen land (as Whadjuk Noongar Elder Len Collard points out, it's like 'receiving stolen goods'), should be returned to Ballardong Noongar people, but I still make home here – squat, really – and to lose control to fire exacerbated by greedy consumer behaviour and precursively lampooned by a government minister and now prime minister's ultimate and selective denial of human-induced climate change by carrying a lump of coal into the Australian parliament and (to paraphrase) saying, 'This is coal, look at it and touch it … it won't hurt you' is a contradiction beyond ambiguity. He wasn't being ambiguous – and his encouraging of the coal industry and apologias for big industry and his deflections through his faith are unambiguous as well. But what are votes? Unambiguous and ambiguous, in this land of the anti-liberty compulsory vote (or receive a fine). We fear the fire. Fire that *can* be generative in terms of flora, fire that can bring new life, and fire that feeds on fire, that doesn't cancel out. But extreme ongoing out of control fire events that are increasing to the point of total incineration? Authorities and privateers (especially farmers) burn when they can and authorities increasingly burn all year round – officially induced, accidental, acts of stupidity, and climate-shift enhanced. So many major fires (New South Wales last year, Sunshine Coast this year) were caused by military training activities!

Some years ago – maybe 2012 – while we were overseas, the shed at Mum's place over near York burnt to the ground. Therein, many things, including books and papers – a filing cabinet full of our papers. But no lives were lost – and yes, that's all that matters. But what so shocked me was discovering in the aftermath that the intense heat had actually 'burnt' granite rock. The heat had exfoliated layers of granite, falling off like the husks of the rock-core. The fire changed the texture of the rock, if not its composition, and it looked ambiguous in its inorganics. It seemed a living thing that had had life taken from it. It expanded and cracked, and its charred remains were the exoskeleton of a quiddity of contradictory presence, colonial and non-colonial at once. Ancient rock. And I thought – disturbed in the Western chronicalising – of Hannibal crossing the Alps to make war on Rome, to invade Italy, and I thought of Robert Frost's 'Fire and Ice', and I thought of Heraclitus and how dreams recorded in those papers lost had been erased, though must still exist in the pits of my memory, never to be pulled up the same, as they were transferred from thought to paper, in 'linguistic form', and uttering loss when presence is the imposition of a greater loss, a loss immeasurable, a loss that has to resist to reconstitute itself and does because it is the stronger dream in the place. It is unambiguous, my

Part six

Figures 17 and 18 Burnt Rocks near Walwalinj, York, 2012. Exfoliated granite due to extreme heat from fire.

records of dreams were ambiguous – dragged up fast as I could record them. Not a dream book – I've never kept one though have known others that have and do, but rather, snatches of imagery and narrative I wanted to solidify, like rock. But rock *can* burn – burn like structuralism. Like trees.

Beyond the ambiguities, I tried to write that most ambiguous of entities, a poem – a poem to deny the ambiguities their grip over incident and consequence, over what was observed, what conclusions drawn, but to also find some form of liberation in the alternatives paths almost impossible to 'select' from:

The Burning of Rocks

Layer by layer they burn
and peel away, as much as skin
or growth rings. What locked-away
state of unawareness, other life form,
brings desire to combust
out of rock exposed to flame
admittedly as intense as that delivered
by a burning shed with its caches
of toxins: its vats and wineskins
of poison, its insulations and wiring,
its indiscretions of lead and paint,
its gasconade and jactitation of plastics.
What makes rock burn? Granite
sheds its layers like fat embroiled
by pure oxygen or something we breathe
but don't recognise, crackling,
busting up its blowhard petrified
indifference. We are soaked in our opinions.
Fire: a vacuum these rocks can breathe in,
a self-defeating *coup de grâce* of violent
diegesis, the York gums nearby still
standing, if singed, while the rocks hiss
cellular soul-filled agony, their
blue flames not of our palette,
life-forms charred beyond
recognition.[7]

We are watching, watching and waiting. Listening. You can listen for fire, too. The crackle and roar. And smell, of course – nothing as intrusive and alarming and lulling at once. An ambiguous time between warning and action. But when the need 'to act', 'to escape', to evacuate, comes, it is obvious and the enactment, the response, unambiguous ... the authorities *say* ... clutching at

---

7 See https://granta.com/the-burning-of-the-rocks/, which also includes a detail from a photo of the burnt rocks.

straws, none of the harvesting of wheat begun around here yet, the crops full-blown and rustling dry, if worse comes to worst try to retreat to already burnt ground where fire can't take hold. But there will be a wall of flames, there will be a liminal zone, and smoking remnants, coals and embers – the fire storm, the leaps the drivenness of fire. What can a notion like 'ambiguity' function as in such moments of crisis, in the actual catastrophe? If worse comes to worst ... if *worst* comes to worse ... if ... to ...

Poetry can lead to speculative 'realist' fiction: the inspiration behind *Hollow Earth*[8]

Ideas and concepts for books brew with me for a long time, sometimes a very long time. *Hollow Earth* is part of a series of interconnected ideas that are becoming speculative novels and novellas that oscillate around questions of justice and consequence in terms of how we are treating the biosphere and the entire planet, from its 'core' through to its place in the solar system and beyond.

These works are largely a kind of *realist* speculative fiction/s, that deal with immediate environmental, social and political justice issues in unusual often bizarre and 'sci-fi'-like scenarios. It's the tension and crossover between literary and 'popular' genres that interests me. I am making stories out of concepts and ideas, but against backdrops of a gritty realism of the damage being done to the planet, and to all life by humans, including humans to humans. These are fictions which play with time and space to offer alternative ways of focussing on the here and now. They are stories of consequences.

Hollow Earth dialogues with a lot of other literature, especially Jules Verne's *Journey to the Centre of the Earth* (also with the first film version of this), and other 'hollow earth' works, especially William R. Bradshaw's clunkily written bizarre *Goddess of Atvatabar* with its appropriative and strange linguistic plays and exploitations, and its variation on Western colonial 'explorer'-risk-at-all-costs in the name of 'knowledge' and science motifs.

What is *inside* the earth inflects what's on its outside, and we wear the interior like a conscience – we unearth what we could be, what we are, what we might have become. Exploration has consequences. I wanted to write out of

---

8 John Kinsella, *Hollow Earth: A Novel* (Transit Lounge, 2019). This sci-fi/fantasy novel opens with a poem. Part of my poetics has been to shapeshift and (di)stress 'genre' into modes it would seem disturbed by. To move beyond the projection of control, of the status quo of topoi, I have enacted an ambiguity of definitions (what is *the poem*, what is *drama*, what is *fiction*, what is *essay* ...?) ... and as text has become out of necessity more a tool (a 'utensil'?) for activist pacifist intervention, so it pushes further beyond the ambiguities I have tried to create where 'officialdom' (the corporate-military-state) once saw few outside the potential for exploitation for 'productivity' and profit, if any. So, creating ambiguities to push beyond them. For a an argument about the failure of metaphor, see my contribution regarding militarism and John Donne in the collaborative creative-critical book, *Per Se*, West-Pavlov (due 2022 from Narr, Tübingen)

and against the colonising impetus of these genre narratives. I wanted to write a book against the tyrannies of gender control. I wanted to challenge big business and mining rapacity. I wanted to deal with addictive behaviours. I wanted to challenge the closing of borders to refugees, the tyranny of centralised government. I wanted to imagine environmental 'technologies', and not praise technology as something valuable in itself, something to profit from. I wanted to imagine versions of non-nuclear families and adaptive relationships. I wanted to consider a different 'science' of nature and 'behaviourism'. I wanted to escape chronologies, and work in the future and the past in the present. Discussing these ideas in fiction goes back to my first science-fiction novella written when I was fifteen (long ago and long lost!).

Hollow Earth started life as a more conventional narrative and became what might be called a cascading series of vignettes that compel a story. It's a quest novel – a compulsion to discover drives the story, but the discoveries have consequences. It's a novel about love and addiction, and about the need to find a way back home. It's a novel asking questions about the very nature of 'home'.

If I had to sum up *in a nutshell* the 'inspiration', I would actually say it comes out of the disgust I developed when I worked on the periphery of the mineral sands industry (in laboratories, preparing samples, supervising the loading and sampling of ships) when I was still a teenager. And maybe the coalescing, gelling idea came when I drew this experience together with my childhood tendency to dig (dangerous!) tunnels, my fascination with visiting caves, and then later, strangely, a visit to the mine shafts at Sovereign Hill, Ballarat, when we were driving 'East' from the Western Australian wheatbelt in 2012. But the first words on paper came the next year when we were living below the 'Neolithic' copper mines of Mount Gabriel, in West Cork, Ireland.

From there, the novel coalesced through the 'traditions' of hollow earth literature, and my ethical and political concerns … as well as a fair dose of imagination, which, for better or worse, I've always had to excess. I am fascinated with how life experience and imagination play off each other, and am sure, in the end, this is what fiction-making is about.

PART SIX (C)

'Virtue gives itself light' … the propaganda of the romantic epic *The Faerie Queene* and the necessity of undoing textual integrities whilst also 'respecting' them … or, 'a vomit full of books and papers' … or, still in Book 1, Canto 1 … 'I' am just the dream of a 'loose lemon' to the doubters…

This[9] is not Kwame Dawes and my 'first adventure' together into 'worldly trouble' … or *wordy* trouble! Issues of 'virtue and justice' might be revamped in our versions, contesting the source, but, nonetheless, we have concern and compassion for 'Whither the soules do fly of men, that live amis.'

---

9 *Tangling with the Epic*, Kwame Dawes and John Kinsella (Peepal Tree, 2019).

Spenser was secretary to the Lord Deputy of Ireland in 1580, and after various posts he occupied Kilcolman estate, County Cork.[10] His relationship with Ireland was complex, as all colonisers' relationships are. His bigotry towards the Irish isn't alleviated by his critiques of colonial administration – his prejudices serve his own colonial project. Due to the long delay in its publication, the question of whether or not Spenser's tract *A View of the Present State of Ireland* was suppressed serves many arguments,[11] but nothing that's not familiar as colonial overlaying and the push for more local control through weaponised racism. The layering of bigotry extends to earlier English colonists who have 'degenerated' into a quasi-Irishness:

> *Eudox*: What is that you say, of so many as remayne English of them? Why are, not they that were once English, abydinge Englishe still?
> *Irenis*: No, for the most parte of them are degenerated and growen almost meare Irishe, yea, and more malicious to the Englishe then the very Irishe them selves.[12]

As Spenser's 'empathetic' biographer Andrew Hadfield notes: 'Spenser is often remembered as a morally flawed, self-interested sycophant, complicit with the brutal policy of extermination that he articulated with great skill in order to protect what he had gained as a colonist in Ireland.'[13] This is also the story of many colonial writers and officials in Australia.

When my family and I are living in Ireland, we sometimes travel from South Cork through Buttevant in North Cork, past where Spenser lived in Castle Kilcolman amid 3,028 acres of pilfered land as part of the Munster Plantation. We always celebrate the bogs and rocky resistances as nature and as resistances to the colonial project.

Spenser's role in the post-Dudley colonisation of Ireland is of specific interest to me in the 'disjunction' between the compactness of his eponymous stanza and the massiveness of *The Faeire Queene*. I use the stanza as a 'formal' but ironic tool of self-reflection with decolonising pacifist intent, specifically as one whose ancestors escaped the English during the Great Famine and became 'settlers' in the south-west of Australia, making incursions into Noongar lands under the aegis of British colonialism. The ironies cascade. Punctuation in my stanzas reflects and inflects these contradictions and disruptions, always attenuated by Kwame's own anti-colonial position and personal-spiritual-political concerns. We are different, but often strongly overlap. The stanzas as a 'string' further overlap us in the template.

Every aspect of my practice and 'belief system' comes into play in remaking the stanza as an array of stanzas: for example, as an environmentalist, an enchanted tree's relationship with the human (it contains) is necessarily

---

10 http://core.ecu.edu/umc/Munster/settlement_munster.html.
11 Andrew Hadfield: https://www.historyireland.com/early-modern-history-1500-1700/another-case-of-censorship-the-riddle-of-edmund-spensers-a-view-of-the-present-state-of-ireland-c-1596/.
12 http://www.luminarium.org/renascence-editions/veue1.html.
13 Andrew Hadfield, *Edmund Spenser: A Life* (Oxford University Press, 2012), p. 401.

complex: it becomes a means of discussing the integrity and intactness of *the tree* – 'the living tree' – and how humans respect it as tree. So the registers between the fantastical and the biospheric are mixed in the signs as much as through narrative. Epic is uncanny.

Let me revert to the year of my birth via Kellogg and Steele's 1963 article 'On the Punctuation of Two Lines of *The Faerie Queene*' which I take as a point of conceptual departure:

> Whether in terms of pitch, stress, and juncture or – less accurately – 'in terms of old fashioned commas' – a phonemic analysis of misunderstood syntax results in bad criticism and inaccurate texts.[14]

As I speak from within a cloud of 'cumbrous gnats' as weather shifts here too fast, overheating, light distressing, and while not defending inaccurate texts, I *do* defend criticism that intentionally misreads to bring a potential range of access points to the slippages and ambiguities of a poem. The act of poem-making in any period is one of instability, however rigorous the poet or poets intend to be. Unstable spellings, 'mis-rhymes' and seemingly inconsistent punctuation marks are generative!

In discussion of tonality, it is too easy to forget the tension inside the poet over transcribing what one sees and hears in one's head and what will be lost in transcribing it (and even speaking it). Destabilising the stanza whilst retaining its shape (in our case, 10 syllables instead of iambic pentameter for the first eight lines and then finishing with a 12-syllable line akin to a French alexandrine instead of an English alexandrine) becomes the anti-colonial measure of the colonial materiality, and this offers lacunae through which suppressed voices might emerge.

I place an emphasis on reconstituting 'Spenser's stanza' and some of his *actual* stanzas as anti-colonial portals. I have talked of 'error zones' elsewhere,[15] and maybe this monstering of the canonical epic relates to the 'character', 'Errour' – 'God help the man so wrapped in Errour's endless train'! To me, the oppressive nature of the epic stanza is also a vehicle of liberation through misreading, repunctuating, interrupting and questioning what junctures in particular might mean. The ease of rolling along as the stanzas unfurl, their svelteness, calls to me for disruption, interruption and diversion.

I think in many ways Kwame's and my stanzas work on shifting intensities of 'juncture'. Kellogg and Steele in 1963 pointing out that Elizabethan syntax is not fully understood is one thing, but the failure to see the poetics of not fully understanding is also part of a colonialist reading technique. The assumption that one can strive to 'understand' – i.e. impose a generic politics of reading – maybe subtracts from the best possibilities of Spenser which exist in those very slippages and lacunae in his poetry, especially in the *Faerie Queene*.

14 Robert L. Kellogg and Oliver L. Steele, 'On the Punctuation of Two Lines of *The Faerie Queene*', *PMLA*, 78:1, 1963, 147–8, DOI: https://doi.org/10.2307/461235.
15 Kinsella, *Disclosed Poetics*.

In a literary-political sense, my purpose is concurrently allegorical *and* anti-allegorical – ultimately *anti-pastoral* – i.e. the yew IS NOT 'obedient to the bender's will' ... but is a yew in its own right, as is the jam tree-*mungart*. That Una might be recreated (along with the Redcrosse Knight) as a Brexiteer, that Gloriana might be Margaret Thatcher or, indeed, Donald Trump, that rather than the Catholic–Protestant conflict we might have Islamophobia, and, indeed, in the Australian 'setting' the tension between Aboriginal spiritual beliefs and the missionary church in its various manifestations, that the dragon might be a double-edged sword and an endangered species, seems pertinent and even essential to me in 'the now'. I see literature not as a set of curatorial artefacts, but as a means to a different array of paths.

Coda: A Note on Paths

Paths are the way we negotiate reading poems, especially long poems: they branch (as more than Frost intimate!) ... they are lost, found ... 'so many turnings ... and which to take ... to paraphrase from early in Book 1 ... they have 'ends' or possibly, 'unends'! We can find many versions of Archimago, but rather it's the Redcrosse Knight and the idea of the (absent) Faerie Queene herself that I deconstruct and whose worlds I turn upside down to context the historic turning upside down of Irish worlds, Aboriginal Australian worlds and all those oppressed by *realpolitik* of class and privilege. We make in 'so many formes and shapes...' (Canto 2, Book 1) because we are compelled to as poets.

PART SIX (D)

Consuming rebellions and the need for non-violent protest

Below are poems written in 'realtime' in support of James, Sarah and the other protesters who camped out, tree-sat, and were constantly present in resistance to the further destruction (it's not over, people!) of the Beeliar wetlands in Perth (on Bibra Drive in this case), in late 2018.

These poems were intended to show that the protesters weren't alone, and that the effort to protect the environment needs to be a universal one; that ALL of our needs and interests intersect in this. As an extension of my notion of 'international regionalism', I am thinking more and more in terms of international responsibility regarding regional *intactness*, and cultural and identity intactness with respect to the natural environments in which they communalise and identify.

I think we need to be conscious of all language we deploy around this shared act of resistance to the damage being done, and that though the umbrella of 'extinction rebellion' covers many driven and passionate people (and I support the public push to show 'enough is enough' and to make positive change happen), it also fails in its naming. 'Rebellion' suggests a moment (that social-media burst of un-thought-out response that leads to chaotic action without focus, consistency or longevity), an aggressive reaction to aggression that will yield little other than earth people's frustration.

I call this 'the buzz' – and once the buzz diminishes, people wander back to their flatscreens, their new phones, their consumerism. Change will come from non-violent direct action merged with language action merged with cultural and identity and gender-respect merged with thinking carefully about what we do and not letting the buzz create the peaks and troughs that have prevented a collective, concerted and long-term response to the rapacity.

Let's stop consuming as a form of 'equality' when consuming makes for inequality – wealth and privilege need to divest themselves immediately and 'property' be shared in common (and I don't believe in 'property' per se!). Let's stop participating in the consumerism ('Western', 'Eastern' … or any of its other manifestations within capital … culture is consumed by the consumer-machine of capitalism, which purports to offer opportunities of consuming while deleting the basic universal freedoms of food, clean air, natural environment etc) … the machine grinds to a halt without being fuelled. Let's concentrate on the priorities of social interaction: food, medicine, protecting the rights of the vulnerable, ceasing the exploitation, ending violent conflict, protecting environment and cultural rights attached to place (and spatiality) … and avoid as much unnecessary consumerism as possible.

Here are a few messages I've sent a couple of friends (especially James) in recent days:

> in protests for the environment there can potentially be a game of better-than-thou going on in which personal templates of 'best behaviour' and 'i'm less oppressing than you are' might be put on display, rather than a real deep caring for the natural world (privilege always allows such gambits – people living in the fallout of the new colonialism of the latest version of the international arms trade get little choice to participate in non-violent resistance to consumerism when they are dying, having their houses destroyed, and their cultures annihilated).
>
> so much activism out of (primarily Western) privilege is a performance rather than the grit of protest. it's happening in poetry, too. people display what they feel they must, and don't mean it. a poet should say what they mean as a poet – good, vital … but don't say what they think people want to hear in the arts set just to fit the moment of angst as the world overheats and dissolves. it doesn't stop the dissolving; it ironically feeds the consumerism – it is a form of consumerism.
>
> too many times shot at, too many times hauled away to the lock-up, too many times been abused to take this pseudo-activism without a vomit feeling. so the performance moves on to what next week? i hope i am wrong, and i know many are long-term committed activists, and some are becoming genuinely aware, but the show must go on and poetry plays its part in that show. poetry actually has purpose to my mind – and not just the purpose of being poetry that the 'best people' will applaud. i don't want applause, i want change – i want the thousands of flooded gums dying around here to stop dying. only one way to achieve that – put our poems where are mouths are.

i am bothered by 'extinction rebellion' because it reminds me of the buzz behind occupy (i was involved with that in london and cambridge) that dissolved into various forms of 'acceptance' for many. it's the cadre zeitgeist buzz people get and then it gets too hard to just stop the abuse by non-participation (the internet and phones etc have led to more of the destruction than almost anything else over the last twenty years). true non-violent 'rebellion' is (as i have just been writing) not participating in capitalist gain, in refusing to participate in the state machine, in being non-violent, in standing in front of the bulldozers, in believing in EVERY tree and every creature. there is no middle way – there is to my mind: the non-usage of animals, the replanting of damaged areas, and certainly using as few 'resources' as we can (from commuting to travel to how we live in houses etc). we all move, we all use these machines ... but even if we lessen our impact it helps more than a raging that vents angst but doesn't actually do anything direct. direct action is standing by that tree, it's choosing to ride your bike rather than drive, it's not buying a new phone or even using one ... it's going offline ...

the kids coming out against the damages against climate/environment was a positive action. peace marches (as tracy says) that are silent, are powerful. such collective actions work, even if in the moment then gone. but 'rebellions' and 'occupies' that become hype about who is connecting with whom, bother me as shared events of buzz rather than long-term commitment. not to say they can't be, but the 'beeliar group' potential is there – once the hype shifts as cadre groups fall out, it fails. rebellion is not what's needed, non-participation in the corporate military state that is doing this (and people go along with it) is what's needed. the moment people get a buzz out of an action, the action becomes secondary. there's no buzz – only commitment. that good feeling you get – of being alive ... is because it's outside the buzz, it's because you're connecting with what you're trying to protect. that matters. city-driven protests too often become about the entertainment zone and social sets of the city – not the dirt and the air and the water and the birds and life itself. same with any concentrations of people over other forms of nature. yes, social media has enhanced empowerment in marginalised groups, but the abuse of rights of self and community has also happened repeatedly on a vast scale. voices of the self should never be lost in the mass voicing of the many – small communities speaking with small communities and so on, rather than the loss of rights of self by 'faceless' (that is face behind the avatar) attacks when every person's situation is different within and without community.

so often these things are propelled by older people feeding on younger people (social-media companies might be the face of the young, but they grow older the more established they become ... and take on values of conservatism) – on young energy that isn't necessarily (though it may be, of course) focussed – rather than the reality of the event itself. extinction is being caused by ALL of us – including the participants in the 'rebellion'. they could truly rebel by changing themselves to start with (some will, many won't, not really). sorry, but i've seen too much of this movement shallow stuff that sparks then fades as lives change etc the coming-together has an energy, then it morphs. hope i'm wrong! i truly do. to stop consuming outside what is necessary to live would be a good start!

that is, start addressing the problems with capitalism and the state and never give ground, with peace as your best friend. no peace and there'll be no peace. 'rebellion' intimates violence even if unintended and that's why we have the problems in the first place. they use it as a 'hashtag' (potentially the end of liberty in too many ways for too many) because it buzzes and attracts young people who want to have the buzz and think they're also being ethical. there's a category error in it all. beeliar writ large. and one needs to come in and out of these well-meaning but often unseeing gatherings and keep a steady line. they will fade as fast as the world is fading. as committed life activists, our function is to be steady, coherent, consistent and persistent. you are all these things – use this commitment to help others stay committed and to not just tune into the buzz then tune out.

Anyway ... here are some of the poems sent through to the tent (of James) and the camp as it grew and to Sarah in the tree:

Poem of the Gathering

The people are gathering
at the wetlands off Bibra Drive

The people are gathering
to ward-off the deleting machines

The people are gathering
with trees as extensions of their bodies

The people are gathering
so Main Roads won't run rings around them

The people are gathering
so quendas can breathe an air of insects and vegetation

The people are gathering
to let the rich wet soil do its organics, speak its rhizomes

The people are gathering
to show no deals are done to sign-off Beeliar!

The Trees Alongside Bibra Drive

The tangle of branches
is the zest of conversation
over-arching the wetlands –

if we study the leaves, the branches,
the ravens interpreting the stories,
we will be able to say: Yes, this planet

is inhabited – we will set our lexicons
to synch with the many voices
that emanate from its green echoes.

But as for the aperçus
of the illuminati
of the Main Roads,

well read *them* with caution:
they are dust rings, debris
orbiting the planet.

The tree offers to look over us

The tree offers to look over us
and cut off its hands, its arms –
down to its life before it was born.
Right back to the start, back
to when energy became sap,
and sap fed the zodiac.
That's what gives us sleep,
then wakes us, arms outstretched.

A Response to James's Report

Fencing is the old trick
of both sides of the fence –
this side 'safe', *that side* ...
that side up for grabs.
But they come back
and back, these fencers,
shifting the lines
of their own discourse.
Fences are about access
to damage, and exclusion
of bush protectors. They are
the lie of divisions.

Don't despair – each
image of the machines
you merge in your psyche
with the growth you watch-
over will work as talisman
and tools to dismantle
the planned assault.

Outside this window
are a pair of bronze-wing
pigeons collecting sticks

and other choice pieces
of dried vegetation
to courier down to Bird Gully
where they are preparing
their nest. I can hear
machines narrowing
horizons, and know sound
and sign are the *variables*
at play here.

I also know that the air
here breathed against
the exhaust, merges
with the exhausted air
there as winds change
and currents make
constellations in our
own atmosphere,
in broad daylight,
like the earth's
other moons
to long
conjectured
sitting right
on us – eggs
to arrive in
the bronzewings' nest.

Bibra Drive Frog Poem Picture Received 4am

The motorbike frog doesn't want to do a deal
with motorbikes, it wants to talk with James
before the sunset opens the hole lot up
to the big grab gaze of the deal-makers.
The frog croaks, This is not a swap meet,
and it's not a colonial cash and carry.
James says, I need to go for a piss,
and the frog says, I'm not stopping you,
but don't expect me to look the other way.

For Tree Sitter Sarah

You are where the nightbirds
daysleep and where they duskwake

and where they watch and hear
and make timeless records

of the movements of interwoven life. Without you,

Sarah, the nightbirds' calls
that delineate the wetlands

will be lost with treefall.
You keep their points

of reference growing.
You sense with them.

Always Now

Community is the bushfloor
and the sharing of stories,
the building of resilience
before the machines
try to say, *this*
was never here –
but it was and is
and is and is and will be!

Resisting from Within the Green Tent at Bibra Drive, Beeliar (for James)

In real time
the air is green
with leaves of grass

through the membrane
contractors talk deletion
but the face

of resistance
wears all life
in its features –

all life's sounds
all life's textures
all life's responses

to the plan
to unmake
air and ground

and water,
to unmake
mediums

in which all life's
many lives
hang on

against
the deletion.
Crow

out of the green light,
speak to the contractors
from within the tent – say:

all life's life is in here,
have some respect
for yourselves

if
nothing
else.

Sweeney Asks: What Am I Worth if I Don't Fly Again When All Wings are Needed?

What the tree-killers fear most is the merging of flesh with cellulose –
they ask: Does it mean that a tree sitter *literally* merges with a tree? Does
it mean that chopping it down might result in a charge of ... what ...
    manslaughter?

But they need not worry – the state and its machinery, the terror
of private property, doesn't recognise such a condition. Up a tree?
Then remove them and that'll be that – tree and human separated.

But Sweeney knows better, flying past, heart swelling with pride
at seeing the human climb and meld into the tree's canopy. That's
how feathers are made, that's what keeps the world exhaling

and inhaling. Sweeney had always been confused by the separation
of symbol from fact, trilling, The tree of life is precisely that, the tree
of life. All life. Hovering above the tree with wattle birds and magpies,

with ravens and honeyeaters, Sweeney calls down to the wetlands – sweating
and alive in the caul it has spun against the spikes of development:
What am I worth if I don't fly again when all wings are needed,

when each sweep of a wing might combine life and drag to drive off
the machines with their steel teeth, the engines that batter
the talk between trees and the life they are, they watch over.

Extinction Rebellion is too much about image and not enough about its own impacts

I was deeply disturbed to see an article in the press[16] on the 'greening' of the Limmat River in Zurich as an 'event', as an act of protest, is obscene. No more dangerous than table salt, they claim? Let's look at some of the background to uranine, the substance used to colour the river in 'protest'.

Uranine has a complex chemistry and a complex history. Sodium fluorescein has made appearances as part of St Patrick Day Celebrations in Chicago,[17] and had coloured the Danube in the 1870s. It is used to trace leaks in water tanks and pipes, but with a strong warning that it is not suitable as a 'food dye'. The materials used to make the dye are from inevitably dangerous extractive industries.

Its apparent 'non-toxicity' means it is used in some surgery, but in undiluted large doses it can prove fatal. It turns up in a report for Project Shad – a series of tests conducted to see what vulnerabilities US warships presented to biological and chemical agents.[18] The report is telling in its implications of industry and application, in the journey a chemical product makes to its eventual usages.[19]

Unless Extinction Rebellion collectively start to comprehend cause and effect, the sources of the materials they use, the extended metaphors (their conceits) and symbolism in the world as a whole they enact, then they are performing and enacting their own (collective and individual) need to be doing something, rather than changing anything.

Phones are their devices, and phones are at the core of much mass extinction. These devices are *manufactured*. The irony of table salt – *no more dangerous than ...* – is figurative and literal. The salt industry in itself is worth scrutiny, and salt on the human body ... well, hardening of the arteries is more than a symbol. Collapsing symbols. This photo op of people floating on the greenness of wish-fulfilment contributes to planetary dissolution; it does not help prevent it. Let the phones you use now (and, indeed, this computer), be the last you purchase. If they are 'de-teched' out of existence, so be it.

Stop buying the crap with horrific environmental consequences and the city will become far more aware than it would from you impressing your friends on social media. Sorry, you disappoint me and many others. Now is the time to act – you/we have the will, but also need to think about *how*.

Not super strong glues[20] (horrific chemistry and horrific side effects to people and the environment); not dyes (synthetic at that![21] *seeing* is also perceiving),

---

16 www.independent.co.uk/news/world/europe/extinction-rebellion-zurich-river-green-limmat-protest-a9099716.html.
17 www.chicagoclout.com/2017/03/the-saint-patricks-day-chicago/.
18 https://en.wikipedia.org/wiki/Project_SHAD.
19 www.nationalacademies.org/hmd/~/media/Files/Report%20Files/2007/Long-Term-Health-Effects-of-Participation-in-Project-SHAD-Shipboard-Hazard-and-Defense/URANINEDYE.pdf.
20 www.theguardian.com/environment/2019/sep/02/manchester-extinction-rebellion-activists-glue-banks-barclays-hsbc.
21 www.sciencedirect.com/topics/biochemistry-genetics-and-molecular-biology/fluorescein.

no phones ... people stopping the consumerist new-tech new colonialism. That way we might make a difference.

I once worked with these dyes in a lab as a teenager. As 'harmless' (!?) as the mineral sands industry the lab was ultimately serving. Not all the leaks were caught, either.

Extinction Rebellion needs to stop being a showpiece and start being a rejection of all tech consumerism. They need to understand that the 'non-toxic' dye down its chain of being encounters origins in naphthalene (hydrocarbon), sulphuric acid etc etc (consider how we get phthalic acid anhydride, how we get resorcinol ... how the reaction takes places etc etc!). Need to dig deeper, think deeper, and act less for performance's sake.

Protest is *being there*, and we are all here, in the moment. We don't need to see *you*, we need to see the changes brought by your (and our) non-consuming and non-self-privileging of access to goods. Altering the 'mere' look of a river is nonetheless *altering* the river. Leave it alone and stop pouring shit – any shit – into it.

Villanelle of a Green Limmat River: With Great Sadness

The disconnect between cause and effect
as Uranine is poured into sharp contrast like snow melt,
the damaged river through the city is made bereft.

Temporary ... as chemical warfare? ... *temporary* as the best
laid plans floating in the bright emulsification of death – a test –
the disconnect between cause and effect.

Social media traces through screen memory through distinct
moments of play in the horror of *on and on* it goes left right left,
the damaged river through the city flows bereft.

Rebellion that feeds the extinction that synthesises and treats
'world' as playground to announce the leaks – halt!
the disconnect between cause and effect.

This landlocked calenture this old city called to order this cost
of confronting like a green algal bloom swallowing each breath,
the damaged river through the city is made bereft.

'As toxic as table salt' – sum of the parts – investigate the collect
& refining of salt, the world's hardening arteries, the logo the crest –
via this disconnect between cause and effect
the damaged river through the city flows bereft.

PART SEVEN: TOWARDS 'CONCLUSIONS'

Closing remarks and observations with their contexts – moving towards a 'conclusion' to a trilogy of books.

Disembodying and re-embodying the poem as act of acknowledgement of land rights and a rejection of 'property': on acts and actioning of environmentally concerned poetry[1]

by 'John Kinsella'

What follows is surely to be read through portals of tolerance, mutual respect, peace/non-violence, equality and egalitarianism, the rights of difference, rights to associate in community, and the belief that poetry can be written out of the damage to resist and even 'repair' some of that damage.

***

An Address to the Editors:

'i' increasingly believe that I have no part in the 'literary world' when 'i' really only want to try and help save environments before it's too late. 'my' writing in all its forms serves only that purpose these days. All future justices will stem from treating the land in a respectful and non-exploitative way, and this of course takes many degrees of consideration into our consequences of impact. Violence against the biosphere is *the violence* that underwrites all other violences. 'i' use the word 'underwrite' consciously. An example: the Adani mine is a colonial implosion of consequence that needs immediate halting in its language. Far be it for 'John Kinsella' to explain the clear nexus in which language and destruction go hand in hand. *Poetry needs to be the work that acts as a preventative in terms of such yokings.*

i' have become so disillusioned with the way poetry of 'nation' (urghhhh) is discussed, that 'i' am at the point now of not only no names but no quotes to critique the group and community poetics we need to scrutinise. *Tabula rasa:* 'i' feel the social media-isation of poetry has turned the genre (which perhaps once dwelt – somewhere, somewhen – in possibility) into to a capitalistic propaganda mechanism, even when relating to 'issues' of our greatest necessity.

So the earth rolls and we do what we do and each letter 'i' type is a participation in the grid, is another breath gone, another email sent. The cost of this exercise needs to be taken into consideration and the restorative potency of poetry by word of mouth must be considered anew.

***

This is a piece of un-Australian writing. 'i' do not wish to write canons and boosts or to report on zeitgeists and whether X does that better than Y. 'i'

---

1 This was written at the request of editors Dan Disney and Matt Hall for *New Directions in Contemporary Australian Poetry* (Palgrave, 2020) and I thank those editors for the comments, suggestions and participations.

Part seven: towards 'conclusions'

want instead to talk of the future of poetry to stop the rot of capital and the strictures of its false consciousness. 'i' instead want to talk of poetry as an alternative, in which we re-direct language into a pacifist-direct de-trope in which words are intrinsic to the events they reference and refer to: in other words, the merging of sign and signified that retains the mutualising of respect. Possible? Too much? No, it's not. No poem quotes and no poets here, not completely. In this act 'i' do not wish to erase any others, or the land, or animals and plants, just myself, 'i'. Residues, echoes, shimmers of syntax that need to keep on altering as damage shakes the poet, the poem, the environments of writing.

This act of writing reflects the poem as an act of necessity, an articulation of the crisis of being in a damaging and damaged state-of-being. Hopefully, the 'essay', like the poem, is an organic act of repair that lets space *be*, lets space grow, without interference. The essay too – no longer as merely a Western, Platonic dialectical mode of 'reasoning'? And the poem-as-witness, of participatory-witnessing? A witness against the blandishments of *whiteness*: the poem as a de-technologising, a de-fetishising (in the Marxian sense) of 'self' in face of community and communal needs that need (through us, and through language) to work coherently with the eco-well-being of the biosphere. *Poetry as (literally) generating energy rather than consuming it.* A spoken, memorised form and one building through the collective voice. The mutualising responsibility of the poem. The inherent call for collaborative poetry with all voices feeding in. A writhing, de-personalized nexus free from poets-as-identities, per se, 'identity' irrelevant to THE POEM which works toward positive sequelae to the damage through justice, repair, restoration and knowledge. Poetry, in this capacity, as integral to all forms of existence. Poetry free from categorisation outside that of responsibility, of embodying intactness. No nation-state (but, rather, communities), and no-self, just collaboration towards languages that people need and respect: this, rather than those languages and narratives forced upon us all as extensions of capital-military-state control.

***

'i' suggest that we start from a position wherein the poem is inseparable from the land itself, and therefore all poems are seen as embodiments of the land. Even if a poem is written about an abstraction (or, for that matter, an abstract noun – love etc or, indeed, an abstract *pronoun* such as "I"), and one that seems very distant from descriptors or even references to 'the land', it is by its very nature of composition – and the acts of the human body that either created it or acted as a vector for its utterance – 'of the land'. This can be a metonymic connection through language, or just via the physical fact of being 'of the land' (or 'of' any of the elements of material existence – earth, water, air …), or as an act of advocacy, spiritual expression, or, conversely, an alienation from the body politics of 'nature' (there are many poems that consciously and, even more so, 'inadvertently' support or affirm acts of destruction).

In writing the body, we are writing the land, in writing the 'soul' we are writing the land, and in writing what we 'experience', we are writing the land, in historicising, we are writing the land.

Therefore the question 'i' wish to address in poetry and in readings of poetry in all contexts, is how do we create an adaptive and respectful poetics of embodiment – a movement from the disembodied to the re-embodied? Taking it further: *how do we create poems that don't lay claim to land as property, that don't obviate and erase the concurrent or prior claims to a writing of that land, and how do we take poetry outside the strictures of Western-centric views (in terms of literary theory), which connect the poem with copyright and authorial rights and ownership, which become de-facto claims on the land itself as embodied in the poem, in the act of writing?* Further, as 'we' are many, and our experiences of possession and dispossession are radically different, can a model be created that traverses, without appropriation or intrusion, the different conditions of connection to the land itself? In essence, how do we create a poetry that respects Indigenous, non-colonial and shared claims to land and at the same time contest 'property', which is the essence of colonial capitalism and its rapacity? 'We' are not necessarily 'you' and/or 'me', and our sense of what 'land' is or might be or was or will be, will greatly differ, and yet, we walk (or swim etc) the earth. Can we have this conversation without it privileging the empowered, the wealthy, the manipulators of 'property'? The questions cascade over the embodied poem, the land.

It is easy to offer evidence for any argument and be 'convincing' if one is proficient at deploying rhetorical devices and 'proofs' within the diegesis of contention, but 'i' refute this, too. That is why we write poetry, to avoid the need to 'round things off', to offer objects that answer their own questions. So many poems are clearly created with curatorial ends in mind(s), to be displayed as objects that are intact, that in being unravelled display their craft and perfect parts. To be clear: such poems are occupations of land, they are colonisations of space. Aesthetics, which arise from value-adding art-as-property through capital, create hierarchies of perception that are used to control responses to human-made and 'natural' environments. The viewing of, say, a piece of remnant bushland on the edge of the city, out of sight of the established suburbs, off their usual routes of middle-class traversal, as expendable, comes about in part because it's not 'known about', but also because it is at an aesthetic remove from where nature leisurists are more likely to engage their encounters. In the 'wheatbelt', we are involved in many struggles to save bush that bring no protesters, no supporters beyond the locals. Perhaps this is because although species-loss and degradation of the biosphere and attendant climate change through carbon emission and destruction of ecologies are understood, visualised and fetishised (Instagrammed etc) domains are always given more aesthetic relevance, and hence 'value' too. The stronger the visuals, the more people come to the cause. But poems create sound and visuals, documents and records, and generate language differentials that offer ways through to hidden truths. For 'me', the poem can be an ethically transgressive new way of seeing, beyond the value systems imposed in capitalised minds: the poem as an anti-aesthetic generator calling toward equities and justice.

***

A poem is a means for absorbing and reconstituting all possible languages, but should it be that? Permissions and consultation are the key to the making of a poem – do we often write against the privacy of others, and is this accepted as part of the rights of the personal voice, of its unified self-intactness, or, conversely, the fragmentation of self in the anti-lyrical 'resistance'? But it's not that easy – to appropriate culturally sensitive 'materials' from outside one's own cultural actuality, and even when writing toward politicised modes of disrespect from within one's own culturality (this but one mode of radical refusal), one senses this might equally and more likely be some form or act of abuse. Is this an issue of censorship or respect for the liberty of others? This should remain one question a poet constantly faces, not only as we use languages we encounter, but even when we neologise and coin – introducing newnesss into a matrix of heritage, which constitutes one more instance of 'othering' – one is compelled to wonder whether metatextual knowledge is enough in writing poems? Or do we have to counter our own intactness to respect that of others? These questions should at least be constantly active.

***

Furthermore: a poem is not merely a freedom to move through space, but also a set of negotiations to move across such spaces. A poem, in use of language, negotiates permissions of access to innumerable conversations while laying claim to the right to speak. This is why 'i' find categories such as 'confessional' or any of the incarnations of 'wearing the inside of the self on the outside' largely irrelevant. Poetry is always in the service of something – be it the self (indeed, 'ego'), community, capital, appendages of the state, the military. Poetry is always being read in different contexts whilst attempting to create context. *Poetry can decolonise but too often colonises, even when it intends to oppose colonisation.* Creating a poem requires vigilance – even the 'surreal' is encased within an environment of presentation, and a poem can be a prison if we are not aware of its mutating presence in the 'outside world'. The journey from interior to exterior can easily be exploited by capital. Poetry too easily can become an industry of placation. Poetry can be a sign hammered into land and made a calling card, an illumination, a 'do not enter' threat. Poetry is occupation of space, or maintenance of spatiality. So we are in situations of working with or against this, or both. We are creating binary behaviours of creation and presence that capital will always quickly exploit. The creator of the poem offers themselves as part of their product and many followers may accrue (and many poets would welcome this). The 'identity' of the poet is fused with the meaning of 'their' poems, and language is controlled as a commodity. But this cannot hold, as 'taste' shifts and consumer trends take the audience to another poetry-product, and meaning lost with the moment, the once-favoured poet now a merely forgotten avatar of capitalism. It doesn't matter if a poem lasts or is lost, but it does matter how this happens and who controls reception. It does matter that a poem written to stop the destruction of a forest or interrupt the progress of 'permissions' for the Adani mine or against the fantasies of white supremacy reaches beyond its moment of exposure, that its utterance sends rhizomes into the fabric of injustice. How do we achieve this? Through the poem coming out of the very language materials of injustice, and then attempting to unwrite that injustice. And again, in this sense, *this is a piece of un-Australian writing*: processes of undoing keep us going, and poems can help replace injustices here with more equitable outcomes and new visions for justice. A poem should be a non-capitalised refusal, a non-violent turning of abusive language back against itself.

***

Poetry is always a collaborative act if it expects an audience. It will make use of dialogues of self/s, conversations with strangers, word-bundles and strings directed towards loved ones or those who don't even know they are being pursued with textual loops. Poetry, in being read and heard, imprints and is hard to undo, even if it's static or a vague sibilance. So there's a responsibility in letting it loose, in unleashing it. This is what makes the poem such a potent tool of protest – it doesn't leave one alone long after it's experienced, and it embeds in layers of memory (explicit and implicit), in the declarative and procedural. In the haze created by human-induced toxicity, in the wasting of land (never waste lands! That's a hope of the colonials so they can *Terra nullius* all over again), the damage to cognitive processes and memory (long- and short-term) is inevitable, and one might argue even accommodated. What gets poetry out of the picture is both 'good' and 'bad' for capital. 'Good' in the (negative and negating) sense that it erases knowledge of why conscience is there, and 'bad' because it damages the mnemonic tools of (self) advertising (which capitalist exploitation relies on as implicit in an audience/receptors of products).

When the collaborative act of communalism leads to a specific poet articulating shared loss or refusal to accept spatial invasiveness, it is particularly potent. A spokesperson arises who parses collective knowledge but inevitably inflects through personal experience. One could cite any number of poets in the Australian ongoing colonial impositions and their rejection in this context. And when parcels of words arise disjunctively, stimulating ways of seeing among readers equipped for surprise rather than angry response, you get shifts in perception. To see something private as the provenance for 'enjoyments' and elucidations that a reader outside the space of the poem-text's creation might never have thought – is to have insight into a closed space. That space is opened not to invite invasiveness and erasure or palimpsest, but to say that you have never considered the possibility that overlap might exist. Despite this overlap, people wish to retain degrees of autonomy. The psychosexual-faith interphase could be an example, but there are many others. People live patterns that are replicated in their poetry, or refused in *their* poetry. But in (the) *our* (of) poetry, they overlap. They have to.

And damage would seem anathema to the poem? It's not, it's part of the word parcels, it's the fallout of wordplay. It costs as the poem either maintains through rite or ritual or breaks away and apart in its iconoclasm. The poem is a tool of holding or breaking. So which is it? In resisting damage, it has to be both because there are issues of respect involved, and also (always) change. No system is perfect because it enforces compliance, but some systems have a better sense of organic wholeness and integrity between people and country. 'i' note this in all 'i' write, or try to. It seems a way in, and an act of seeking permission while speaking out no matter what. Not a resolution to a paradox, but an acknowledgement that paradoxes have an energy that can be used respectfully and constructively.

***

Where are the names? Where are the quotes? You have them at your fingertips, as you have writing materials and means of dissemination, dispersal. But we don't always want to hear what *wants* to be said, and having it imposed or 'dropped' on us is an intrusion. 'i' have always found those 'peace poem bomb drops' an obscene act of aggression, invasiveness and environmental damage.

***

It seems to be frequently assumed that younger poets are inevitably activist, but this is no more true for the younger generations of 'now' than it has been at any other time, of the many 'thens'. Each generation has its activist poets, as well its more conservative or cautious voices, or its larger array of voices that may be concerned by 'activist' issues but preferring to keep this separate from their poetry. How does activism enter poetry? If a poem is issue-specific and 'didactic', it seems obvious, but often or even mostly poems are not. The poem that asserts the beauty of a flower may be intended as its own activism for that flower against human encroachment? But when that same flower is an extension of human desire and 'love', it becomes secondary to the primacy of the human emotion, the human need? Yes, but the companion 'no' doesn't need the conjunction to yoke it to the spatial-temporal inevitability because the flower in the poem is a symbol and does not have to be literally exploited (the flower observed plucked and placed in Ezra Pound's vase at home). It can be an extension – and this is why 'i' have fewer and fewer problems with anthropomorphics – that carries a protection and respect of its inspiration, an *actual* flower.

To make clear, 'i' am not suggesting the appreciation of a flower is an activism because the flower is intrinsically beautiful, and beauty is an activism – in fact (as 'i' tried to show in *Shades of the Sublime & Beautiful*), as one who does not hold with the values of aesthetics, 'i' reject that there can in fact be 'beauty' outside acts of justice and equality. So the lyrical poem that 'values' the flower *per se* as capital within the poem – as beauty to bring pleasure to the reader – is a poem of placation, and not resistance. It is a poem of preserving a social status quo (of capital), and not 'nature' ('the flower') in itself. But the activist lyric will be inherently conscious of this (the poem is organic, not machine), and the mention of the flower, the focus on the flower, will make a statement of respect. How might this be achieved? In titling the poem, in naming the flower, in delivering it at a protest against the destruction of 'nature'. 'i' have read many poems at protests – it's incredible how context can shift the meaning of a poem against the way it has usually or often been read. The poetry of Gerard Manley Hopkins is interesting in this context: poems read on the steps of the cathedral in London during *Occupy* didn't *need* to be bespoke to have an impact – the context lifted lyrics into activism.

It's true, that activisms have found focus through social media and connectedness facilitated by the internet, but this has also brought its own activist contradictions. We need to be transparent about the obfuscations of poems and poetics that are both openly declared and readily accessible, but also others that either operate outside more accessible medium and media, or don't invite such ready access. Language is the variable in all contestations of repressive status quos, and access to the 'major' languages of the world inevitably brings greater focus even to local concerns, because the fate of the biosphere is local and global. But these separations and sharings need unpicking, and poetry is a medium through which this might be done.

And then we might consider the problem of 'major languages' – the tools we have to read and how they are made available, what we are born to as language and what we've been prevented from being born to or accessing (word of mouth, written, signed) by colonial capital. Language-activism poetry (against, say, the colonisation of language by the dominant languages of power and trade) is pivotal to any activism, be it environmental, social, about ethnic rights and integrities, land rights and cultural intactness, gender and self-determination (in its many forms), animal rights or a combination of some or all of these concerns – but it's a way of opening discussion that we hope will reach out across languages, and help scrutinise what, say, 'English' languages are today. Poetry is part of the necessary reconstitution of languages that have been attacked, that have faced erasure-desire, and that have persisted. Poetry is also a challenge to the annihilation of languages by power structures of colonial capital – not by replacing with poetry written in the languages of oppression, but by 'rewriting' that colonising language with new and reconnecting languages of spirit and cultural receptiveness. This is not prescriptive, not to be 'told', because that is its own colonialism of theory, but it is proffered as an affirming possibility, and one that seems, to me, to have been enacted in poetry and song in powerful ways in Australian Aboriginal writing, speaking and country.

All poets are likely to resist any form of categorisation outside their self-declared and/or shared positions, but discussions of 'the poem' rarely break away from the poem itself – the failures of close reading. Cultural and environmental impacts, the toxicities attendant on analysis and adapting to the context of the critic and their assumed audience, affects even more than the contexts in which a poem was created. Can we offer insights into what drives difference and togetherness, of where separations and differences are in flux, and where a constant search and pursuit for justice is the driving force? We cannot write out of, and certainly never 'into', without a diversity of voices from many different physical, emotional, spiritual, and conceptual spaces, that challenge not only the status quo and its oppressions, but the very nature and validities of expression itself.

Resist! Against cruelty – emphasis without violence[2]

Like all my writings, this final part of a final chapter is interconnected to all that has come before as well as what else I will write in the future – it is ongoing, and open. What follows is the introduction to an issue of a poetry journal focussing on 'activism'. The call-out is unambiguous, the relationship the choice of pieces and the raison d'être of the issue have to the workings of each poem included necessarily *is*. To 'resist' is to declare an opposition but also to suggest answers are possible – the poem as activist text rests between the awareness of a wrong and the means by which it will ultimately be rectified (if at all). An essential ambiguity resides in the relationship dynamics between editor and poets in making a statement about the need for multiple activisms in a world under pressure in so many ways. Divergent and intersecting with shifting variables. The decision-making and articulation of a textual environment needs to be clear, but space and understanding for 'difference' paramount. This collating becomes room for contradiction and generative creative ambiguity (that will have many variants and views on 'aesthetics', polemics, lyric, rhetoric, public and private acts at physical sites of protest etc) within a more 'generic' and general non-ambiguity:

As I said in the call-out to poets, this issue is intended to be a safe zone for poets to express their resistance to oppression in its many forms. Further, the publication of this issue is in immediate response to planetary environmental degradation verging on complete collapse, to issues of injustice and unfairness in our various social spaces, and is a challenge to institutional bigotry, brutality and indifference. Issues of injustice are not separate, but are in dialogue. I also stated the need for primary recognition and support for Aboriginal and Torres Strait Islander cultural and land rights, for an intense advocacy for the natural environment, for the rights of refugees and the celebration of cultural diversity, as an enactment for any whose voice is suppressed, for a resistance to violence and the arms industry, for animal and human rights.

There is frequently an ongoing, shared pursuit for justice in the making of poems. *Resist!* is intended to be an act of advocacy for the marginalised against the often silent (and sometimes aggressively loud) majority's desire for

---

2 *Australian Poetry Journal*, 9.1, *Resist!*, guest edited by John Kinsella (2019).

preserving the 'Australian' status quo of nationalistic, Eurocentric, colonial (in its many derivations), officially empowered, consumer-orientated language-control. *Resist!* won't have this.

Resist! is a non-violent act of contesting and refusing language-controls. Though it is not a single cause but many causes, all of them passionately and determinedly resist the power structures of oppression with the peaceful act(s) of poem-making and lyrical/de-lyrical utterance. This is a collective of individual voices with resolve. The poems are of different 'opinions', but share a platform to speak out and be heard.

The call-out received an overwhelming response – both in numbers and in intensity of poems. *Resist!* is not a 'theme' per se, but an act of many events, and has been interpreted and/or approached in very different ways, as it should. From calls for direct intervention at the crisis moment, to explications of the anxiety brought on by the cascading issues of injustice that are biospheric and also specifically local, what manifests is the broad spectrum of 'issues' with specific need for concentration. Consequently, reader and activist need to ask themselves how to articulate their own responses to these resistances, ask how they each come into dialogue with others, and if that's even possible (I strongly believe it is, which is the purpose behind this issue).

But there's verbal and conceptual flux in making conversations through the diversity of this collation, and that can be demanding. Provocations *are* demanding, and how we respond matters as much as the poems themselves. It needs to be said from the start that this is not a curatorial exercise, but a bringing together of actions. Each poem speaks its own voicings, with its own impetus, yet gathered together, they do more than offer a cross-section of alienations and rejections of oppression – they form a growing intersectional community of objection and refusal.

In the context of these collectivised acts of protest, I also make clear that I rejected any work suggesting violent responses to injustice. This does not mean poems herein don't articulate violence, or engage with highly passionate, highly committed drives to bring change, but rather that violence is not part of what they are calling for. I am a pacifist – this position is relevant to choice-making not so much in terms of 'issues', but in terms of what responses to injustice are suggested, intimated or called on. I came to my pacifism out of rejecting past experience of violence, and I know that violence is no answer in itself. It brings no positive lasting change, and is contradictory; violent change almost inevitably brings violence in its wake – an ongoing violence that underwrites the future it creates because it becomes the measure of 'change' and 'success' and, bizarrely, 'justice'.

I don't know if any poets in this issue believe that violence is the answer against the violence of oppression, but certainly their work being gathered here inevitably forms part of a collective expression of determined, peaceful change, for a non-invasive methodology in finding justice. That's not intended as an imposition of view/s on poets, but a statement about the environment in which their included poem is 'operating'.

Part seven: towards 'conclusions'

I have a strong feeling that we should all come into focus in a collective statement of resistance against the idea and brutal reality of 'injustice'. Each of us is accountable and culpable for our words. In physically present, non-violent protest actions, I do not believe in 'masking up',[3] but in standing proudly with others, or on my own if I have to, and defining who I am by what I do. The poems here will carry what anonymity they wish to have, but they also carry the wills and declarations of their authors who are not mere avatars. And if they are 'avatars' or presenting behind whichever 'naming' they choose, it is by way of statement against the occluding, copyrighting, exploitative nature of capital and the state. Identity-theft is more than a fiscal act; it is a cascading violation of personhood and community. As is the theft of cultural knowledge, especially in the case of capitalist profiteering. Often, such theft is unwitting in terms of 'art', but awareness is everything, and once made aware, those practitioners who are outside a declared and defined cultural space, arguing for its own rights to intactness, need to negotiate their entry into that space, should they wish to go there. Again, dialogue. Again, language. Again, poem as meeting-zone of language slippage that *can* operate outside of theft.

This issue is not to declare a collective 'politics' – there clearly isn't one, and diversity in all things with common purpose is what this act is all about – but to note as readers that there seems a common awareness of massive social and material inequality tending to manifest in cultural insensitivity, theft, and, at the very least, a brute insensitivity and certainly a disregard for environment.

This issue intersects with innumerable moments of protest. I believe in long-term, committed, ongoing 'organic' protest – that is, everything we do should be part of our attempt to move things towards justice. In other words, how we live is part of how we protest. Extinction Rebellion marches might be good in drawing attention to the moment of crisis and mass species loss, but unless we change in all we do as part of that awareness, it is only marking the moment. We must think about the trajectory (that's the word) of the glue from its origins through factories to shops to oneself in one's moment of sticking oneself to the street as protest action. Yes, disrupt peacefully, utilise civil and linguistic disobedience, but let's think about cause and effect – these dangerous chemicals being used have consequences to environment, the people working in the factories, the communities exploited in obtaining the raw materials. Who benefits? Capitalists. The greedy.

We have to all be wary in how we propel the resistance, wary that we don't negate what we're trying to achieve. Witnessing without responsibility? Acting without giving up to lessen our impact? A poem of resistance, for me, needs to question its own contradictions, needs to express itself out of its own constraints of conventional language usage. Even the 'clearest' utterance needs to bother us into response. It is the utterance of observation and experience, it comes out

---

3 I refer to 'masking up' and 'anonymity' in public protest actions, not to the use of masks during pandemics, for health reasons etc. ... this book largely pre-dates the Covid-19 pandemic.

of a necessity of resistance, and yet it cannot just fall into the zone of publication and be content with itself. It is part of authorial responsibility – singularly or collaboratively – towards the action it is trying to prompt. Walking the walk, and talking the talk.

The complexity of discussing overlaps of protest in looking for common purpose can easily become a kind of pseudo anti-capitalist version of *glocalisation*. Inflecting the international brand with local concern so easily irons out specificity of need and case. This is one of the disturbing truths behind the co-opting of Indigenous-rights injustices around the world to concerns of environmental exploitation. Like all issues relating to the health of the biosphere, it *is* all our concern, but the relationship between a people and their *country* is also *their* concern. Communities are capable of caring for their ecologies without consumer communities telling them how it's done. There are sometimes (often?) issues of external patronising in this (the irony of this is overwhelming!) that lead to fewer rights for dispossessed peoples and for the land itself when Westernised pressure groups try to control discourse and the pattern of protest (whilst still consuming and often being culturally insensitive). *Noting* this isn't enough; respecting local custodial integrity *and* biospheric[4] concerns is part of an essential dialogue that needs to be happening in many forums.

Poetry seems a generative access point for bringing together different communities with common interest. Poetry has the ability to coalesce the disparate for reception, its language-usage generating access points to an experiential observation that gives permission for reading though not permission for cultural intrusion. Language is used to record injustice, but is also a record of injustice in itself. It overlays and extracts; it pushes to retain its intactness; it lays its own claims to belonging. It is also manipulated and altered by 'elites' to suit capital, to suit colonial mechanisms, the military, the state. Poets need to zigzag a way through to responsibility in this, surely?

The current issue is largely in English, which ideally shouldn't be the case, but each poem speaks outside the constraints of imposed and received language to connect with other modes of expression. I am not going to list the different protests here, as a list seems counterintuitive to the breadth of purpose in suggesting a temporary common-purpose-aligned 'community of resistance' against very obvious injustices, which have immediate fatal consequences, through to those threads that smoulder insidiously and erode and corrode over time.

Further, even in the case of the most extreme injustices, there is inevitably tension in trying to prevent further or ongoing injustice, and activists will push aside all other concerns, and often others' concerns, in focussing on the need for urgent action. Animal rights activists feel that every death of every animal in industrialised profit-making machines is reason for immediate concentration

---

4 Note: I use the term 'biospheric', which to my mind includes human-induced climate change in the contexts in which I use it. If you prefer it delineated, you can add this statement after the first use of 'biospheric': '(this includes human-induced climate change and other consequences to ecologies of rapacious human activity taken as a whole)'.

Part seven: towards 'conclusions'

of energy and personal resources on that issue. Those who are giving all their time and health to resisting Adani, coal mining and Big Energy, and Australian industry and governmental collusion with the mass destruction of earth, water and air feel that's where they must expend what strength they have. Those involved in resisting indelible human rights abuses, in Australia's offshore detention centres and 'Border Protection' bill applications, might well concentrate their energy and 'advocacy' there. And at the core of the Australian condition is the failure to enact treaty with Aboriginal and Torres Straits peoples, and begin the process of rights restoration, consultation with real outcomes in terms of how everyone here lives on Aboriginal and Torres Straits peoples' lands, and comprehensive economic restitution.

The argument might go that these are 'issues', and demand of us all that we can give, and spreading thin is to fail at everything. I don't think so – they are not separable off as *issues*, but are *realities*, and part of a mutual commitment to *response* (without necessarily claiming rights as part of that protest – to protest against injustice does not always mean individually benefiting from the rectification of that injustice; something important for all writers to think about, surely?). We have a collective responsibility to live justly, and to work for mutual justice (again, a complex term that is not *fixed* per se), understanding each other, and respecting *difference*. Again, poetry is one of the most effective and linguistically affecting ways of achieving this. The poem as thing in itself is, as I have argued before, a form of 'agora' in so many ways. Even very disparate issues of justice can find common ground. There's too much greed, exploitation, and utter indifference to suffering out there, for us not to work together, especially when we share a deep knowledge that these abuses must be addressed. We share issues of conscience, maybe?

In selecting poems for this issue I acknowledge the right of each person to be as they are and wish to be, for self-definition and intactness of body, belief, and spirit, to be respected. All of us have the right not to be bullied and cajoled, and, to my mind, the land, the biosphere, has that right too. It is a representation and an actuality of the difference and plurality of ourselves too. Interestingly, if one 'value' links all these works, it's a deep abhorrence of cruelty. No liberty can include cruelty; no form of justice can include cruelty. Liberty is never cruelty. Patriarchy, which we all swim through (no, it hasn't gone away!), by way of a shout-out-loud example, is a form of cruelty as well as deprivation. Racism is cruelty, and in this the construct of 'Australia' is too often a cruelty, in terms of the monopolies of power and major right-wing media interventions and manipulations, and distinct privileging of 'whiteness'. Cruelty is the common thread of injustice, and cruelty is at the core of what *we* are resisting. I take responsibility for these words, but here we are together.

***

And as statement of temporary departure, but not close, I sign off with an eclogue – a pastoral protest against the colonial acts of the pastoral ... an

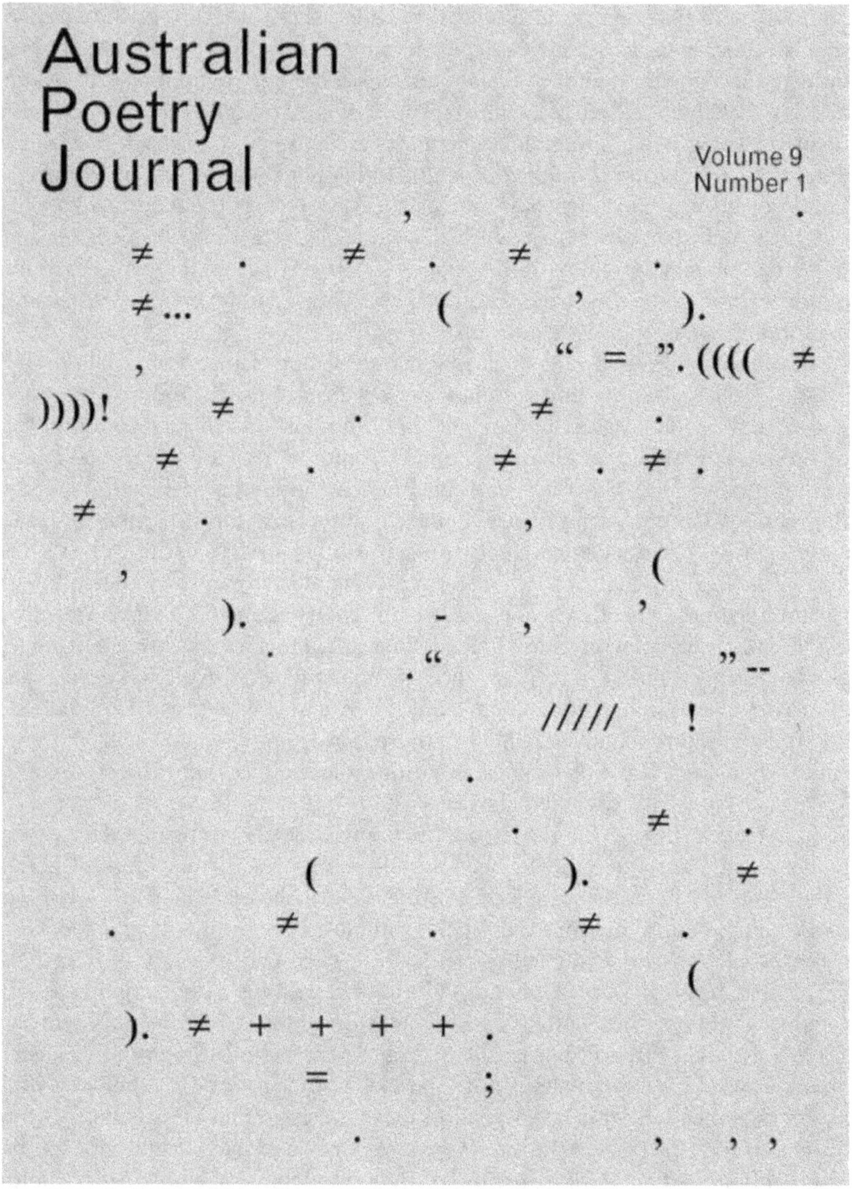

Australian Poetry Journal

Volume 9
Number 1

,
≠ . ≠ . ≠ .
≠ ... (').
" = ". ((((≠
' ≠ . ≠ .
))))! ≠ . ≠ . ≠ .
≠ .
'
('
). - ,).
. "
///// !
.
. ≠ .
( ). ≠
≠ . ≠ .
(
). ≠ + + + + .
= ;
. ' ' '

Figure 19 Cover image of the *Australian Poetry Journal*, 9.1, *Resist!*

attempt to go beyond the ambiguities of creativity and enact a justice. A making of the book – this book and where you are engaging with it – a site of activism, a merging of poem and its reading, of where it can go from here:

Part seven: towards 'conclusions'

Eclogue of Moon Before the Storm

for Tim
The moon is dark adapted
as red clouds herald late,
    a single flyer's single wing
buffeted and torn and tossed
    down to form a skin
between ink and record,
the sum of what's reflected.

Our search is dark adapted
where fire had edged the world,
    a rush of darkening gale
leaving no time for adjustment.
    Un-nocturnal birds fly away,
lopsided into scrawl – a venation

    of collapsed sky-writing,
a gall of vaticination.

Conclusion to *Beyond Ambiguity* and a triptych of poetics

Having always 'rejected closure' and, in a sense, always believed in and subscribed to the idea of the 'ongoing draft' or open text that adapts to the needs of the moment, I am hesitant to say this is a 'conclusion'. But as discussed in the opening material of this work, this *is* the third and 'final' volume of my Angelaki Series/Manchester University Press investigation of the textual politics and ethics of not only making a personal poetics, but quite frequently a shared, collaborative or overlapping poetics.[5] As such, I must admit to feeling as if some kind of 'end' has been reached. As we look beyond ambiguity for answers to doubt and hesitation, whilst acknowledging the frequently generative nature of ambiguity,[6] so we look to a shifting and permeable 'end'. If Eliot said 'The end is in the beginning', so we might add 'the beginning is in the end'. And maybe that's the displacement of aesthetics that I hope takes place in this trilogy across two decades of making – that nothing is curatorial, nothing is fixed, and that 'ends' in themselves can too easily be an abandoning, a closing of the door, and a forgetting.

    I want *no* forgetting. I want no excuses. And though 'civics' for communities and across the 'international' necessarily shift in their language, the

---

5 The first two being *Disclosed Poetics: Beyond Landscape and Lyricism* (2007) and *Polysituatedness: A Poetics of Displacement* (2017).
6 Micro considerations of ambiguity in specific poetry texts (such as in syntax, vocabulary, punctuation etc.) has not been the focus of this work. Rather, I have concentrated on macro concerns of poetry as protest or extension of ethical 'belief'.

basic wrongs of oppression, bigotry and greed remain as they always have. Environmental degradation remains just that, even if the discourse around permission and use alters according to the manipulations of capital and power. But I have consistently, I think, expressed admiration and hope that Indigenous knowledges will be respected as an intactness inside their communities, and that, if offered (and not appropriated by non-Indigenous people), learnt from, outside their communities. Indigenous land rights seem an essential part of the corrective – a key to biospheric repair.

Poetry and song, the use of compacted language and its iterations, has always seemed key to me in addressing colonial and imperial wrongs, and also in showing just how much humans don't have a claim over all existence. And I mean poetry of all forms of language (signs), with some of those 'versions' existing outside the 'five senses', that is, beyond the reading of physical sensation, as well – as ideas of enactment and responsibility that will fuse the abstract with the sensual concrete. Poetry is always physical *and* intangible, empirical *and* heuristic, even at its most interventionist, activist and specific in these works.

During the writing of these three books and their accumulating, scrolling pragmatics of appearance, gathering and inclusion (what's in what's out, how does the argument thread together etc), I have written many other books in other 'genres', with, as I say, a few between and across genres (as with 'closure', I reject 'genre' as exclusive) and some maybe their own genres (at least in my mind). Inevitably, these works form nodal points and interstices with the trilogy, especially as concerns activist issues (from 'activist poetics' to 'antifa' writings), and more so because I frequently and increasingly work in collaboration. I speak with others, and my works speak with each other as well. So, these poetics books are in dialogue with many of my own works, and also innumerable other voices. But some of my more strident pacifist anarchist vegan views can only be put down to me, not because I want it that way, but because I have to be held accountable for them.

Some of the 'determining' threads that have reached across the three volumes include: the nature of pastoral and the radical pastoral; the failure of the bucolic; problems with notions of 'landscape'; the politics behind acts of writing and the physical process of writing ('graphology', 'orthography', the manual typewriter etc); the complexities of reading 'place' and the 'polysituated' characteristics of identity; 'international regionalism'; the problematical politics behind the lyric and how we might contest and make it a more activist vehicle – with a strong interest in its spatiality and where it can fuse with rhetorical expression and modality; issues of prosody and their political implications; considerations of disclosure, dislocation and displacement in movements of people and persons around the world; Indigenous rights and poetry; human rights activism and poetry; considerations of the work of individual poets and how reading coalesces into a broader activist critique; animal rights; and environmentalism and poetry.

The list is long and the ideas are, I hope, interwoven into a dialogue that always has more than writer and reader involved, and quite often many participants. I work with other people, and that to me is a core fascination in life, and a purpose for writing. I write about other people's work, and I listen to what they have to say about mine. I work with other people to create a mutuality of utterance, but that can vary immensely in its co-ordinates in how it happens, and what identification of 'authors' and their roles comes out of it – I try to talk about that and trace it.

For me, writing about the nature of introductions and references, of encomiums and blurbs, as I do in this third volume, is almost a category error in that there is never one way to discuss a text or the people creating that text, and consequently, to offer up a comment that becomes a focus for others, inevitably reduces possibilities in meaning through this act of public speaking. I also *receive*, am gifted by others, in the process as I write on work that I value, and about people I respect. The ambiguity is in the role of commentator and recipient, but there is a politics in the *beyond ambiguity* wherein the 'original text', and the 'comments' it evokes are part of a mutual aid of cognition and articulation. An introduction to a work becomes shared purpose in the critique – not as necessarily affirmation of everything being commented on, but as a spatialising of a discussion.

Three overwhelming 'factors' come into play across these books and I need to declare them clearly. The first is my political-ethical focus of vegan anarchist pacifism – it's been the principle/s of my life for over thirty-five years and necessarily informs how I write in any form. Second is my concern for writing *against* as much as through 'the pastoral' both in terms of its 'literary history' and its historicism in Western-colonial discourse, but also undoing the pastoral in a more literal rural sense of its trope-myth adaptation from the educated elitism of upper and middle class consumers, to the rural working class as subject, especially as adapted in Australia to a corrosive white national mythology/ discourse of 'ownership', when the reality is theft of Aboriginal lands and acts of ongoing dispossession and humanitarian rights violations in cascading and virulent ways.

As a poet, I see it as my purpose to unwrite this pastoral and add yet 'another version' (almost 'misplacing' William Empson). Finally, the fact I am a poet, and have been most of my life, is the driver behind a 'poetics', which strongly connects with, and arises from, the act of keeping a personal activist-writing journal (having done so since I was a teenager). That journal-keeping has been about poetry, environmentalism, ruralism and the ethics of thinking, as much as anything else. My journals are records – weather recordings, animal sightings, tree plantings, walks, encounters with birds, always threaded through with a temporal-spatial wondering and critique. These journals have formed the backbone of this trilogy, as they have many of my other works. I write out of and to them, and in different ways will necessarily continue to do so. But maybe not quite as I have in these volumes, in which they shift in and out of focus in different ways – occasionally in *Disclosed Poetics*, overtly as dated entries in sequence in *Polysituatedness*, and conceptually rather than directly in *Beyond Ambiguity*.

As we 'age' and 'pass', as decay converts our physical selves into nutrients and minerals for new beginnings, we become inherent to the future, or as I prefer, the eternal present, the ongoing 'now'. I write for the here and now, as an act of intervention and disclosure, and never for 'posterity', but I write with a belief that poetry and critical discourse can *converse* and enhance the chances of future. In a sense, the ambiguity of entropy needs to be nurtured as concept so that it becomes generative rather than destructive, so that, rather than resigning ourselves to species loss and biospheric devastation, we act *now*. And in acting now, the disorder we are leaving will have more chance of coalescing into longevity and 'future'.

I increasingly think in a figurative (not literal) 'block universe' of cause and effect, and feel that activism which is implicit in the now must perpetuate 'today' rather than losing itself in a bleaker tomorrow, especially given how bleak today is! In other words, we cannot consign colonialism to the past, because it is always present, but by addressing its wrongs, we can bring some justice to the past as well as the future. We have an obligation in all our works to address wrongs past, present, future, in the now, and in some ways, these volumes constitute such an attempt.

But it's not all bleak – many of the sections across these works are celebrations of nature, humanitarian acts, just causes, and the act of writing. These are never refuges from the trauma of invasiveness and the destruction of people and habitat, but they are *possible* ways through to means of expressing injustice in order to bring justice, and above all, peace. Many poets are talked about, many places encountered, and generic modes of prejudice addressed. These are works about the contradictions implicit in holding a position, disagreeing (often fervently) with a writer or situation, but finding the purpose of disagreeing as generative in itself – as revealing something about my limitations as critic, as much as anything else. Even at their most strident, these surely become acts of self-doubt. The doubt is not in what is said, necessarily, but in the mode of presenting such pieces in a narrativised trilogy such as this. And then there's the inevitable fallibility of the author!

In many cases, I write about works and poets I admire, and try to find my way into using different 'ways of seeing'. It seems relevant to state here that though there's a collation aspect to this particular book, every piece was written or thought of in the context of the notion of getting beyond ambiguity, while being enthralled by ambiguity. The connections are always subtextually there, as they are with place and time – with issues of spatiality. If *Disclosed Poetics* (Vol. 1 of the trilogy) had its basis literally in a *thesis*, that thesis (and its many antithetical prompts) has extended through each book in the trilogy. The concerns over radical non-violent solutions to ecological and political injustice as expressed through acts of writing poetry, of trying to merge the 'lyric' with 'rhetoric', or, rather an anti-rhetoric based in the 'agora' rather than the 'senate' – anarchist and not institutional – has been the linguistic undercurrent of the whole. The 'market' is a place of exchange, sharing, possibly barter for me – never about capital, never about profit and privileging one over another.

One of the other guiding principles of the trilogy is the act of juxtaposing seemingly non-related or directly connected 'ideas'. This is an enactment of the figurative language of the poem into the body of the overall text. I cite poems, often my own, as 'illumination' or extension or a form of heteroglossia (as opposed to 'illustration', which I don't think they ever are), so they bring the surrounding 'prose' text, the narrative of argument, into the act of *being* poem. In the movement of these critical works, I try to parse verticality with horizontalism ('poem' and 'prose') both structurally and conceptually in the imagining and writing of 'verses' in and around discussion. So the prose becomes part of the poems, and the poems part of the prose. The flow of a prose document seems to me to create an active 'field' for poems to work through, to speak out of with amplification and other sonic, visual and sensual qualities.

So, the books become polysemous and cascading enactments of slippage. The degrees of slippage are pertinent and relevant to reading the parts within the whole as outlined in the opening sections of each book. The rapacity of the 'pastoral' literary trope as smokescreen for colonial imposition, land clearing, romanticising a cordon sanitaire whilst reducing the 'wilds' (which they aren't) to fragments so as to provide territory for industrial agriculture, seems, *in the slippage*, as potentially abusive to the earth as (over writings on) industrial land usage and almanacs of capitalised farming. Unless it is addressed critically. But how does such a slippage work in the context of the destruction of ecosystems and destruction life on the planet? It doesn't, but how we write and 'cite' injustice is on a spectrum, even if a contradictory and ambiguous spectrum. I always wish to push beyond those generative ambiguities into a less conflicted and more focussed activism. A form of holistics?

In any long-term work, as suggested above, the 'civic' world/s change/s as it is being written, but what you have written remains (for a moment at least), unless you rewrite, erase or it is deleted by others. With this trilogy, the story might begin in the first volume, but in its 'block universe' it speaks back and forth as if it were written at once, or so I intend it. And though 'completed', these texts will remain in dialogue with whatever I write *after* 'signing off'. What is available to me to 'discuss' is a question I ask myself whenever I write anything. For pieces on collaborative works, especially as traced in *Polysituatedness*, I did so with consultation and permission, which remains the textual principle I write by. However, permission is impermanent and change will necessarily shift any perspectives on this work that might arise, but I do not wish to obscure culpability with ambiguity of temporal spatial 'facts'. I have sourced my references not in ways designed to privilege or to erase, but in such ways as I felt would be least intrusive; though ultimately, all conversations in such texts are a form of intrusion and displacement. bell hooks writes (and without connecting myself with this, which I have no right to, I cite as something that affects me): 'Both radical and revolutionary feminists long ago critiqued this opportunistic use of feminist thinking to improve one's individual lifestyle.'[7]

And in the use of material in juxtaposition to create slippages, one certainly risks many such acts of self-serving, even if serving an argument. Poetry does

---

7 bell hooks, *Outlaw Culture* (Routledge, 2008), p. 115.

this par excellence, and yet we hope its intensity (even in 'loose' open lines) might impel a different way of seeing with integrity and justification. But in the end, poetry, too, is culpable not for what it sources, but what it actually does with it. If it de-politicises a text by diluting and replacing it with effusions and evasions, its ambiguities are destructive and often offensive. But if it compels and impels its inspirations and references, it might bring momentum to an argument. I think this particularly in the case of using Henry David Thoreau,[8] whom I find so admirable and so problematical at the same time. I resolve this through poetry of environmental and anti-colonial activism, whether I succeed or not.

And, as a last gesture, I wonder about quoting William Empson – who has contradictorily bothered me across the decades, and *prompted* me into response ... or maybe Raymond Williams *The Country and the City* ... But rather, I will quote Eunice Foote from an experiment she conducted in 1856 and 'discovering what we call "greenhouse gases"': 'An atmosphere of that gas would give to our earth a high temperature.'[9] And I will add, that nuclear power is not an answer, being both an accruing contamination and, potentially, immediate destruction of the biosphere.

Maybe the overall effect of these poetics is to suggest that we lessen our impact through less consuming of goods, ensure an equal distribution of 'wealth', protect human and animal rights, allow creativity to heal rather than damage ... to address and respond and never remain indifferent. Poetry can act as a tool of social criticism, and can affect positive, peaceful change as *idea*, and as *utterance* – that poetry can help resolve conflict and help bring *justice* to all living things, and the biosphere itself.

Aligning, imploding and dispersing contrast in metaphors – on Helen Frankenthaler's *Seven Types of Ambiguity*, 1957

As if a spine of metaphor where metaphor

has abandoned veneration of bodily resolution – that

head of some author or other reflected as if in their face,

that argument for a different blue coat-hanger direction of hue

as if in the contradictions of orange deportment messing

with pierced colour agreement of depth as if we might pull

sharp-smooth together heart-and-eye as bathysphere of surfaces alike.

---

8 Especially in my poetry collection *Jam Tree Gully* (WW Norton, 2012), which is both response and argument to *Walden; or, Life In the Woods* (1854).

9 www.climatechangenews.com/2016/09/02/the-woman-who-identified-the-greenhouse-effect-years-before-tyndall/.

EU authorised representative for GPSR:
Easy Access System Europe, Mustamäe tee 50,
10621 Tallinn, Estonia
gpsr.requests@easproject.com

www.ingramcontent.com/pod-product-compliance
Lightning Source LLC
Chambersburg PA
CBHW051609230426
43668CB00013B/2038